# ERASING
# RACISM

"A very skillful and powerful illumination of the dark corners of real life. . . . I do not know how anyone can address the presence of racism/white supremacy without the kind of deep understanding that is conveyed by this work."

—Asa G. Hilliard III–Baffour Amankwatia II
Fuller E. Callaway Professor of Education
Georgia State University, Atlanta

"By surveying the special status of blacks throughout the history of America's racial order, *Erasing Racism* recenters the role that white supremacy played and continues to play in our national status quo. Asante's arguments are quite provocative, particularly in a time when postmodern analyses of race typically discount its reality or overestimate its fluidity."

—Darnell M. Hunt, Ph.D.
Director, Center for African American Studies
Interim Chair, Afro-American Studies
Professor of Sociology
University of California, Los Angeles

"Reparations is a central issue for the new millennium and Molefi Kete Asante takes the debate to the next level in his passionate and informed call for racial justice."

—Dr. Charles P. Henry
Professor of African American Studies
University of California, Berkeley

"Dr. Asante has tackled a 500-year problem, the problem of white supremacy. What is most helpful about his book in addition to his analysis is the concrete steps that he offers in terms of addressing this 500-year-old problem and taking positive steps so that both the racists and the victims of racism can begin the healing process. . . . This is 'must' reading for persons of faith and persons of good will."

—Rev. Dr. Jeremiah A. Wright Jr.
Senior Pastor
Trinity United Church of Christ, Chicago

Revised and Expanded Second Edition

The Survival of the American Nation

# ERASING RACISM

## MOLEFI KETE ASANTE

**Prometheus Books**

59 John Glenn Drive
Amherst, New York 14228-2119

Published 2009 by Prometheus Books

Inquiries should be addressed to
Prometheus Books
59 John Glenn Drive
Amherst, New York 14228–2119
VOICE: 716–691–0133, ext. 210
FAX: 716–691–0137
WWW.PROMETHEUSBOOKS.COM

13 12 11 10 09    5 4 3 2 1

Library of Congress Cataloging-in-Publication Data

Asante, Molefi K., 1942–
    Erasing racism : the survival of the American nation / Molefi Kete Asante. —
Rev. and expanded 2nd ed.
        p. cm.
    Includes bibliographical references.
    ISBN 978–1–59102–765–2 (pbk. : alk. paper)
    1. United States—Race relations. 2. Racism—United States. 3. African Americans—Civil rights. 4. African Americans—Social conditions—1975–
5. African Americans—Reparations. I. Title.

E185.615.A8 2009
305.800973—dc22

2009020492

Printed in the United States of America on acid-free paper

# CONTENTS

# INTRODUCTION
# EXPANDING THE DREAM

The 2008 election of President Barack Hussein Obama changed forever the arena of race relations in the United States and simultaneously highlighted race and racism in many other multi-ethnic, multiracial, heterogeneous nations. These two facts alone have introduced a new dynamic into the discourse on race unpredicted by the earlier edition of *Erasing Racism*. It is probably rare for a writer to admit that he or she could not peer deep into the future to predict radical changes in the public arena centered on the issue of race. I humbly submit to my readers the truth that I would have never assumed in 2002 that a person of African descent, regardless of the mixture, would be elected president of the United States of America. I wish I could have been so precocious but, alas, my humanity could not anticipate the irony of the situation.

There are reasons for my lack of political foresight regarding the election of Barack Obama. First, I was born in Valdosta, Georgia, a place where in the early twentieth century a black woman named Mary Turner was violently murdered and her unborn fetus ripped from her womb and stomped to death, because Turner protested the lynching of her husband. Thus, the uncontrolled hatred against black people was palpable, real, immediate, and violent in my father's, as well as my own, lifetime, and I never forgot the meanness with which whites in Georgia approached blacks. Therefore, in the first edition of *Erasing Racism* I wanted to state for the record some of the most heinous crimes committed against African Americans to remind the reader that we are living in a nation with a split personality. This much remains true. One cannot gainsay the triumph of reasonable politics over ignorance in the case of the election of Obama, but by the same token we must not be too eager to dismiss the continuing crisis of race in the country. All is not resolved by the election of a black man to the presidency; indeed, I guarantee you that Obama himself knows this very well, and if he does not, he will certainly learn fast. One can hardly forget that even with his Harvard Law degree and experience as a University of Chicago law professor, Obama was still referred to as "well spoken." There is obviously a racial component to calling a brilliant law professor "well spoken," which is something one would never say about a white professor of law who had also been editor of the *Harvard Law Review* as a student.

The second reason for my disconnect with the possibility of the election of Obama during the writing of the first edition had to do with the nature of American politics or, perhaps, the character of black politics in America. In the United States black political relations in have been confrontational, combative, difficult in regard to the attempt to point out the hypocrisy of whites who say one thing but do another, and provocative in the sense that the objective was always to push the white racist to see his own image in the mirror of public criticism. Barack Obama stepped onto the stage from another, totally unsuspecting direction and surprised the nation with the appeal of his politics of togetherness. Obama did not have a civil rights inheritance: he never rode on a bus into the segregated South; he was never spat upon as a child worker; he did not know the cold, hard facts of personal physical abuse; he never had to deal with anyone in his family or from his circle of friends being lynched for being black; he could never completely identify with the generations of poverty and violation that shackled the minds of millions of African Americans. In that sense, Obama offered a new, innovative voice that sought to try something different. What Obama had was a sense of shared history with the sufferings of the masses of black people brought about by a combination of factors such as an open-minded mother, an international upbringing, and the experience of living and working in South Chicago. He may have been biologically black and white, but he became culturally and politically black. Few whites would have suspected his biracial heritage by examining his political and social choices. His Chicago politics were clearly based in his core black constituents, political bosses, and their political issues and perspectives. His national politics enlarged and expanded his reach into a wider group than he ever would have imagined when he was first elected to the Illinois state legislature. Born in Hawaii and raised in Indonesia and Hawaii by a white parent and white grandparents, Obama brought a different view of America to his politics. He saw a multiracial America, "not a black America, not a white America, not a brown America, but a United States of America." Such rhetoric was electric, inspiring, and visionary in the way that all of the talk about justice, fairness, and equality had been forty years earlier. When Martin Luther King Jr. gave his "I have a dream" speech he was hailed as the greatest articulator of the sentiments of black America. Obama's Philadelphia Speech in 2007, the so-called Race Speech, will be hailed by generations to come as one of the most authentic attempts to deal with the real character of our race problem by any politician.

The fact that I did not predict Barack Obama's or any black person's election to the presidency of the United States does not invalidate any of the claims made in the first edition of *Erasing Racism*. The thesis in the book remains sound, although I am the first to admit that the dynamics have shifted. I argued that America was two nations and that this separation could be captured by the metaphors of the Promised Land and the Wilderness. This remains the case. In fact, the election of Obama may have shown us different ways of under-standing the fault lines.

I was in Starkville, Mississippi, on November 4, 2008, to speak at Mississippi State University as a scholar-in-residence. I had already voted in Pennsylvania, but here I was in a hotel room in the reddest of the red states where men in denim overalls drove around in trucks with signs that said "It's a White House, Dummy!"

I phoned my wife, Ana Yenenga, and said, "I am not going outside the hotel tonight; this is still Mississippi." I must admit I yet retained some of John Lewis's and Jesse Jackson's trepidations about the red states. My history is like theirs: I have demonstrated, marched, and seen the fires of hatred in the eyes of white American citizens. I also read the editorials in the newspapers across the southern part of this nation. When the dust settled in Mississippi only 12 percent of the whites voted for Barack Obama; furthermore, I know that those who voted for him were largely considered liberals and progressives and were probably verbally abused by their neighbors. Most of those whites who voted against Obama likely did so because they saw him as black.

We are not yet in the Promised Land where race does not matter.

The political contest was far from one of class coherence and solidarity in the South. The black poor and working classes voted differently from the white poor and working classes. The issue was race, pure and simple. Among African Americans, a person who is biologically black and white is accepted as black because of the social and political history of racial classifications. In a society that was based on the idea of the "purity of the white race," it was unthinkable to whites that a person with African ancestry could be considered white. With African Americans—the quintessential Americans in the sense of having a genetic combination of races, cultures, or ethnicities as a part of the African American community—race purity is not a problem and has not been a problem since the first time a white slave owner sired a child by an African woman and abandoned that child to be raised by the black mother. Henry Louis Gates Jr. declared that nearly 65 percent of all African Americans have some European or Native American ancestry,[1] and nearly 30 percent of all black Americans have white paternity.[2]

The Wilderness people, those often kept outside of the Promise of America, saw a new type of optimism in the election of Obama. There was a keen interest in what was possible. The transference of Obama's victory to themselves gave them a temporary shot of psychological electricity that may have been enough, in some cases, to jolt young men and women to action as it brought old men and women to tears. When one saw Jesse Jackson standing at Jackson Park in South Chicago with tears in his eyes, one knew that the breaking of the chains on the Wilderness was happening right before one's eyes. In serious and righteous ways Jackson has defended the poor, the downtrodden, and the discriminated against neglect, discrimination, and despair. What he felt with the election of Obama was the weight of history shifting from one generation to another. He was the grand old man in defense of the Wilderness dwellers, but here was a new man ready to find the source of togetherness. To say the least, the rhetoric was genuine and authentic, but the difficulty is always in the execution of the details. Freedom is more than a slogan and so is the erasing of racism.

The second part of the impact of Obama's election is the direct shake-up of race relations and the discourse about racism in other nations. I was traveling in Colombia during part of the campaign season; I lectured at the Universitario del Pacifico in Buenaventura and visited the Universitario del Valle in Cali. The excitement among the Afro-Colombians was obvious whenever I mentioned the campaign or the name of Obama. While talking with the students, I discovered how desperate the Afro-Colombians are for an American president who understands the condition of blacks in their country. Many claimed that President Uribe of Colombia was a racist who has sought to ensure the inferior position of blacks in education, the economy, and social life. Yet he was considered by President Bush to be one of America's best friends. The Afro-Colombians would like to see a new policy toward Colombia that would consider the fact that one-third of the population is African.

Obama's political election has probably affected France and Brazil more than Colombia or any other nation. I think that the whites in Colombia have not arrived at the idea or language of a society of equals, whereas the rhetoric of both France and Brazil is one of racial democracy. Nevertheless, the high-sounding tone has not produced any great number of African leaders, neither in France nor in Brazil. People within those two societies have begun to question their own governments and their policies toward race, given the fact that both nations in the past have seen themselves to be more liberal and progressive than the United States.

When I studied French in Angers in France's Loire Valley, I was told, "In France if you speak French and adopt the culture, then you are French and we make no distinctions." Of course, it did not take long for me to see that this was not the case. There were too many black French people who could not get jobs or positions in the industrial or the corporate worlds because they were black. There were too many well-educated French scholars who would not be hired in the universities because they were black. To be black in France is a limiting experience, despite public statements to the contrary.

The Brazilian situation is similar. Nearly half of the population of Brazil is African and yet the blacks of the country do not appear in large numbers in any sector of the society other than sports. There are few government ministers, few high-level executives at top companies, and few people in positions of leadership in education who are black. Brazil, like France, is a country of empty rhetoric when it comes to the equality of its citizens.

Now that Obama is president of the United States he has become the most public face of the American nation. That fact in itself is akin to radically shaking up the established script about America. People all over the world have reacted with awe at the power of American democracy but, more than the democratic institutions, it is the moral power of antiracist thinking that has captured the imaginations of the world's people. But this is to be understood in light of the many blows that have been launched against enslavement, segregation, and discrimination in the United States by strong, firm, determined cadres of generations after generations of Africans who refused to be assigned an inferior place in human history. Barack Obama's election is the result of the latest stage of this ongoing struggle for normalcy. What is necessary to further advance the case for normalcy is antiracist education.

George Dei, the leading Canadian expert on antiracist education, has written poignantly about what a society must do if it is to prepare its people to live with difference.[3] He defines integrative antiracism as the study of the dynamics of social difference as mediated through race, class, and gender. What Dei seeks to establish in Canada is a context for antiracism. This is a remarkable objective but few in Canada could say that antiracism is truly fully engaged.

In the United States, even with the election of Obama, we do not have a national education system that is antiracist. We have other concepts and other disciplines, such as multiculturalism and pluralism, but not antiracism as a form of education. Our schools of education do not teach antiracism. We have diversity training and we often see support for multiculturalism, but antiracism is something different. I think that one of the most critical loci of our problems is in the education sector. Our system remains, for the most part, shot through and through with negativity toward Africa and blackness at the level of teacher, curricula, and supervision. Education in the United States does not rid people of racism; if anything, education often enshrines racism and racial domination in its system.

This is true at every level of the educational experience. In the elementary schools it is rampant. But it is also found at the secondary school level and at the university level. We are all victims of a pattern of racism that must be broken to have a truly liberated nation free of racial unfairness and political provincialism.

Take the idea that education in the United States is the locus of divisive and volatile racial discourse. What is necessary is that those in charge should acknowledge the inclusiveness and diversity of American society. Difference does not mean that we have to fight with each other. What appears to grab the attention of some Americans is the shifting identities and locations of people along a continuum of racial understanding. Because the educational site, at whatever level, is the place for producing and maintaining ideological hegemony, it is also the location for teaching patriarchy and racism. I believe that it is possible to rewrite the discourse on race and place on the table of our national discussion a feast of possibilities for dealing with the difficulties of race.

Many critical race theorists in the United States believe that racism is normal in the United States and that there is nothing color-blind about American society. Consequently their view challenges the idea of a raceless society and at the same time suggests that white identity cannot be positive in such a context. Of course, there are those who feel that all identities can be recognized without hierarchy. The view I have advanced, which I call Afrocentric, acknowledges the profound influence of the enslavement of Africans on the entire ideological apparatus of American society. In addition, Afrocentrists believe that it is necessary to turn the page of history so that those who participate unconsciously or consciously in the privileges or in the abuses of the system understand precisely how we got to this point. But this is not an easy course because even liberal whites or those who one could reasonably expect to have progressive ideas are often beguiled by the racist arguments that constitute the emic paradigms of racial understanding in American society.

For example, during the frenzied aftermath of two significant moments in liberal thinking about race in America, the venerable Marvin Harris stooped to pick up the debris left by Arthur Schlesinger Jr.'s *The Disuniting of America* and Mary Lefkowitz's *Not Out of Africa*, two books notable in the 1990s for their attacks on the now extensive and mature Afrocentric intellectual school of thought.[4] Schlesinger opined that black intellectuals who created their own theories or took a different approach to phenomena than their white colleagues had created the possibility that his "America" would be disunited. I recall a debate featuring Schlesinger, Cornel West, and myself at Stroudsberg University in Pennsylvania where I said that "the nation has always been divided and the divisions are old, deep, and long."[5] America was born with divisions, with strong furrows of class, race, and region. On the other hand, Mary Lefkowitz attempted to challenge the emerging African and African American scholarship on ancient Egypt. She failed at her attempt to "dismantle" the scaffolding that had been erected by the Kemetologists (those who study African civilizations Afrocentrically), but she generated a lot of excitement among white scholars who had been looking for someone to counter the Afrocentrists. I shall demonstrate how a social scientist like Marvin Harris took the propaganda of Schlesinger and Lefkowitz and made it a part of his own thesis about Africa and Africans.

In his book *Theories of Culture in PostModern Times*, Marvin Harris introduces the emotionally charged term "Afrocentric Ethnomania" to describe what ultimately is neither Afrocentric nor manic.[6] Harris charges, "What began as an argument for equality has escalated into an argument for supremacy. Leaders of nonwhite movements now urge their followers to think of themselves as more beautiful, intelligent, musical, athletic, generous, earth-caring, and human than people of European descent."[7] One is not sure what Harris is referring to when he claims it began as an argument for equality and then escalated into an argument for supremacy. There is nothing, not a single line ever written by an Afrocentric scholar, to warrant such a baseless charge. This is the kind of nonsense that leads African Americans, Latinos, and Asian Americans to claim that some whites will do anything to maintain advantage and privilege. Who are these "leaders of nonwhite movements" that are urging supremacy? They do not exist and have never existed; this is a classic case of questionable scholarship but, more important, disingenuous discourse based upon hearsay, propaganda, and the Whittle Communications communiqué that was circulated to thousands of white institutions, corporations, universities, and think tanks in the 1990s to stifle the Afrocentric movement. Furthermore, Harris has confused "Afrocentric" with what he calls "African American leaders," the former refers to an intellectual school of thought and the latter to those engaged in political or social policy. Unbeknownst to his readers, perhaps, the two are not the same and their agendas would be different, but Harris does not bother to explain his mixing of apples and oranges. Instead he goes further into a bizarre territory with this comment: "Black American scholars, authors and radio-talk show hosts urge people of African descent to see the world through African American eyes."[8] One wonders, through whose eyes should black Americans see the world if not their own?

Marvin Harris takes positions against the Afrocentric movement without ever once describing what the movement is or what constitutes its principal assumptions or main publications. Where he mentions anything resembling a critique he distorts the intellectual idea. One is curious why there are no citations referencing the Afrocentrists who are said to contribute this or that idea. At least, the readers would have been able to study for themselves the works of the Afrocentrists and other ethnocentric scholars such as the Asiocentrist Yoshitaka Miike to learn something about agency and action, had Harris obligated himself to provide the whole story.

Harris declares, for example, "one of the principal objectives of Afrocentrism is the inculcation of respect for black Africa's history."[9] The fact that enslavement maimed and brutalized African history and culture should be uncontestable. Why wouldn't Afrocentrists or anyone, for that matter, seek to inculcate respect for African history? Indeed, since Africans have been in the English-speaking America for nearly four hundred years, it is only because of racism that African history has not been taught. Erasing racism will never occur until African Americans, Latinos, Native Americans, and Asian Americans are able to view themselves as agents within their own history and until whites like Harris and others are willing to accept that type of agency as a normal process of human development.

Americans tend to fear a discourse on race. I find that both blacks and whites have apprehension about the way we discuss race. Whites feel that the discussion will focus on transgressions and blacks feel that the discussion will not bring out the true feelings of whites about blacks. Everyone fears that the discussants will tiptoe around the nitty-gritty issue of America's racial history. The one element missing in all of the dismal discussions about race is courage. Once you have a couple of individuals with a sense of courage and a willingness to lay bare their own feelings about the sorry state of race discourse in society, there is an immediate benefit to the conversation about humanity. It is not a conversation about race that the nation needs, but a conversation about our common humanity. Until we can, with the insight that comes from our best reflections, free ourselves from racial fears, which ultimately are about survival, neither whites nor blacks will be capable of imagining the future of a united America. This will involve the utmost attention to human detail because Americans will become whom we decide we should be. Our objective must always be openness to learn everything that we do not know about others. I want to know how you see yourself, your history, and your philosophy, as well as our common journey on the human road.

In the contemporary play by Von Washington Sr. called *Conspiracy*, the playwright has a black female graduate student named Arleta confront her white history professor, Henderson Lane, and her white dean about a paper she wants to present in class on Greeks in antiquity. The history professor quickly sees that the paper will be a deconstruction of the role of Greeks in human civilization and immediately discusses it with the dean, who then "conspires" with him to have the one black professor in history, Dr. De'Bwa, advise Arleta about her paper. The two whites hope that the professor, who is slated to give the annual lecture on Greek classics, will counsel Arleta against her paper's direction. Surprisingly, Arleta is able to convince the black professor, who is in line to deliver a Eurocentric account of Greek history and philosophy, that much of Greek philosophy had been stolen from Africa. What unfolds in the play is the unraveling of the conspiracy and an important lesson about ancient African history.

Washington's choice of the title of *Conspiracy* contains something of his view that the role of the established order seems to conspire against genuine communication. Neither the white professor nor the white dean wanted to have the conversation with Arleta that would have been necessary for a true understanding of how racism functions to prevent authentic interaction. Of course, the black professor, Dr. De'Bwa, also had a problem. If he were to be accepted by the white establishment as a smart black, he would have had to give a lecture that the whites approved. It would have been a speech devoid of any reference to the fact that Aesop was black or that the ancient Egyptians, from Africa, taught the Greeks astronomy, medicine, law, politics, architecture, art, mathematics, geometry, sculpture, music, and religion. In the end he could not do this, and consequently he found himself able to speak confidently about his own history. Having learned the lessons from Arleta, who was inspired by her deceased son to research the subjects, Dr. De'Bwa was convinced that he had behaved in an authentic manner; there was no psychological space for inauthenticity because truth had to be spoken.

There are many whites and blacks in our own circles who are faking it, when it comes to communication, because they fear the consequence of speaking their minds. How we overcome this burden of pain, this saddle of guilt, is the beginning of racial wisdom. What many whites secretly wish for are blacks who lie to them. There are always those who believe that the lie is easier to deal with than the truth.

The African American civil rights author Louis Lomax once wrote about how some blacks "fool" whites in their discourse on race. They refuse to tell whites the truth because they have become clever enough to know that whites appear to be pleased with lies and have been known to be infuriated with the truth.[10] As a legacy of the Great Enslavement when an enslaved African could endanger his life for telling the truth, genuine discourses on race in America are rare. Indeed, whites have their own version of evading the hard realities about the conditions in society, education, industry, and economics.

In some senses the two inauthentic responses to racial issues mirror the fear and distrust we have of each other.

The theorist Ama Mazama refers to African Americans who perpetrate "clean" lies as "malevolent agents" whose purpose is to win favor with the white supervisor, administrator, university provost, or CEO at the expense of truth.[11] They are clever enough to know which stereotypes of Africans exist in the minds of white folk. When people do not tell the truth and when we do not want to hear the truth we create some of the most dangerous moments in racial discourse because we operate on false information and attitudes. Eager for black approval or black love, there are whites who are faking their behavior as well. They articulate an appreciation for blacks, but in reality they demonstrate an appreciation for the caricature of black culture and history. Like the black malevolent agents, these whites are really corrupting weasels who play the interracial and intercultural game with the malevolent blacks or Asians or Latinos to the disadvantage of authentic communication. It might be said that everyone is "fronting."

A friend of mine, Arthur James, a pediatrician and obstetrician skilled in medical sciences, has often run into trouble in his community by trying to bring a meaningful discourse about the quality of black life to his city leaders. When you live in a city where the infant mortality, teen pregnancy, and low birth weight rates, and the number of children who enter kindergarten and graduate thirteen years later from high school all reveal a gross disparity between black and white children, the only discourse you can have, particularly when white children in the same municipality have some of the best quality of life factors in the nation, is about structural racism. Of course, a discussion about structural racism to city leaders is often fraught with pain. No one seems to want to hear about how racist one's own institutions are in a city. Had Arthur James lied, smiled, and told them that all was right in the city, he might have been tolerated, but the underlying racism would have remained unresolved. However, because of his efforts, several new interventions were put in place to create opportunities for communication and cooperation, and avenues for equality.

A discourse on racism is not a discourse about the moral values of black people. It is not a discourse about the intelligence of black people. It is not a discourse about the culture of black people. It is a discourse about race and politics or race and the possibility of reducing racism. But reduction of racism can only begin when we announce our assault on all forms of prejudice, even the prejudice against the black body itself.

Ronald L. Jackson II has written an intriguing book, *Scripting the Black Masculine Body: Identity, Discourse, and Racial Politics in Popular Media*, about the messages of black bodies, particularly black male bodies.[12] What Jackson does for discourse on the black masculine body is to bring it into the open as a topic for conversations about racism. The physical identification of the body with race and racism at the intersection of sexuality is one of the forbidden themes in the racist imagination. This is why the pioneering analysis of Lillian Smith during the segregated South in the United States had such a powerful impact. Smith's book of essays, *Killers of the Dream*, was one of the most biting critiques of racism written by a white person from the South.[13] She believed that segregation was one of the most dehumanizing systems ever devised and said so in no uncertain terms. However, it was the white woman—placed on a pedestal by white men, who in their own private lives had too often raped and abused black women—who became the symbol of the purity of the white race. To keep the white race pure became the standard cry of the white racists in the South during the 1940s and 1950s. This insanity eventually erupted in the violence perpetrated against a fourteen-year-old black boy, Emmett Till, in 1955, for whistling at a white woman named Carolyn Bryant in Money, Mississippi. Till was killed, his body mutilated and hidden in swampy water. Roy Bryant, Carolyn Bryant's husband, and J. W. Milam were charged and tried twenty-four days after the murder. A twelve-man white jury acquitted the two white men, Bryant and Milam, in about one hour on September 19, 1955. The attitude of the South was contained in the simple dictum that no black man, not even a man-child, could be allowed to whistle at a white woman for fear that the white race would lose its purity.[14]

On the other hand, the racist script of the black woman's body contained myth and mystery of another kind. Pat Reid-Merritt writes in her book *Sister Power* that black women were described stereotypically as "sexy, sultry Saffires, or they were Aunt Jemimas."[15] Furthermore, the image of the black woman's body was captured by a racial cartography of one and the other. Thus, the racial dualism (where white was pure meant that black was impure; white women were good and black women were evil) posed problems of signification and re-signification. Black people had to constantly reassign positive signification to themselves and their children while whites often accepted the idea of white superiority as a proper signification for whiteness. The white race held positive views about white women and their values, and negative views about black women and their values. There was this need to paint the black woman as sexually promiscuous. The fact that black women had more children than white women simply added to this spurious dilemma of madness in the white racist mind. Is the black woman having children because she is sexually promiscuous or is she sexually promiscuous and therefore having too many children? The quandary was indeed false.

The black woman was the pure representative of Africa, the "dark" continent, and an intricate, complex, and detailed articulation of sexual fantasies were at the heart of racial thinking. The black female body was seen as a form of darkness as in the case of Saartjie Bartmann, the Khoi-san woman, who fascinated Europe in the early twentieth century. In fact, the European audiences gazed upon Saartjie as if she were an animal. They caged her and used her as a curiosity. The size of her genitalia and buttocks were thought to be examples of the excessive sexuality and "primitiveness" of the African woman.

Of course, the body, whether male or female, is an interface between one's self and one's environment. I mean, if truth can be told, the black body has been iconic in its visibility in American society but at the same time invisible among certain groups, such as intellectuals, scientists, dramatists, and presidents. With Barack and Michelle Obama in the White House one might expect a difference in the nature of the icons of the black body. Still, how do we get beyond the iconography of the black body in the racial discourse in America?

A script tells us something about messages. If you are able to read a script, you should be able to say something about the message that is being conveyed. How does one learn to read scripts, especially those scripts that are physical bodies? I think that in erasing racism we must tackle the complexities of corporeal reality itself and that means using our own bodies to normalize discourse about all human activities and possibilities. Ultimately this is the meaning of any form of interracial communication.

To a large degree it is society that teaches us about the scripts we use, and we use them in ways that teach others that our usage is correct. I can give you a whole lot of scripts about black bodies that can be read, and indeed are read, by society in general. We can discuss this scripting with an eye toward developing new ways of writing with our own bodies or new methods of interpreting what it is that we see when we see bodies and so forth. No one is locked into a script, and the bodies themselves may change and become something else. Nevertheless, to erase racism in American society we have to change the nature of our scripting of bodies. When South African apartheid ended in 1994 with the election of Nelson Mandela the country had to change its laws regarding black miners. Before independence black miners lived in male-only hostels, were separated from their families, and went to work five miles underground only to end each workday standing stark naked for a full body search by white men.

The black body, whether male or female, conveys numerous messages about the power, intelligence, status, sexuality, health, and virility of the black person. Almost all black people know that when listening to or watching sports the sports announcer will eventually use words that are coded in such a way that they could only refer to a black person. One of the most common is to say that a person is truly "athletic." One wants to tell the announcer not to mention "athleticism" or some other word that is intended to diminish the skill of the competitor. What we object to is not the word itself but the racializing of the word. I have seen this use of the term in other racially organized societies such as South Africa, France, Colombia, Britain, and Brazil. The black body, with its centuries of social and physical contortions in the face of oppression, has become, in the antiquity of racism, novel, indeed, exotic to those who made it so. To erase racism in any society is to begin the process of destroying prejudice itself.

President Jean-Bertrand Aristide of Haiti asks in his book, *Eyes of the Heart*, "How do we wash away the dirt of prejudice?"[16] Although the president was writing about the conflict between the elite and the masses in his native Haiti, he was asking a universal question that has importance for any discussion on racism. Of course, the answer must be that we get rid of prejudice with a cleansing flood produced by a common family of resisters to all forms of discrimination.

Perceptions matter. A few years ago a white university dean told a gathering of African American department faculty that she did not believe there was a black community in Philadelphia. Of course, there was objection to this line of thinking and it made many people in the audience wonder in what universe was the dean living. She had just arrived in Pennsylvania from Louisiana and spoke without knowledge of the historical situation in the old black community. When she was questioned about her statement she became agitated that someone would even question her. I think that this is at the core of black-white communication in the nation. The dean assumed that she knew something that she did not know and refused to accept the truth as told to her by faculty members. I see this as a matter of perception and, obviously, arrogance. Let me explain what I mean.

There are two arrogant models of behavior that operate in racial situations. One model shapes itself in the racial dialogue by assuming knowledge. Many black people believe that whites assume they are the authorities in all matters that relate to black people. This is called the *arrogance of ignorance* model. The dean at the university was a perfect example of this model. Coming to a Northern university with a long history of self-confident black people, the Southern dean felt that she had the right to say anything and do anything. She was met with an immediate and definitive negation.

There are whites who think they must lead blacks in any situation that involves blacks and whites on an equal footing. This is called the *foolhardy* model. It is as if white parents and institutions have instructed their children from the earliest age that they, even if they are not as gifted as the black child, must not be placed in a position where they take leadership from blacks. Indeed, many black supervisors, presidents, CEOs, professors, army officers, managers, and coaches have run into problems with whites who assume that they know better than the person leading them. A considerable amount of racial conflict gathers around the *foolhardy* model of human behavior. However, the election of Barack Obama should serve to complicate the racist notion of leadership. When a man of African origin rises to the presidency of the United States it means that the highest position in the American polity serves as a model to other social behaviors.

Of course, we should all be aware of what this really means. The election of Obama must be seen in its totality to make sense in the drive to erase racism. After all, the achievement is not a miracle, as some have proclaimed, but the result of hard work on the part of masses of young white and black students, progressives of the Old Left, liberals, disenchanted and disaffected Republicans, womanists and feminists, and religious social activists.

Then there is the factor that Noam Chomsky mentioned when he talked about the fact that the country is more civilized than it was forty years ago. In Chomsky's opinion, the historic election illustrated the civilized nature of the country. While I am also extremely pleased, I happened to be in Mississippi on November 4, 2008, when 88 percent of the white vote went against Barack Obama. The issue of change in the character of the nation can be problematic when we do not understand the full extent of the resistance to civilization.

What I would like to see is the constant struggle for civilization coming in every sector of society. I know that we have not seen the full extent of this change in national character in the educational sector because I work in it every day and see the results of the rumpled spirits that are unable to climb out of the barrel of ignorance yet wish to keep others back. When each person, or a significant enough number of Americans, fights against all forms of racist insult, ignorance, discrimination, and prejudice, whether in spirit or in action, in voice or in writing, then we will be on the road to becoming a civilized nation.

We can never claim this status so long as "citizens" permit, allow, or acquiesce in racial attacks on other citizens or simply other people because of their racial background and physical features.

I am not the first to be disappointed about the lack of national unity on the necessity for the Obama doctrine of change. Actually, I went to give lectures at the University of Witwatersrand in Johannesburg, the National Chengchi University in Taipei, and the Shanghai Normal University in China a few weeks after the election. Just the mention of the fact that Obama had won gained me thunderous applause in those three separate places. However, I told the audiences that we must not read into this election what is not in it. The 2008 election of Barack Obama, as important as it was, has not effectively changed the racial hierarchy and economic structure of American society. We are different as a society, to be sure, but we are still not what many in the United States and around the world think we are. Less than 50 percent of white voters voted for Obama on the national level. And, as I have noted, there were some states, called red states, where white voters rejected Obama.

The reason this is important is that Obama should have won by an enormous landslide if we were looking at all the rational evidence for his victory. In the first place, the incumbent president, George W. Bush, had an approval record of less than 30 percent during most of the campaign, the economy came apart at the seams as banks failed and employees were laid off in massive downsizing, the Iraqi and Afghanistan wars ground on to no objective conclusion, and the American electorate said it wanted change in every national poll. Yet Obama, the candidate for change, did not win by a landslide; he won a good victory, but a victory that should have demonstrated the absolute moral outrage of a people fed up with war, racism, and prejudice.

# CHAPTER ONE
# THE TORTURED DREAM

Since September 11, 2001, there has been a general impression, maintained by media surveys, that the United States is more united than ever. People from every ethnic group, all social classes, and many religions were impacted by the spearing planes launched against the World Trade Center and the Pentagon. The national reaction, like that of the international community, was one of horror mixed with solidarity. There was cohesion in the national spirit that was marked by outpourings of assistance and expressions of the "national will." Yet clearly, unity around a common tragedy is not patriotism—nor is it as simple as it seems.

A reporter called me soon after the attack to ask if I would comment about the loyalty and true patriotism of the African American people. I told him that the common expression of horror and patriotism had little to do with each other. The terror that befell New York City; Washington, D.C.; and the Pennsylvania countryside did not trigger the loyalty of African Americans. Indeed, African Americans are not only patriotic but willing to defend their homeland against any external or internal threat.

There has never been a credible question about the willingness of African Americans to defend the interests of their country, even while being attacked by their fellow Americans. We have participated in every war against those defined as enemies of the nation, yet we have an abiding issue that sits at the table during every discussion of national unity. Justice, for the descendants of the millions of Africans enslaved during that terrible period of American history, has eluded our society, and discussion of it creates unusually harsh reactions from many Americans. The lingering effects of the enslavement are current and immediate in almost all sectors of American life: health, education, employment, housing, and law. Our patriotism as African Americans does not lessen our criticism of the way our nation has treated us.

The implementation of justice is the most difficult of all national tasks. How do you bring about real equality except, as the ancient Egyptian priests said, to do *maat*, justice? Through the numerous protests and calls for political and racial justice, we have seen how fully denial is entrenched in American society. Even before September 11, many Americans, black and white, knew that something more *must* be done.

I have always been convinced that the nation could resolve the remaining issues of injustice and advance society through a philosophy of fairness. African Americans are not a beggar people; we simply want the nation to confront its own history and do justice. Sitting in the Birmingham Church of the Advent, the Episcopal cathedral in Birmingham, Alabama, waiting to hear Archbishop Desmond Tutu deliver a message of hope for humanity on April 19, 2002, I noticed an anonymous African American man making his way to the front of the church. He was wearing a white T-shirt with the word "ERACISM" on the front and back. No more fitting message could have been brought by any speaker than that delivered by the young man who braved the large, mostly white audience to take his seat in the third pew. No orator could have spoken any more clearly about what the national mission ought to be at this time.

In his provocative book *The Debt: What America Owes to Blacks*, Randall Robinson speaks eloquently about the crimes against Africans in America, stuttering only when he discusses payment for the debt.[1] I believe that reparations can be paid in a variety of ways, which I will explain in this book. However, Robinson raises the issues that must be placed squarely before the American people if we are to truly come together in the spirit of unity: African Americans live inside a fog of accumulated abuses. Until we understand the nature of that fog we will never be able to resolve adequately our national crisis. From political elections to international conferences against racism, African Americans have a number of grievances that further add to centuries of abuse.

In the 2000 presidential contest between George W. Bush and Al Gore, the most startling allegations of abuse occurred among African American districts in Florida. Kwesi Mfume of the National Association for the Advancement of Colored People (NAACP) charged that in Broward, Duval, Palm Beach, and Miami counties, African Americans were prevented from voting, blocked by police from going to the polls, given false information regarding their registration status, and had to contend with misplaced ballot boxes. To say the least, there was anger, outrage, and distrust within the African American community to a degree that had rarely been seen after a contemporary election. Many African Americans, among others, still believe that the 2000 election was stolen.

On a Philadelphia radio talk show the morning after the Supreme Court of the United States ruled that the counting of ballots in Florida had to stop, black callers raised the question of a conspiracy. Some claimed that had a similar situation—where the brother of the presidential candidate was the governor of the province that would decide the election and the candidate's father had been a previous president as well as a former national intelligence director—occurred in another, less democratic country, there would be no question in the minds of the public that the election was stolen. Others opined that the majority of the justices had ties to the Bush camp, either having sons or relatives working in law firms supporting Bush or being beholden to former president George H. W. Bush for their judgeships.[2]

The vilest and most severe criticism from the African American community was leveled at Justice Clarence Thomas, whom some callers thought appeared to be the proverbial Uncle Tom. Thomas's style of not asking any questions of the lawyers arguing in the Court angered some blacks, who believed that he was appointed by former president George H. W. Bush because he had no depth in the African American community and would support white, often racist, interests against his own people. The late Supreme Court Justice Thurgood Marshall, they said, would not have sat on the bench without opening his mouth. Of course, Thomas, as always, voted with the conservative side in the 5–4 decision that gave the election to Bush.

In August 2001 the Bush administration refused to send Secretary of State Colin Powell, the highest African American official in the United States, to the United Nations Conference Against Racism held in Durban, South Africa. This refusal by the Bush administration was a demonstration of the resiliency of anachronistic views in the American government. This was a childish reaction to the possibility of criticism of America's racial history. Furthermore, refusal to attend the conference suggested that the American government wanted no part in a meaningful discourse on racism. The official reason President George W. Bush refused to send Colin Powell to the conference was twofold: He feared the possibility that the conference would declare Zionism to be racism and that is would develop a resolution calling for reparations for the enslavement of Africans. To the majority of African Americans, however, the refusal to even take part in this conference was also a slap in the face.

The United States government did not initiate, promote, or profit from the Holocaust; it did initiate, promote, and profit from the enslavement of Africans. Furthermore, whether or not Zionism as practiced in Israel discriminates against Arabs in the same way that racism in the United States causes discrimination against blacks is a legitimate issue for a conference concerned with racial hierarchies. The refusal of the United States to show up was a troubling reminder to African Americans that victory has not yet been realized.

One cannot forget that the American delegation walked out of the conference just a few days before the attacks on New York City and Washington, D.C. African Americans, always ready to defend the honor of their nation, rallied against the enemies of the state—the very state that just turned its back on issues critical to African Americans. The black community saw America's action as a tragic situation because Secretary of State Powell, the most visible African person in a leadership position in a Western nation, had been rendered speechless and invisible in the dispute in Durban. The United States, the nation that had gained the most from the enslavement of Africans and the one that had done the most to obliterate the disadvantages of that condition, refused to take leadership or to even meet in the same room as other world nations.

Add to this record of abuse, the refusal to discuss reparations for the enslavement of Africans, and the lack of a commitment to end racism, and one can see why anger still exists in the black community. I want to vividly depict the sustained brutality against African Americans in order to retrace the steps that may lead us to the fork in the road where our nation took a wrong turn.

This book will not be an essay on Patrick Dorismond, Amadou Diallo, Abner Louima, Rodney King, or scores of other black victims of police brutality and killings. This is also not an essay about blacks losing their minds and advocating attacks on whites out of some notion of vengeance. This is a story that is more than the periodic urban revolts that occur over police murders of African American men in city streets. This is more; this is about a dream that a dreamer named Martin Luther King Jr. once had. It is a human story that can be resolved only by humans engaging in the most open discussion about purpose and will.

On May 4, 1969, James Forman and his supporters interrupted a worship service at the well-known Riverside Church in New York City to present the "Black Manifesto" and a demand for $500 million in reparations to African Americans. Since that time, low-level discussions about reparations have been held in seminars, workshops, and churches. Books have been written detailing what the settlement should or should not be. Soon after the Black Manifesto was issued, Arnold Schuchter, in his book *Reparations*, assigned a leading role to the church, seeing it as a bastion of revolutionary activity.[3] He was sadly mistaken about the role the Christian church would play in bringing about justice, for, like the rest of American society, the church has been afraid to confront the sin in its own soul of supporting slavery and discrimination for so long.

In more recent times, attorneys have filed suits against Aetna and other companies said to have profited from the enslavement of Africans. But this meaningful and well-intentioned movement must not lose sight of the healing that is necessary in the nation. It is so easy to slip into a mode of bitterness that leads us away from erasing racism. We must confront racism at its origins, defeat it in the American soul, and move toward a new beginning in national relations.

Reparations for enslavement and discrimination are critical issues. Yet discussions about reparations have not detracted from the countless seminars and workshops on race relations. There are many forums for talking about how we ought to live together in this society. Like a lot of people, I am exhausted by some of the discourses on race and racism in this country. I have been particularly offended by the sociological explanations of racism and the "do nothing" or "blame the victims" attitude that many of those analyses imply.

Racism often becomes somebody else's problem when it is really a national concern. What is often presented about American racism is a detached, sterile view of racial animosities in this society. I believe this is one reason Robinson's *The Debt* resonates so well with those who care about the future of America. It is not filled with invective, but with a sustained rage against a known evil. Unlike Cornel West's more celebrated book *Race Matters*, Robinson's work clearly identifies white racial domination in all sectors of society, including education, as the greatest obstacle to racial harmony. West, on the other hand, is memorable for his discourse on black nihilism.[4]

The election of George W. Bush as the forty-third president of the United States is a watershed in the lives of African Americans, one way or another. It shattered the notion of fair play. It reopened the sores of segregation laws and the evils that surrounded voting in the South during the twentieth century when millions of African Americans were disenfranchised by racist policies. Despite the hype of the War on Terrorism and the subsequent rhetoric of the war on Iraq, historical criticism of the Bush administration will focus on the 2000 presidential election, which forced the nation to discuss how presidents are chosen, voting rights, and constitutional provisions for resolving election crises.

Clearly, the election, inter alia, showed the extent of the political disconnect between the African American and white populations in the United States. Furthermore, private investigations in Florida uncovered voting malfeasance reminiscent of the beginning of the 1900s, which resulted in voter disaffection. To write about race in America, one must write about power, force, custom, social will, law, and double vision. Indeed, the reality of our national injury can best be understood by referring to the Promise and the Wilderness, political and social metaphors current in American society. What is implied by Promise is an express assurance that something good is to be expected. What Wilderness implies is something difficult, perhaps unknown; a place where one does not know what to expect. Indeed, the Wilderness may reveal something beautiful—but it is equally possible for it to deliver something evil. A declaration that something will be given—for example, life, liberty, and the pursuit of happiness—is the crux of the American Promise. The 2000 presidential election was one more piece in a long list of evidence that African Americans had not escaped the Wilderness.

A disproportionate number of blacks remain at the socioeconomic bottom of American society. This has nothing to do wtih intelligence, with industry, with the ability to perform a task, or with cultural values; the Wilderness experience is shaped preeminently by the economic deprivation caused by racial discrimination.

I am reminded of H. G. Wells's *The Time Machine*, which was written during a period of rampant and uncontrolled capitalism, industrialization, and monopoly economics. Wells envisioned two groups of people living in some way-off century that held opposing views because of their experiences. In Wells's era-shaped imagination, the genteel Eloi were the descendants of the upper classes and the cannibalistic Morlocks were the descendants of the lower classes. Whatever the meaning embedded in Wells's mind, what we have now is the legacy of this binary thinking as a part of the social and racial history of the Western world.

The entitlements of the Promise exist because of the structure of racism in American society, not because of any special talents or superior intelligence; it is merely the participation in the Eurocentric domination of other cultures that creates the entitlements. Indeed, those blacks, Asians, and Eastern and Southern Europeans—groups not normally thought of as white—may be "Promise people" if they accept ideas such as that whites are superior and blacks are inferior, that America is an Anglo-Germanic nation, and that Christianity is the religion of civilization. On the other hand, one is assigned to the Wilderness because of previous traditions of servitude, skin color, and, sometimes, political perspectives. Of course, one can also *choose* the Wilderness, but in doing so one is seeking identification with a social, cultural, or political reality. As in Wells's book, it is possible to highlight the duality in our society by stating clear definitions of the ongoing struggle. A chasm of misinformation exists between the two visions, the Promise and the Wilderness, and because it is too large to cross in casual conversation, the chasm often leads to racial hostilities. We have seen this in recent years with the debates about Jewish racism and black anti-Semitism. We have witnessed discussions about black-Korean relations or black-Cuban relations ad infinitum. Most often, however, this is the arena of black-white relations throughout the country.

The 2000 presidential election in Florida turned on the fact that the number of African Americans voting was at an all-time high and the attitude was one of revenge against George W. Bush's brother Gov. Jeb Bush, who had campaigned against affirmative action in a state with a known history of racial discrimination against blacks. The overwhelming burden of Florida's racial history, the competitiveness of the election between Al Gore and George W. Bush, and the African Americans' complaints about Jeb Bush's policies combined to mobilize the African American community as it had never been mobilized before. It is usual to think of two fundamental American conversations about race as the dispossession of the Native Americans and the historical mistreatment of Africans. All other discussions are derivatives.

Thus, the ethnic cleansing of the land to make way for European settlers is an unspeakable act, though it is the backdrop for thousands of circumstances. The Native Americans and the Kanaka Moloi of Hawaii lost their lands, their country, their ancestral mounds and sacred forests, and were left with ancient memories because of what is called *European expansionism* but which was, in fact, the theft of the land. Africans almost lost their identity, all familial connections, and an entire continent, and were often left with devastating isolation and terrible anomie. Both conversations, the dispossession of the Native Americans and the enslavement of the Africans, are interconnected in any real discussion of race and the future of America. Do presidents and national legislators really want to hear the issues as they are being put forth by the African American Wilderness dwellers?

Former President Bill Clinton, in one of the defining moments of his second administration, claimed race as one of the conversations that he wanted the nation to have in order to resolve old habits and prejudices. Clinton recognized the inevitability of the clash of races in America if we did not move quickly to engage each other honestly about the lingering effects of the enslavement of Africans.

Indeed, Clinton's creation of the National Committee on Race, headed by the venerable John Hope Franklin, was a significant step in the right direction. But the failure of this committee could have been predicted because it did not deal with the fundamental issues impinging on race. Too often, national leaders have skirted the core and played around the edges of the issues. To discuss race means to tackle white racial supremacy as an ideology, conscious or unconscious, in the American psyche; it is to discuss the issue of "African agency," that is, an America in which African Americans do not have to abandon their cultural heritage in order to be Americans. Unfortunately, the good intentions of the National Committee on Race fell on hard ground because the issue was defined as "race relations" rather than eliminating white racial supremacy. Nevertheless, Clinton knew that something had to be done; what was tried was ineffective because it omitted the core issues.

In response to Clinton's engagement, President George W. Bush chose the path of disengagement with race, although he had in his cabinet the highest-ranking African American in history. National Security Advisor Condeleezza Rice has reached one of the highest levels of government service of any African American woman, yet her international advice and policy recommendations have been criticized as conservative and often reactionary. Thus, Bush has had his own critics for choosing blacks for his administration who were often seen as lacking in identification with the Wilderness struggle for equality, human rights, and the elimination of racism.

Strong and powerful antiracist intellectuals such as Derrick Bell, Joe Feagin, Maulana Karenga, Manning Marable, Cornel West, Marimba Ani, Andrew Hacker, and Jonathan Kozol have come down on one side or the other of the raging debate over the future of race relations in the United States. They have been armed with poignant studies showing that African American males are incarcerated at a rate far out of proportion to their number in the overall American population. They have reports indicating that one-third of black American men in their twenties are under the control of the criminal justice system. In California, where blacks make up only 7 percent of the population, more than 42 percent of African American males in the state will be imprisoned, on probation, or on parole in the year 2003. This contrasts with the fact that only 5 percent of white men in their twenties and 13 percent of Hispanic men of that same age group were in the criminal system in California in 1999.

Since the 1980s, when the so-called three strikes rule went into effect in California, the prison terms of black men have become even more disproportionate. Certainly drug arrests constitute a sizable proportion of the arrests, but even discounting the arrests for drugs, other factors seem to come into play. According to the *New York Times*, African Americans were charged seventeen times more often than whites under the new California law.[5] But these facts suggest the *result* of discrimination; the act or process itself is far more insidious, subtle, and difficult to ferret out.

Despite what is evidently the result of social, racial, or economic bias, we have been entertained by conservatives such as John Bunzel, Dinesh D'Souza, Stephan Thernstrom, and Linda Chavez announcing, among other things, the end of racism. Even the once clear-headed Jim Sleeper has come out with a call for "an end to blackness," by which he means an end to African Americans viewing themselves as people of African descent. It is as if one called for an end to Jewishness or Frenchness or Chineseness. Ted Koppel announced a decision in 1996 to produce at least one program per month on racism in the United States, indicating that the respected host felt that racism had not ended and in fact that it was a serious issue to which he should devote attention. But even Koppel, the contemporary Edward R. Murrow, could not sustain such a discussion for long, and after less than a year the idea was abandoned.

One of the biggest issues to be confronted by the American democracy is the historical tendency to denounce anything and anyone that calls attention to the country's dreadful past. It is like talking to someone who has killed his mother: How do you have a real conversation with that person without stumbling over the issue? We have to raise the case for reparations on historical and moral grounds without calling for individual guilt to be expressed by individual white people. I see a collective guilt of the American nation, some corporate institutions, universities, and churches. Those whites who were complicit in slavery and segregation and those who have partaken and benefited from the largesse amassed by the profiteers of racism have added to the warrant for reparations.

African Americans know some things about the conditions of race relations firsthand. Yet our knowledge has not brought us liberation in the sense of equal justice, social and political equality, economic justice and opportunity, or equity of education. Many promises have been made—usually during periods of national guilt brought on by the persuasive rhetoric of justice initiated by black civil rights activists —but those promises have been broken numerous times during periods of forgetfulness. In the cycles of knowing and not knowing, the African American has been a constant reminder of the nation's racial past and its potential future. The key to our survival as a people has not been compulsive optimism or self-delusion, but a prophetic sense of justice, a belief that one day wrong will be righted and truth will triumph across the American landscape. There is no greater vision of harmony than that realized by the proponents of reparations.

Several political appointments have been made that merit close scrutiny. President George W. Bush's appointment of Judge Al Gonzales of Texas as White House counsel, Colin Powell as secretary of state, and Condoleezza Rice as national security advisor, among other Latino and African appointees, was an attempt to ameliorate the fury raging in the emotional heart of African Americans. Part of the problem for this Bush administration is the memory of the previous Bush administration and its lack of aggressive support for civil rights.

Conquering the past has become even more treacherous in recent years because of the rapid increase in the number of people who know nothing substantive about American history. If we are ever in danger of losing a sense of national identity and mission, without the focusing brought about by national crisis, then it seems that the danger comes from a lack of education about the nation's past, not from new discourses around race and racism. I shudder to think that schools, universities, churches, and other institutions committed to some notion of truth are often the greatest impediments to justice. They have been quick to identify with the populist, self-serving, and dehumanizing values of society.

Yale University students discovered in 2001 that their institution was founded with money made from the dirty business of the slave trade. But Yale is not alone; profitting from the enslavement of Africans was a national project, not merely an individual corporate or personal one. There were individual whites who had nothing to do with the enslavement of blacks per se. Of course, most whites participated in the privilege that came with whiteness in a racist society, and there is culpability when one receives the rewards of someone else's suffering and degradation. The fact that one of the most prestigious universities in the nation has a history interwined with the slave trade only demonstrates the extent of the crime.

"I am not white; I am Polish," a recent immigrant once responded to me after I gave a speech about white privilege. I felt the sincerity in his voice, the attempt to announce his retention of culture, and his dissociation with slave masters, but I knew as I walked away from the discussion that it would be only a matter of time—a short time—before the newcomer realized that he had privilege because he was defined as white. And the fact of the matter is that when he realized it, he would use all the privileges that came with it in America. In fact, the conflicts that African Americans have often experienced with new immigrants are caused by a misperception about African Americans and the history of America. There are few measures in place to ensure a proper understanding of American history. Immigrants typically learn American history as national self-compliment and gain no coherent understanding of African Americans except in stereotypical terms.

The United States of America is a country comprised of many cultures and a multiplicity of national identities, which are often complicated and compromised by history. Jews and Germans, Poles and Germans, Spaniards and Basques, Turks and Kurds, Ibo and Hausa, Koreans and Japanese, and so forth all live in one political society. In addition to this complex mix of nationalities and histories, there is the abiding African presence in the land. One cannot consider the periodic fury in the African American community, defined by responses to perceived or real broken promises, such as the prospects of political justice, without an appeal to historical experience. Like all political complications of American society, often challenged and debated, cursed and praised, African Americans' actions are based also on perceptions of national identity.

*E pluribus unum*, "One out of many," was conceived as an expression of early Americans' desire to see one central government instead of thirteen separate governments. This was not, as some have thought, an attempt to create one race or one culture that could be called "American." There is neither one American culture nor one American identity; there is only one American citizenship, which covers a multitude of cultures, religions, political attitudes, and races.

While it is true that we are linked by certain social and political commonalities that force us to perceive our situations in similar ways, each cultural group has its own historical traditions. This does not mean that there are no commonalities, because there are definite civic, political, cultural, and economic symbols of unity within American society that emerge from our daily interactions with each other in language, literature, and law. We are, in a sense, making American culture, but it is not yet made.

There is something troubling about the national picture, bringing into focus the disparate voices of the many Americans who have entered into the compact with each other. Some voices are harsh and disgruntled, seeking to overturn the federal government; others are critical and vocal, seeking to find accommodation; some are tired, desperate to maintain the old order; and still others, largely African American, are insisting on finding the pieces to a broken dream. In Martin Luther King Jr.'s day the dream was to have proper lodging after a long day's journey, to have residential mobility, and to be able to vote for the candidate of one's choice. These were reachable, palpable goals.

The African American relationship with the American nation has always been tinged with suspicion. The 2000 presidential election in Florida only added to this distrust. We have seen too many trap doors, too many booby traps, and have felt the lash of national ignorance so many times that the masses of African Americans often anticipate racism at the door of opportunity. But the idea of erasing racism appeals to us from a moral and ethical standpoint.

Two visions tend to encompass the entirety of the many views. Martin Luther King Jr. dreamed of America as the Promised Land. But his writings and speeches give every indication that we were not yet in the Promised Land. In fact, we were still in the Wilderness.

When Sen. Trent Lott praised Strom Thurmond, the arch segregationist senator of South Carolina, on the occasion of Thurmond's one-hundredth birthday in December 2002, it set off a chain reaction among Republicans and Democrats alike. Lott, at the time the majority leader of the Senate, expressed his view that Thurmond should have been elected president in 1948. Certain symbols of racism have come to represent a belief in the maintenance of white racial domination. Thus, attachment to the Confederate flag, praise of the segregationist era, acceptance of white-only policies in clubs, and membership in white supremacist organizations are understood by African Americans to indicate a belief in racism. This is why Trent Lott got into trouble. The nation has moved beyond the public acceptance of brute racism by national officials. Making the two visions one is going to be a long struggle, but I am optimistic that this can happen.

I think for African Americans the test of faith comes down to how we believe our fellow citizens, those who constitute the majority opinions, have treated our dreams of the Promised Land. If we feel unfettered, without the possibility of discrimination and unoppressed by society, we are either close to the Promised Land or have sympathies that tie us to the Promised Land.

On the other hand, those of us who experience discrimination, consistently bad treatment from authorities, redlining of property, ethnic and racial profiling, loan discrimination, insurance discrimination, educational maltreatment, and racial or religious bias often see nothing but a barren future.

There is a sense that Africans from the seventeenth century, during and after the enslavement, have been, by and large, people of the Wilderness. While others may have experienced disillusionment based on political ideologies—such as federal gun laws, use of federal lands, environmental pollution, oppressiveness of big government, and the like—only African Americans have continuously experienced the stark reality of being outsiders in our own country.

Europeans arriving in America from the disunion and anarchy of despotic and sometimes brutal governments in the old European countries felt that they had indeed discovered a Promised Land. For them, the biblical "city that sitteth upon a hill" was found when they landed in North America. Sharing the land with Africans, Hispanics, Asians, and others has often been problematic because of the doctrine of white supremacy. There remain in the United States whites who believe that America is a white land, delivered—promised, as it were —by the Bible.

While there have been periodic outbursts of white violence against the government shaped by the sense of being betrayed by the

Promised Land, these actions have often been attempts to assert their own view of the American Promise. This is true whether one speaks of the eighteenth century Shays's Rebellion in western Massachusetts, the Whiskey Rebellion in western Pennsylvania, or the more contemporary militia and paramilitary operations throughout the nation.

On the other hand, those from a hundred different ethnic groups who came to America aboard thousands of slave ships had a necessarily different perspective than Europeans who dissolved into whiteness and, hence, privilege. Africans found here no abiding faith in the human spirit, no sensitivity to the demands of ethnic and cultural diversity, and no Promised Land—only an unfamiliar and lonely Wilderness, without freedom and, after the Civil War, without equality. The irony of all of this is that the nation was not a Wilderness made by Native Americans but a Wilderness of spirit made by whites looking for a promise. They enslaved, segregated, discriminated against, and pushed Africans to the fringes of human history, often denying our humanity in the process. Our psychology was, therefore, formed on the margins of the Promise. Only those who were rebels, revolutionaries, and resisters fought against this psychology to carve out a reasonable independence of mind and some modicum of human dignity.

But the real contest in the United States, of course, is whether or not we are able to define a common vision, a uniting perspective of reality. In fact, quite a number of white writers have decried the breakdown of common purpose and common objective in our society. I am of the opinion that such commonalities never existed in the first place. As certainly as I would love to see a more egalitarian society, nothing in American history convinces me of such a radical democratic assessment.[6] Finally, when I see widespread revulsion against racism and the vestiges of racism, I will have a greater degree of optimism about the future of a united country.

In fact, the dynamic tension between different racial visions is the ideal content of our national project. In his rambling monograph *The Disuniting of America*, Arthur Schlesinger Jr. reasserts the liberal democratic idea of a common culture produced by integration of Africans, Native Americans, Puerto Ricans, Mexicans, eastern and southern Europeans, and Asians into what he obviously believes is the northern European core America.[7] This vision of the United States created African Americans who often disliked themselves, disparaged their continent of origin, believed in white superiority, and blamed themselves for their own enslavement. Frantz Fanon understood this phenomenon and identified it in his book *Black Skin, White Masks*, and Albert Memmi examined it in detail in his book *The Colonizer and the Colonized*.[8] Both knew that the horrible details of racism affected the psyches of the victims. Suffocating and stunting cultural growth, racial oppression thoroughly and emphatically undermines self-concept, identity, relationships, and attachment to ancestors. Acceptance of the idea that white supremacy is the standard by which African Americans should live would mean the abandonment of African histories, and the obliteration of culture and the commonality of the national idea of pluralism.

Other, more conservative, writers have argued in a similar vein that the American society is essentially a white society. The conservative view suggests that the African American would have to divest himself or herself of any relationship with an African origin or culture and accept white cultural history and values in order to benefit from the economic possibilities in American society. These are the radical Europeanists who would recreate America in their own image. And obviously in such a society the "whiter" you behave, the greater the economic benefits. Admittedly, some whites feel disaffected from the Promise or hold to it so dearly that they would destroy it to protect it.

The April 1995 bombing of the Alfred P. Murrah Federal Building in Oklahoma City by Timothy McVeigh was a clear indication that some Americans are so embittered toward the US government that they are willing to murder innocent people. This is an anger fueled by antifederalist propaganda and a siege mentality encouraged by militias that believe that the federal government is at war with its own citizens.

The votarists see the government shootouts with members of militias; the siege on the Branch Davidian sect in Waco, Texas; and the appointment of Mexican and African Americans to cabinet posts as crimes against their view of the US Constitution.

In contrast to African Americans, Native Americans, and Mexican Americans, for example, the disgruntled white extremist groups do not point to historical discrimination against them. Their anger is fueled by suggestions that America is a multiracial and multiethnic society. It is the inclusion of others that often triggers the outbreaks of antagonism toward the federal government. There are few parallels between the rage that one finds in the heart of African Americans and that lurking in the hearts of whites disaffected with the federal government.

Our disaffection stems from a crisis of confidence in the social and relational compact of neighbors. One can find African Americans who believe that the federal government has often demonstrated more good faith than ordinary private citizens in correcting past injustices. There are still white Americans who harbor deep racial resentment against Africans. Indeed, this is a further reason for black disaffection, because there is nothing in African American history that indicates a reason for such white resentment.

Nevertheless, as African Americans our souls have been split. This is not, as W. E. B. Du Bois saw it, a psychic problem but a political one. We are plagued not by a double consciousness but by a tug between supporting the government as our best hope for ending discrimination and loving the country for which many have died, as opposed to social nihilism, alienation, and anarchy. There are no cyclones to carry us away into some magical Land of Oz. There are no tin woodsman, no scarecrow, and no lion looking for the Emerald City. We are abandoned to ourselves, becoming, in effect, our own wizards.

What African Americans have had to ask each other in regard to this is the Lion King's question in terms of success: "Have you sold your soul?" Obviously, those who have a paternalistic and chauvinistic attitude toward the African American community seek lost souls wherever they can find them. The attack on the idea of a multiplicity of cultures, diversity, and multiculturalism as "divisive" is truly anti-democratic. Just paying us for the damage done to our psyches would be a moral victory for the nation, but in the end there must be a combination of adjustments—that is, back pay—for psychological, physical, and political deprivation. We are not yet out of the woods in terms of the destructive power unleashed against our defenseless and innocent people. Our experiences are the nightmares at the core of the American Dream.

Some commentators—liberal and conservative—have predicated their attacks on multiculturalism, Afrocentricity, feminism, and other pluralistic ideas upon the false belief that the dominant motifs of happiness, economic justice, fair play, and equality are fundamentally European male conceptions of society, and that any discussion of "fixing" what others consider to be inequalities is divisive. One reason that reparation is frowned upon by some white reactionaries is that it exposes, more than most issues, the hypocrisy at the center of the American ideal. But I believe that the issue of reparations has the potential to unite the progressive forces in America toward a final push for equal justice. We must be willing to confront the terror and to terrorize those who snipe at every advance made toward justice.

All the whites I speak with know that my experience in the United States, for the most part, has been quite different from theirs. I suspect that deep in their hearts they also know that privileging whiteness racially and culturally undermines a national transformation. This remains a source for a furious relationship.[9] Whatever my position in the American society, and whatever my achievements, my joys, and my rewards, I realize that I have been punished, denied opportunities, and categorized negatively by many in the majority because of my racial origin. Of course, "still I rise" is Maya Angelou's African American anthem to racial hatred.

Thus, while race has characterized American social, economic, and political issues since the seventeenth century, class and gender have been used to underscore certain racial constructions. For example, "middle-classness" remains more closely identified with the white race and "lower-classness" with blacks in the United States. This is exacerbated by the persistence of the employment differential between whites and blacks. It is greatly agitated by the fact that the wealth accrued to white males during the period of African enslavement and racial segregation remains the driving force of the American economy. Poor black women with children continue to be disproportionately represented among the most destitute in the nation, further augmenting the gender inequality.

I recognize the subtleties of ethnic distinctions and the growing populations of Hispanics and Asians in the United States, but I believe that race in America is defined by the expression of and resistance to white supremacy. The initial inequality of the slave master and the enslaved, the dominator and the dominated, the oppressor and the oppressed, is the single factor driving our discussions of class and gender and setting the agenda for discourses on race.

Even now, after the September 11, 2001, terror, many of the paramilitary groups that train to attack the federal government have as one of their tenets an intense hatred, particularly of African Americans and Jews. Their rhetoric harks back to a line of argument for white supremacy formed during the enslavement of African people and the historic European antagonism toward Jews.

Claiming, as some do, that the American nation is an Anglo-Saxon creation, they fail to appreciate that America has never been a static idea. Indeed, it may have begun as a primarily English experiment, but it quickly added diversity even from the European continent. When the Revolutionary War ended, nearly 61 percent of the whites in the new country were English. Another 17 percent were Scottish or Irish. Nine percent were German and about 3 percent were Dutch. Of course, there were smatterings of Finns, Swiss, French, Swedish, and other European groups. However, by the turn of the nineteenth century, the country had already lost its English character and was becoming, at least in states such as Pennsylvania and New York, increasingly German and Dutch. Of course, Africans and Jews also lived in the colonies during the pre–Revolutionary War era. Layered in the same time frame as the new arrivals from Europe and Africa were the indigenous people already here, who represented a diverse population of Native Americans. In some senses, the continuing fight to eradicate the last vestiges of racism is a part of a long struggle against inhumanity. African Americans may represent, as Andrew Hacker understood, the principal test of America's ability to do justice and respect diversity.[10]

Thus, in the minutiae of cultural discussion—the folklore, the humor, and the philosophical discussions of race—one finds ever present the negative references to Africa and Africans. I know, as I walk through the streets, that I am a principal obsession of many in white America. The significance of this obsession does not escape the attention of the most distant Idaho hamlets, where paramilitary forces gather to play in the dark. In its failure to confront its past and deal justly with African Americans, the American nation, by its attempt to ignore history, creates a passive obsession. It is as if one spaceship is lost in the universe and another has been sent on a journey to some distant planet, knowing all the time in its travel through space that the lost spaceship is somewhere out there. But of course I am equally obsessed with white America; that is our national drama. Like many African Americans, I strain to understand the varieties of white hatred and can only conclude that the racial animosity that one still sees is a guise to cover up guilt. Anyway, what has our history been but a persistent struggle against all forms of oppression?

Growing up in Georgia and Tennessee, my earliest memories are of a society without whites, segregated, self-contained, and filled with the Holy Ghost. Nevertheless, we all knew that distant whites had created the miserable world in which we lived. We knew this because from time to time they entered our world, and their entry was vile, oppressive, arrogant, and brutal. They were bill collectors, police, night riders, and others looking to harass African people. And so our misery was not for lack of human kindness or family spirit or laughter or good times, but due to economic, social, and political oppression.

During the early days of television, the entire community would rush to the television sets to see Nat King Cole or Eartha Kitt or Harry Belafonte. Such a society, strictly defined by race, was the norm in the American South and was often replicated in the North. Racial covenants that prevented African Americans from living in certain neighborhoods, job discrimination that made African Americans the last hired and the first fired, and school segregation were prevalent in the North during the period when the South was under heavy pressure to desegregate.

Notwithstanding segregation and discrimination, African Americans created cultural, educational, and economic opportunities often without the support of any major municipal or state institutions. No taxpayer dollars supported the teaching of African American culture in the way that government entities funded the promotion of European music, choirs, dance concerts, and dramatic productions. Like the general attitude of whites in the South after the Civil War about African freedom, we were on our own. This is not to say that we were ever left alone. To be on your own does not mean that others will leave you alone or will not interfere negatively in your life. Being alone was not so much the problem as was maltreatment, brutal and subtle discrimination, and the denial of citizenship rights.

We were victims of the most horrendous and vicious racism, denied economic opportunities and yet condemned for our poverty, refused admission to colleges and yet blamed for our ignorance. And when we protested, we were called vile names, assaulted with sticks and cattle prods, and often murdered. Those among us who demanded to vote were asked to recite the preamble to the Constitution, present the receipt for our poll taxes, or to interpret various articles of the Constitution. In all things and in every place, our way was blocked.[11] Our crime in a society dominated by white supremacists was that we were black and hated white supremacy. Those who accepted the idea of inferiority committed crimes against their own communities, not against the racist establishment. And the internalization of inferiority caused wide intracommunity violence in one urban city after another. Blacks killing blacks, as whites had done with impunity in the nineteenth century, became a Saturday night special performance in most cities in the late twentieth century.

While it is easy to claim, as some will do, that my descriptions are of another, more primitive America, the police beating of Rodney King in Los Angeles; Colin Ferguson's rampage against whites on a Long Island commuter train; the New Jersey State Police's assault on young black male motorists; and the various murders of individuals just because of the color of their skin in New York, Georgia, Pennsylvania, and California, by either police or plain citizens throughout America's history, is enough to remind me of the salience of race as a factor in human relationships. The extent of these crimes is not confined to the large cities, however; this is a national crisis. My desire is to see this seemingly intractable issue between Americans resolved in ways that will respect the rights of all Americans. This is a tremendous task, but if it is achieved, it will establish a significant foundation for what we do as a united people in this country.

Ellis Cose writes insightfully of the *Rage of a Privileged Class*, but the story I tell is not simply a tale of black corporate executives or rich investment bankers angry because they cannot get into the country club or get their children in the right private schools.[12] There is a story there, and Cose tells it brilliantly. But my concern is with the anger that has welled up among all social strata of African Americans. One can isolate the rich, the upwardly mobile, and hear their pain but I contend that their pain, is of the same cut and fabric one finds in the lives of the poor, the working classes, the *lumpenproletariat*, the shut out, and the economically shunned. It is the reality of the Wilderness.

In *Race Matters*, Cornel West writes of nihilism and the search for social justice. No one has dealt so ably as West with the manifold ways the American society has avoided dealing with the ethical dimensions of white racial domination as ideology and black inferiority as practice. He brings to bear a philosophical inquiry into the nature of race in a profoundly important manner, but I believe he overstates the case for nihilism, particularly in its meaning that one sees everything as meaningless, worthless, and lifeless. What West calls "the numbing detachment from others and a self-destructive disposition toward the world"[13] is a different assessment than my knowledge and observations of the African American community.

My experiences are those of a person who knows both the wandering in the Wilderness and the search for the Promise. When I write, I am writing as an African American, one who has grown up with the Wilderness experience, yet I have never suffered strivings in "one dark body" of "double consciousness."[14] I do not now, nor have I ever had, strivings between my citizenship as an American and my cultural roots as an African. I believe that my experience is that of the majority of people of African descent in this country.

Whites who live in America are the most consciously white people in the world, the most actively white people in the world, because their lives are defined by the images they have created of the African people. This is an image of power and of revenge, of fear and of suspicion, of hate and domination. Many whites seem to think, "What would blacks do in our place?" The whites in South Africa have begun to realize that their own sense of whiteness as power, as status, is ephemeral. In the United States, where white Americans have lived with the images of Africans as free much longer than whites in South Africa, there is the recognition that the two communities are linked in racial twinness: two worlds, two systems, interlocking and dependent.

The ideas I had as a child, which were encouraged in me as a young adult by many people—the richness of African culture, the beauty and grace of African people, the memory of the Spirituals, the need for activism against racial injustice, the common destiny of human beings, and the necessity of constant vigilance against those who would deny our freedom—have come to serve me with a quickening insight. I am, as a reflection of many African Americans, the quintessential product of the American Wilderness experience: shaken, but eternally optimistic about what can be if a national will existed to create a constructive human transformation.

Racial separation, antagonism, and suspicion, which have existed from the inception of the American nation, can be transcended only if we retrace the steps to our present condition. National transformation, like the renewal of a lost romance, can be achieved only through honesty and diligence.

# CHAPTER TWO

# THE POLITICAL MEMORY

The election of Barack Obama to the presidency is often hailed as something that could only happen in America. While this is an exhortative piece of rhetorical optimism and belief, it is remembered by historians and politicians that just in the contemporary era, we have seen equally momentous occasions in politics, such as the election of Evo Morales, an Indian, in Bolivia, and Hugo Chavez, an African Indian, in Venezuela, and several female presidents in Africa, Europe, and South America. Beyond the more recent election of these individuals to positions of leadership, there have been other similarly momentous historical events in politics.

Historically, the rise to power in the Roman Empire of the African emperor Septimius Severus was not without its surreal quality. In the Roman period Africans were among the mightiest soldiers of the empire and they helped to establish the Roman civilization in many places. Some of the distinguished African political figures included military hero Antonius Pius, who lived during the reign of the Roman emperor Hadrian, and a senator named P. Salvius Julianus, who was chosen as a *consul ordinaries* (a judge appointed at the beginning of the year as opposed to later in the year) in 148 CE, which was a very special honor, during the celebration of the nine-hundredth anniversary of Rome's foundation.

Notable Africans were present not only in the political arena, but also in the educational sector of Roman society. Several African teachers are on record, such as the tutor of Aurelius Caesar, whose name was M. Cornelius Fronto of Cirta. Another, known as Sulpicius Apollinaris from Carthage, was a professional teacher in Rome. The famous author of *Metamorphoses*, or *Golden Ass*, was also from Africa; he was Apuleius of Madauros.[1]

The most famous of all the African leaders of Rome was Lucius Septimius Severus, who moved swiftly up the ladder of power, crossing the boundaries of the military, the nobility, and the Senate to become Caesar, which meant, in his time, the ruler of most of the world. Severus had his fingerprints on history, and his name can never be neglected in the fields of history, civilization, religion, or classics. Lucius Septimius Severus was born April 1,145 CE, at Leptis Magna in Tripolitania—on the continent of Africa. By ascending to the throne of Rome, Severus, a complex, yet effective and charismatic military leader, probably captured the imagination of the world less so than Barack Obama because Severus's rise to power came long before the enslavement of Africans, the colonization of Africa, and the white doctrine of racial purity and superiority.

## AN ACT OF TRANSFORMATION

Barack Hussein Obama's victory in the longest presidential race in the United States' history was a transformative act of global proportions. In one of the most stunning representations of generational change, a relatively young candidate defeated a national military hero to transfer not just political power, but symbolic power, to a new generation of Americans who will oversee the diminishing of race as a factor in US human relations. Nothing is guaranteed but everything is hoped for.

Many who voted for Obama actually thought that the nation would put race and the negative connotations surrounding blackness in its past. And some people will continue to believe in that possibility, but we must never be fooled into thinking that ignorant bigots have altogether disappeared. President Obama is the son of a white Kansan mother and a black Kenyan father. Throughout American history, almost since the very beginning of the discourse on race, any person who had African ancestry was considered black. This defied all biological reason, yet it was a construction established to support the enslavement of the illegitimate children of white slaveholders and to "keep the white race pure."[2] Obama's personal history, therefore, converges with his political history. This man, whose biology is derived from a combination of Africans and Europeans, has now assumed the presidency of the United States of America as the truest representative of the long-standing battle to define what an American is. As a person who sees himself culturally as an African American, he has broken the barrier of ethnicity and culture, and pointed the way for Latinos and Asian Americans as well. Obama can be the transformative person who gives all Americans an opportunity to change racial and political discourse. But even he recognizes the complexity of racial text because there are still people, black and white, who see him as different from those who have a history of enslavement, which is something that does not exist in his biological history (although I would argue that his father, a colonized African, shared some of the same humiliations as enslaved and segregated Africans in the United States).

Does Obama's election mean that racism is over, that racial profiling is gone, that institutions will no longer discriminate? No, this is not the panacea for all that ails the nation in the area of race. I do not see in the election of Barack Obama an end to inequality in healthcare, employment, infant mortality, or bank lending. However, his election is definitely a point of strict departure from what we have had and where we have been as a society. Therefore, I see the beginning of a progressive discourse about race and privilege in American society. Obama is pivoting us toward the goal of erasing racism, but his victory as a president is not the final object of the game.

There are those who believe that the way to interracial salvation is through the political arena, and they continue to invest their lives and their resources in this goal, only to discover that politics itself has limitations. Quite frankly, nothing in recent years has generated political excitement among the youth in American society like the Barack Obama presidential campaign. It was rather phenomenal that millions of people put their most optimistic hopes in the candidate for change, which signaled a shift in the nature of our political will as a nation. But all were not pleased that an African American candidate was running for the highest office in the land. Some found their deepest prejudices emerging from the depths of their souls to confound their reason. They were eager to vote against a black candidate, saying, as one woman did in an interview, "I just can't bring myself to vote for a black person for the presidency of the United States."[3] Such personal, emotional paralysis meant that this woman, and others like her, had no intention of confronting their prejudices; rather, they would allow those prejudices to override their reason.

This did not mean that reasons behind prejudices were not given; they were, and most of them had to do with issues of value, religion, and personality. For example, one often heard comments about Obama's religion, and there were some who actually believed that Obama was a Muslim even though this was repeatedly denied. In one dramatic instance at a rally for Senator John McCain, a woman in the audience leaped to her feet to explain that she had a difficulty with Obama because "he is an Arab!"[4] In defense of Obama, and it was a spirited defense, Senator McCain, either in a slip of the tongue or because of a deeply held opinion about Arabs, said, " No, ma'am, he is a decent American."[5]

On the one hand, McCain was defending the character of Barack Obama, but on the other, he allowed the idea to remain that somehow an Arab could not be a "decent American" when, in fact, being American requires nothing more than citizenship, not biology. In the end, enough whites, nearly 46 percent—more than the 43 percent who had voted for Bill Clinton in his first election—decided to cast their ballots for Obama to help place him in the presidency.

There were those who voted for Barack Obama believing that an individual who was fresh in his perspective, devoted to his family, international in his vision, and gifted with the ability to connect to a new, technologically inclined generation would bring about a great leap forward in racial reconciliation. The expectations were richly embedded with possibilities and new characterizations, not so much of Obama, but of ourselves as a nation. Having endured a president who was widely considered one of the lesser performing individuals who have held that office, the nation was ready for intelligence, science, skill, courage, eloquence, and generosity. The fact that these qualities seemed to fit the African American candidate for the presidency more than any others running in the 2008 presidential campaign underscored the contrast present in the election. A black man, a university law professor, a community organizer, presented himself magnificently as the anti-Bush.

Even those who supported Obama for president are bound to be disappointed at some point with some of his political decisions; this is the nature of the political process. We are irreversibly political, and the road to optimism at the political level must go by the sites of our most secret social and racial fears. One person cannot carry the weight for the entire society. Obama's campaign demonstrated the power of branding in the new approach to racial politics. He was the new, young, intellectual, progressive orator. These were terms that voters could use to contrast Obama and Senator John McCain.

The presidency was long regarded as beyond the reach of any person of African descent in the United States, although little black children were urged by some of their black teachers to "work hard, study hard, and learn everything because one day you might be president." There was an obvious contradiction in the myth of the nation regarding "the American Dream" and the Wilderness reality. Martin

Luther King Jr. had famously recited a litany of dreamable objectives for a new society in his 1963 march on Washington speech:

> I have a dream that one day this nation will rise up and live out the true meaning of its creed: "We hold these truths to be self-evident: that all men are created equal."
>
> I have a dream that one day on the red hills of Georgia the sons of former slaves and the sons of former slave owners will be able to sit down together at the table of brotherhood.
>
> I have a dream that one day even the state of Mississippi, a state sweltering with the heat of injustice, sweltering with the heat of oppression, will be transformed into an oasis of freedom and justice.
>
> I have a dream that my four little children will one day live in a nation where they will not be judged by the color of their skin but by the content of their character.
>
> I have a dream today.
>
> I have a dream that one day, down in Alabama, with its vicious racists, with its governor having his lips dripping with the words of interposition and nullification; one day right there in Alabama, little black boys and black girls will be able to join hands with little white boys and white girls as sisters and brothers.[6]

While there was nothing in this series of dreams that intimated that a black person would seek the presidency, there were enough signposts in King's dream about equality to suggest that nothing was out of bounds for the America that King envisioned.

## THE DEFINING MOMENT

Prior to Obama's 2008 presidential campaign, overwhelming prejudice wrapped in the fabric of social possibility concealed the real nature of African Americans' ordinary lives. Youths who adopted hip-hop as their standard lifestyle and Lil Wayne as one of their torch-bearers often felt alienated from the possibility of a political kingdom that would speak to the constant grind of their daily lives.

It is into this climate that the change campaign of Barack Obama, the junior senator from the state of Illinois, entered the race to become the Democratic presidential candidate in 2007. Announcing his entry into the contest at the Illinois capitol building in Springfield, Obama recalled the life and words of Abraham Lincoln, who is long remembered and often honored for his role in keeping the Union united and fighting against the slaveholding states of the Confederacy. Aligning himself with the tradition of social liberalism, Obama presented himself as the candidate for change.

He eventually transformed the rhetoric of race in the American nation. I cannot think of a more defining moment for the erasing of racism than the election of Barack Obama as president. There are many reasons for this assessment, despite the obstacles that he might confront in office.

Some of the reasons for this new moment in our national history have been forged by Obama himself, others have been thrust upon him, and still others are the result of his own natural, biological, and social being. What he forged, that is, the brand that he promoted, was a multicultural mantra of togetherness. He claimed positions that would bring the nation together and end the old divisions of Democrats and Republicans, Jews and Gentiles, Christians and Muslims, blacks and whites, and so forth. This was a new rhetoric. Furthermore, it was a rhetoric that could not be easily utilized by any other candidate but a black one. There was a moral imperative in his intense desire to demonstrate, not just emotionally, but intellectually, the possibility of America being precisely what black dreamers had seen in their clearest visions. Indeed, he would seek to bring into play the most powerful symbols of this vision by selecting cabinet appointees representative of the national spectrum. Talent, that is, political talent, would not remain limited to white males, but would be extended in a deeper way than before to a wider racial and ethnic class of women and men. Thus, tapping the best and brightest of America's intellectuals and political administrators, Obama announced a revivification of the national image.

With resonances of the eloquent discourses of Martin Luther King Jr., the national hero of justice, Obama articulated the language of justice against injustice, faith against despair, and optimism against pessimism in his run for the presidency. We were to be a nation at ease with a new type of political person.

The issues that were thrust upon him had as much to do with his career as a student, community worker, churchgoer, and social activist as anything else. He was bent toward assisting the poor and down-trodden. There was in him the ability to compensate for his own success and social mobility by performing good deeds for those less fortunate. This is where the church community at the Trinity United Church of Christ came into the picture. Obama had been a member of this church in Chicago since he was in his twenties. He was unapologetically Christian, but also unapologetically culturally and socially black, his mixed biological background notwithstanding.

Dr. Jeremiah Wright, the famed pastor of the Trinity United Church of Christ, was one of the most sought after speakers and theologians in the African American community when the Republicans went through his public archive of thousands of speeches to find one or two in which he criticized the American government for its international policies. There was nothing controversial to Wright's congregation about his moral castigations against America's broken promises. Yet the media repeatedly played one of Wright's most concise critiques of Bush's philosophy, which he delivered as passionately as he usually would when condemning immorality. In essence, it revealed the media's capability of turning truth into folly. The media's Big Lie strategy (a propaganda technique in which a statement is repeated many times so that the public believes that no one would be so bold as to repeat something so often unless it were absolutely true) was to play the clip in which Wright concludes "not God bless America, God damns America." Jeremiah Wright's sermon, couched in terms of his own military service to the nation and compelled by his strong attachment to values and morality, was a stunning rebuke of a nation that sang "God Bless America," when in fact its deeds around the world created violence, such as torture in Iraq, hunger in Africa, the abuse of prisoners at Guantanamo, and the displacement of millions of people in Asia and Africa. In this context, the preacher assumes that what he sees is "God damns America." If the mantle of the pulpit in the black community could have been transferred from Martin Luther King Jr., there is no stronger voice for national justice and community strength than Jeremiah Wright. It is shameful that in the last months of the 2008 political campaign this brilliant moralist and nonconforming voice of authenticity was silenced.

Indeed, Wright's résumé was impeccable as a pastor at Trinity United. He had served in the the US Marines and was honored by the United States in several capacities; he was even invited to the White House by President William Clinton. Even among scholars who are not noted for following pastors, Wright established himself as a historian and linguist, and a comprehensive intellectual devoted to overcoming all forms of racism. So Obama's membership at the church of Jeremiah Wright, a progressive, antidiscrimination, and justice-seeking preacher for sure, was not un-American. Wright's tradition in the pulpit as a prophetic voice in times of crisis goes back to the days of Henry Ward Beecher, John Jasper, and Martin Luther King Jr. Wright would never be satisfied with stepping softly over tough turf when the times called for stronger, sturdier mettle. But was he abusive, racist, ignorant, pushing for the destruction of America, or disloyal to his ancestors' dreams of justice?

The racist nature of American society, filled as it is with hate radio programs and Internet sites that preach violence against blacks and others, found in Jeremiah Wright's criticisms of the American political arena a reason to attack Barack Obama. Here was a situation thrust upon Obama and his campaign. Regardless of the merits of the attacks on Obama or Wright, this situation could only have happened in a racist society, and it suggests that we have not overcome the sensitive nature of the racial divide.

Obama answered the challenge of this situation with a two-pronged assault. He had to deny his preacher and his preacher's influence. In fact, he was forced by circumstance to "reject and denounce" Reverend Wright. There are some in the African American community who have not forgiven Obama for sacrificing his relationship with the famous pastor for what surely appears to be political opportunity. Alas, those supporters have asked, "Is the presidency more important than the personal relationship?" In my own judgment, Obama's team could have sent surrogates to the media to dissect, almost in a rhetorical analytic manner, the statements attributed to Wright. This would have taken more time, but it would have revealed the anemic nature of the reactionary attack on Wright, and it would have sent a strong message to the public that Wright's position was that of a prophetic voice speaking against evil as he saw it, and that even had Obama been present when Wright was making these statements, he had the wisdom nonetheless to sort out for himself what his own role should be in the political arena.

What does the Wright episode tell us about the state of the racism discussion in America? It told us that society was not ready to have a discussion about the oppressive type of racism that made the truth-telling Wright viable and necessary. There was nothing said by Reverend Wright that did not have substance in the lives of his parishioners. They believed in what he preached and they were moved by his identification with their sense of abandonment by the society for which they had pledged their lives. Subsequently, Wright went on television before a group of national journalists and confirmed many of the media's worst portrayals of his style and attitude. However, one can assume that Wright's strategy was meant to disarm those who wanted to use him as a whipping post against the Obama campaign. By providing journalists with a rhetorical feast of sorts, Wright could have meant to deflate the national debate. In the end, his handling of the questions created a temporary firestorm while deflecting attacks on Obama.

Racism is an ever-changing octopus with tentacles of two feet and six hands. Barack Obama found this to be the case when he entered the presidential campaign. If he minimized his African heritage, some people considered him a sellout; if he emphasized his African heritage, other people considered him "too black." When he decided to discuss his grandmother's prejudices, some saw it as insensitive; but when he spoke of his father's death as being a missed opportunity, they said he was whining. When he was strong in his assaults on indecency in Washington politics, he was called inexperienced. When he pledged to use the same kind of judgment he used in opposing the Iraqi invasion, he was called a grandstander. When he spoke about a new vision for a new century, he was called an eloquent speaker with great flourishes of rhetoric but no substance. Like an octopus's tentacles, responses to Obama were nuanced, diversionary, multiple, and engaging. He could not dance to the music of a multitude of demands, however rhythmic his rhetorical flourishes. The point is that just as racism is tentacular, it is also chameleonic; it changes its color in order to meet the demands of its owner's prejudices. All one has to do is examine the contours and trajectories of race and racism during the last half of the twentieth century to see the nature of this change.

What we are currently dealing with is the aftermath, the long, bitter, and often sordid aftermath, of 246 years of enslavement followed by another one hundred years of racial segregation and inequality. Our voices were muted, our behavior distorted, and our minds twisted by the irrationality of the system of racial brutality. Both blacks and whites were transformed by the legacy of enslavement. Not only were we Americans two peoples, and sometimes three, four, or five different peoples, caught in the vice of the old system that allowed for the opposing sides of the Civil War, the promise and failure of the Reconstruction, and the witness and perpetration of lynching; we were also people who understood the legacy of systematic denial of voting rights, the abuse of power, and the brokenness of communication between races. These in turn lead to false starts, superficial engagements, and mythical interactions that became fetishes of communication devoid of authenticity. We were afraid to really engage each other on the question of race.

# PRIVILEGE

Putting our interracial communication on a solid foundation will mean taking genuine stock of what we do when we interact with each other. What are the stereotypes that we carry? What privileges exist for whites that do not exist for blacks? How does society translate privilege into economic, educational, and political advantages? Privilege, a concept explored by antiracist writers such as Peggy McIntosh, Joe Feagin, and Tom Wise, sits at the entrance to all discourses on race in America.[7] What is it that gives one group of people the right to more easily succeed in social and economic terms while others have to suffer the consequences of their color, race, religion, perspective, gender, and/or point of origin?

In a brilliant essay written on September 13, 2008, and posted on his Web site, the social critic Tim Wise explained what white privilege is in the American context. Wise writes:

> White privilege is when you can get pregnant at seventeen like Bristol Palin and everyone is quick to insist that your life and that of your family is a personal matter, and that no one has a right to judge you or your parents, because "every family has challenges," even as black and Latino families with similar "challenges" are regularly typified as irresponsible, pathological and arbiters of social decay.[8]

One of the most popular white writers on race, Tim Wise believes that racism often blinds people to the realities of social and political privilege. Even those who might accuse Wise of overstating the case of Sarah Palin's privilege know that an African American with Sarah Palin's qualifications, education, and credentials would probably have never been selected to run for the second-highest office in the land.

Indeed, Wise touches one of the principal nerves in the ideology of racism: white superiority. When whites discover that they are no different from other human beings, they are often quick to make excuses that seek to turn their weaknesses into strengths. It is almost a knee-jerk reaction, and many blacks say that they can predict when it will happen. Indeed, one of the most remarkable things about Tim Wise's perceptions is his honesty in reinforcing the genius of those black seers who could have shown you the hypocrisy surrounding the fact that Palin attended four different colleges in six years—actually failing in one of them and having to make up work in a community college before returning—yet was still considered an intelligent person of outstanding qualities. Wise comments, "Persons of color who did this would be viewed as unfit for college, and probably someone who only got in, in the first place, because of affirmative action."[9]

Wise contends that "white privilege is being able to be a gun enthusiast and not make people immediately scared of you."[10] This was particularly important to say in the context of the political campaign in which Palin emphasized the fact that she liked to go moose hunting. A black person who showed as much enthusiasm for guns, whether for sport or for protection, would have been looked upon as frightening and perhaps violently inclined. Finally, Wise writes:

> White privilege is being able to attend churches over the years whose pastors say that people who voted for John Kerry or merely criticize George W. Bush are going to hell, and that the U.S. is an explicitly Christian nation and the job of Christians is to bring Christian theological principles into government, and who bring in speakers who say the conflict in the Middle East is God's punishment on Jews for rejecting Jesus, and everyone can still think you're just a good church-going Christian, but if you're black and friends with a black pastor who has noted (as have Colin Powell and the U.S. Department of Defense) that terrorist attacks are often the result of U.S. foreign policy and who talks about the history of racism and its effect on black people, you're an extremist who probably hates America.[11]

What Tim Wise leaves unsaid, because it is unnecessary to say it, is that racism is behind this cloak of white privilege. When one accepts the activities of some white people, even activities that are considered normal, as correct, just, fair, and positive, you must rethink the entire process of racial interaction when there is a history of institutional or personal racial abuse. There is no innocence about racism in American life; it permeates everything from the corporate world to the academic world, from religious institutions to the best schools, and it is found every day and every moment in the most intimate trenches of personal declarations. Consequently, one must guard against its insidious nature in every sector of society. One of the greatest crimes of racism is to make the victim believe that the criminal is acting fairly and without bias.

## MASKING GUILT

In effect, the fact that chauvinism, xenophobia, and prejudice are sustained by institutions in society that participate in victimizing certain individuals is one of the basic reasons for the continuation of racism. The institutions are used to justify the crime; the idea of fairness is couched in regulatory or legal terms that conspire against authentic fairness, especially when it comes to race. Without critical abilities we are at risk of misnaming the actions of racists and claiming easy victories. By this I mean that there are some activities that are racist but do not initially appear as such. They could actually appear to be counter-racist. Take the situation that occurred in a large Eastern university when the white dean of the college of liberal arts at the institution consistently supported a black administrator of a department despite the fact that there was expert testimony that the administrator was incompetent, disorganized, and often vindictive to students and faculty. Her response to these accounts of his incompetence was only to support him more fervently. When confronted about the gravity of the situation, the dean maintained her support for the administrator despite the dissatisfaction of the students and faculty and their accusations of the professor being ill equipped for the job. To support an incompetent person because he or she is black is one of *the most racist actions* that one can take. Such a position assumes not only the inferiority of black people but also the stupidity of the black masses. The *clarencization* process, that is, named after Clarence Thomas, must be called what it is: an assault on the best interests of African people in the United States. In the old days, such people were called Uncle Toms and were used by white segregationists in the South to protect white racial interests. They interfered with the authentic and legitimate aspirations of the masses of African people and demonstrated no vision based on the genuine, organic realities of African history. Whites would "empower" the "Tom" and "Aunt Jemima" figures, give them the authority to attack their own people, and then defend them as representatives of African people in the United States. Of course, on the plantation there were always blacks who did not accept any form of racism and oppression, and who despised the incompetence, weakness, and self-negating "Negroes" who thought that their "playing the game" would amount to self-aggrandizement.

Thus, at the large, urban Eastern university, there were black faculty members in the college of liberal arts who warned the white administrators that the black administrator was not doing his job. Instead of doing what she would have done in the case of a discredited, incompetent white administrator, the dean decided to give her full support to the black incompetent. This is a form of self-deceit on one level, but also a gross form of racism in the traditional sense of "giving" institutional credibility to the person who best serves the interests of white racism.

The meta-ideology that drives this racism is the belief in black inferiority. Indeed, this is where the history of racism in America reveals itself to be deeply entrenched in the institutional culture of the corporate, educational, and political structures of society. Support for incompetence, far from being supportive of African Americans, is a slap in the face of African American achievements, accomplishments, and legacies of nobility. Denial of this legacy demonstrates the uncertainty of white privilege and the instability of a racist administration. Only by neutralizing this tendency to support self-hatred, blame, and persecution of others can we truly mutually transform society.

One of the continuing facades of racism is the cowboy or cowgirl personality in which an inauthentic toughness is seen to be nothing more than the masking of the guilt of responsibility, that is, the lack of taking responsibility. Behind this mask there is an attempt on the part of the racist individual to escape from the awesome consequences of an encounter with himself or herself. The consequences are self-delusion, lack of control, and psychological disorganization. This is precisely the mental state of those racists who asked, "Can a black man really be president?"

The level of human communication required for erasing racism comes with problems that are complex, but not unfathomable. Guilt shifting plays a large role in how those in charge of the institutional brand seek to defend their positions. For example, someone is walking down the sidewalk in a large city and, while not looking straight in front of himself, stumbles over a child's wagon. The walker, in denial of his own responsibility to look where he is going, can blame the child for not minding the wagon, or the parents for not looking after the child, or the city for not giving adequate warning that children are at play—anything that would shift responsibility off of himself and onto the other person.

We rarely speak about the problem of low self-esteem among "Toms" and "Aunt Jemimas" because we have never really experienced a national self-disclosure discourse. Instead we have bits and pieces written by intelligent and wise authors who have made their observations in books and articles written largely for the African American community. The only reason one can be a Tom or an Aunt Jemima is because he or she assumes the geography of survival demands surrendering dignity, whether it is an authentic African name, body, reputation, character, or style of dress. During enslavement the idea was that the best of the worst food, the best of the worst treatment, and the best of the worst punishment and abuse was reserved for those "dearly beloved Negroes," whether house or field slaves. Some field hands were also victims of low self-esteem and would run to the master with fantastic tales about other Africans to amuse the puerile interests of the master or to gain favor from the master as a "good Negro." Such "good Negroes" were despised by the masses of Africans who worked in either the house or the field. The masters also despised them as weak, ignorant, self-hating cowards. Of course, the self-delusion of the master meant that he never trusted the genuine voices of the black masses. When the revolts occurred, as they often did, the Toms and the Aunt Jemimas suffered the same fate as the slaveholders. This is the logic of the narrative of Nat Turner and other slave revolts.

## SELF-NEGATION AND RACISM

Black self-hatred is not a thing of the past; it is present in contemporary society in more ways than we recognize. To some extent we speak of it in concrete terms of human relationships, but not nearly enough when we consider the problem of interracial and transcultural communication. Obviously there have been enlightened discussions of this attitude in numerous sociological studies, literary analyses, African American studies, and other disciplinary works. I am not writing about something that is unknown or that has escaped the attention of the social scientists and humanists interested in creating a more livable society. If anything, I am trying to discuss self-negation and racism in the context of the new realities of racial discourse in the nation. I am influenced in this style of writing by Derrick Bell, Kola Boof, Michael Tillotson, Ama Mazama, and others who have tried to understand the nature of self-hatred among black people.

There are two types of blacks who harbor self-hatred: those who seek to deny their blackness altogether and those who accept their blackness but despise their mothers and fathers for bringing them into a white-dominated world. As handlers for these two concepts, the first group might be called *Deniers* and the second group, *Despisers*.

## Deniers

The Deniers discover their reasons for denying their blackness in biology, historical myths, and skin color. These are individuals who are trapped in a racist society; in so many words, they are up a stream, without a paddle, and hence confront chaos everywhere the boat turns. There is an uncomfortable nature to their lives and their experiences are seen to bear out their frustrations. Wherever they turn, they are reminded of their blackness, but they are in complete denial that they are black. In some ways, one understands how the enslavement process has created this disjointed, confused mental state. Yet one rushes to say that if Deniers knew some limited history, had some earlier guidance, or listened to the elders of the communities, then they would not have been so confused as to deny their blackness, which, in effect, is to deny their Africanness.

Let us commence at the beginning of this discussion. If Africa were seen as a positive location, understood to have been the mother of humanity, the mother of human civilization, the place where humans first came to consciousness about the unknown and where they first created rituals and ceremonies to hold back chaos, we would have a different view about claiming African ancestry. However, in the world of the Denier, all of Africa is bad. The continent suffers from poor political administration, bad wars, internecine conflicts, lack of education, HIV/AIDS, child soldiers, mosquitoes, too much rain, too much sun, dangerous deserts, inhospitable forests, and black people. The first response of the Denier is to say, "No, I do not have anything to do with Africa; I am not black."

Now one of the problems with such a declaration is usually that no one in American society would believe it. Most Deniers I have met are phenotypically black; they live in predominantly black communities, they work at jobs where they are seen as black, and they attend churches, mosques, and synagogues where there are black Christians, black Muslims, or black Jews. So when a person such as this says that he or she is not black, it creates suspicion that the person is trying to escape his or her historical or social situation. Indeed, it might even be an attempt to escape a political situation.

The wages of blackness in a racist society are severe. The Denier seeks to move away, as far as he can, from any association with blackness as it has come to be defined in American society. For instance, the old segregationist idea that one drop of African blood makes a person black is disputed by the Deniers. They see this, as it has always been, as an anachronistic way of looking at blackness biologically. I recall a young, well-dressed black man who came to hear me give a speech at a university in the South and who said to me after my speech, "I am Italian. I am not black." My first reaction was, "But you do not look Italian. You look very black." He said to me, "But my grandfather was Italian and I have decided to claim my Italian heritage." In the end, you cannot criticize the young man for wanting to claim his Italian heritage, which is obviously a part of his genetic makeup, but you can cringe when he says "I am not black." In the United States he will always be considered black before he is considered Italian, despite his denial of his blackness. To him, and to other Deniers, being anything but African appears more attractive. In fact, mentally, they feel that one way to overcome the pain of enslavement is to discover any genetic string that ties them to some other racial or cultural group.

This brings to mind the case of Homer Plessy. In the late 1890s he challenged the segregation law on public transportation in New Orleans in a historic case that was called *Plessy v. Ferguson*. In 1896 the United States Supreme Court ruled that "separate but equal" treatment was upheld by the Constitution in public transportation and public accommodation. A group of African Americans intent on defeating the 1896 law passed by the state of Louisiana as ACT III—which required separate railway cars for Africans and whites, in contrast to the freedoms they had enjoyed during the Reconstruction—chose Homer Plessy, who was considered an octoroon, which meant at that time that he was one-eighth black, to be the test case. Plessy was light enough to "pass" for white; therefore, the legal case was meant to test the "science" of detecting one drop of African blood.

In June 1892, Plessy boarded a railcar and sat in an area designated for whites only. Although he was one-eighth black and seven-eighths white, under Louisiana law he was considered a black man and was therefore required to sit in the "colored" car. Plessy was recognized as a "colored" man by one of the conductors, and he was asked to move. Plessy refused to leave the car in which he was seated, and he was consequently arrested and jailed. In the court trial, Judge John Howard Ferguson ruled that the state of Louisiana had the right to regulate its railcars as it saw fit. Subsequently, attorney Albion W. Tourgée filed legal briefs with the Supreme Court. When the Court ruled against Plessy, it meant that the African American community would have to continue fighting until the 1954 *Brown v. Board of Education of Topeka* case finally demolished the "separate but equal" doctrine. *Plessy v. Ferguson* did not resolve the issues of race and biology inasmuch as these are outside of the Court's capability; these are primarily social and political decisions. In South Africa, for example, in 2008 the government passed legislation to make all South-African-born Chinese, black. Indeed, both the South African case and the historic American case demonstrate the flexibility of the ideology of race.

Another twist to the Deniers' logic in America is that if they can somehow claim Native American ancestry, they could also escape the problems associated with Africa and African history in the United States, and perhaps even stake a fundamental claim for ownership of the American territory. Historically, Africans became Native Americans in three fundamental ways: marrying into a Native American group; escaping enslavement and living among Native Americans, *exempli gratia*, the Seminole case; or being held in bondage by one of the so-called Five Civilized Tribes, *exempli gratia*, among the Cherokees.[12] In 2007 the Cherokee Nation officially declared that blacks could not be Cherokee, despite the fact that some African Americans claimed Cherokee ancestry legally by virtue of being on the rolls and others had declared themselves Native Americans by ancestry.

The debate over the legitimacy of the Africans' claims to be Cherokee brought legal action by Congresswoman Diane Watson of

California, who submitted a bill to Congress to deny the Cherokees the right to discriminate against black Cherokees. This was in reaction to the Cherokee Nation passing a law requiring every current Cherokee to have at least one Indian ancestor listed on the 1906 Indian census, called the Dawes Rolls. The 2,800 back descendants of freed Africans who had been owned by the Cherokee protested this ruling by the Cherokee Nation because most of them would lose their citizenship. This would be due to the fact that they were often not included on the Dawes Rolls, the official listing of tribal membership used by the federal government to decide the size of the reservation land to be set aside for a tribe.

Watson's bill sought to cut off all federal funding to the Cherokees, amounting to nearly $300 million annually, and to suspend their right to casinos, if they continued with discrimination against the black Cherokees who were brought up as Indians and lived among the Cherokee as individuals who participated in the culture, spoke the language, and followed the customs and ceremonies of the Cherokees. Watson's bill, by curtailing the licenses of the Cherokee to run its seven casinos, would hold up another $300 million in earnings from the gaming business. The case of the black Cherokee is strong because the Treaty of 1866 signed by the Cherokee Nation and the United States government stated, "all freedmen who have been liberated by voluntary act of their former owners or by law, and their descendants, shall have all the rights of native Cherokee."[13] The new citizenship requirement—much like the old grandfather clause introduced in the South to prevent blacks from voting in elections—is discriminatory and meant to block any claim that African American Indians would have on the Cherokee Nation.

In addition to introducing the bill in Congress, Diane Watson and twenty-five of her colleagues sent a letter to the Bureau of Indian Affairs seeking to push the federal government to enforce the 1866 treaty, which stated unequivocally that the freedmen should be treated in all regards as Cherokees.[14] Because the Cherokees held a larger number of enslaved Africans than any other tribe (about 7 percent of families held enslaved persons), there may be as many as 50,000 descendants of Cherokee freedmen. Chad Smith, the principal chief of the Cherokee Nation, defends the citizenship provision by saying that the 1866 treaty never guaranteed that the descendants of the freedmen would have citizenship. Part of the problem is centered on sharing the nearly $1 billion combination of benefits and awards received by the Cherokees from federal assistance. The African Americans who have pushed for citizenship in the various Native Americans nations have often done so out of the firm belief in their legitimate rights as descendants of Native Americans, either through birthright or inheritance from being a descendant of a freed African. On the other hand, there are some African Americans who declare themselves to be Native American as a way to minimize the idea of Africanness. The line given by such Africans is that they heard someone say, or they saw a picture of someone who looked like an Indian and they knew, that they were descended from that person. Because race is complex and shifting in the American nation, it is not always clear what is meant by this claim, except to suggest that the person may assume that being Native American is of higher status than being African American. If this is the mind-set, it demonstrates the wickedness of the racial hegemony that creates in blacks a need to declare themselves something other than black. Thus, we have in increasing numbers African Americans claiming their Native American ancestry, but Native American organizations are pushing back by declaring that these African Americans are not on the proper census rolls and must not be accorded citizenship.

## Despisers

The Despiser is a person who maintains a negative emotional reaction to his cultural line. Thus, the Despiser despises himself. Although he has accepted the material fact of his blackness and has no difficulty with the historical reality, the Despiser has a psychological problem with the fact that he is living in a racist-dominated world that despises him. In fact, this condition causes him to have a form of cultural self-hatred. He is able to demonize the condition that has made him a Despiser, as well as himself for his cultural weakness. One way to demonstrate how much the Despiser hates himself is in the way the he demeans African cultural forms. In demeaning one's own culture, one perpetuates social and cultural repercussions that are present in schools, books, policies, and social interactions.

When the Despiser is not able to appreciate his own culture and his own history, justice becomes something that will always remain unfinished in his mind. Does the Despiser have a problem because he is burdened by the inability to alleviate the fear, rage, and intimidation he feels in a racist society? Without being able to express frustration and guilt to alleviate his suffering, the African person often turns on himself. He despises his color, his nose, his mouth, his hair, his physical image, and his association with other black people. To underscore the despicable nature of his life he expresses dislike for African food, his ancestors' lack of good judgment by allowing colonization and enslavement, and his own isolation from the European experience that he desires. He becomes, among his family and friends, a cultural laggard who refuses to join the movement for culture.

Many Despisers are middle class. Instead of the black middle class promoting African American culture in a massive way, Despisers leave it to those called "nationalists" who tend to have less money and less professional stature in the community. Thus, the Despisers are willing to abandon their sense of culture because they see it as a drawback to their personal ambitions; in their eyes, to relate to the poorer nationalists would be to indentify with them. By running away from African culture, the Despisers, especially the middle-class Despisers, ensure the continuing tension between those addicted to "white culture" and those who support their own ancestors and culture. Consequently, the Despisers are a part of the racial hegemony. Without expressly identifying their behavior in that manner, they undergird the idea that white culture is somehow better and superior to their own African traditions. This is a racist position. Whereas I might be burdened by the history of brutality against African people and the wrongs done to my ancestors, and I could use this history as a foundation for asserting my own cultural traditions, the Despiser is troubled and burdened by his inability to alter the situation of oppression and therefore becomes too depressed to ever consider the possibility of liberation. Why seek liberation when it is possible to abandon all thinking about Africa and the past of enslaved Africans? What pours forth from the Despiser is anger, self-hatred, and internal rage against his psychic situation. But one cannot be free simply by seeking an escape from responsibility that emerges from the existential condition. In the end, even the Despiser of culture must see that the dominant antiracist and anti-discriminatory practices cannot be eliminated without the active participation of the Despiser himself. In fact, the Despiser is essentially, by definition, anti-African; therein is the problem of many in the African American middle class. Despising themselves and hating their cultural origins, these Despisers participate in the same anti-African behavior of the whites they detest, while simultaneously seeking to adopt white cultural forms and styles. The condition of the Despisers is a sickness, a type of social illness, that robs the African American community of some of its brightest minds.

Therefore, the African's dilemma both in and outside of Africa remains the same. After five hundred years of European domination, African people are still attempting to learn how to deal with negation, abuse, racial prejudice, and doctrines of inferiority. There are certainly enough voices in the African American and African communities who are cheered on by the white elite for denying and despising Africa. I will never forget the extent to which white academics, and some blacks, praised Paul Gilroy's *The Black Atlantic*, a book thoroughly without an appreciation or love of African origin.[15] Indeed, Mark Christian, author of *Black Identity in the 20th Century*, justifiably called the book "Africaphobic," meaning that Gilroy appeared to crave consideration as an "accepted" black man, in the sense of being accepted by white people as good enough to be included in white culture.[16] One easily discovers the source of Gilroy's intellectual problem in writing a book and calling it *The Black Atlantic* when the entire term is off center, that is, dislocated and disoriented. The Atlantic is probably best referred to as the West African Ocean, and it is certainly neither black nor white; it is an ocean that connects cultures from Africa and Europe, but one should not assume this connection only in the Northern Hemisphere, which Gilroy seems to do. In fact, more Africans landed in South America than North America during the enslavement, and the largest population of blacks in the Americas is in Brazil.[17] I find myself agreeing with Christian; Gilroy's writings tend to evade the real issue of white supremacy and therefore, in his postmodern analysis, he is able to force fluidity on everything, even the words with which he writes or speaks about Africans. To an extent, one finds the same tendency in the writings of Anthony Appiah. His book *In My Father's House* should have been called *In My Mother's House* because, unlike Barack Obama, who appears to cherish both aspects of his mixed heritage, Appiah seems to be running away from his African traditions to embrace those of his English mother.[18] These are clearly individual choices, and one cannot impose any external pressure on people to choose one parent over the other, but one can criticize unbalanced reporting of the African culture by an individual who claims Africa only when it is convenient. It reminds me of the writings of the Indian author Dinesh D'Souza, who claimed for a while to be a minority person while continuously writing against African people.[19] Of course, because he was Indian, he could claim that he was one of the colored people, but his analyses were anti-African. They all seem to be knee-jerking, button-pushing rants that are comprised of xenophobic, homophobic, racist, and chauvinist signal terms that might be used by demagogues to rouse the most venal emotions in humanity. As an assault against anti-African writings or other racist attitudes and actions, we have to seek the compelling reintegration and resolution of racial conflict as a provocative, yet creative activity.

Let me put it this way: all forms of racism stem from the individual urge to demean, criticize, humiliate, and marginalize. Using language to eliminate, ridicule, ignore, and discredit is an attempt to obliterate the other person or group. When demagogues take this line of rhetoric and whip up emotions against the group that they are discriminating against, the masses who have their own set of complaints are often used as tools against the legitimate rights of the group that is being effectively marginalized. This is what happened during World War II in Lima, Peru, when the shops of Japanese Peruvians were wiped out by an enraged mob because Japan had gone to war with the United States, an ally of the Peruvian government. Peruvians, disregarding the little information that the Japanese had been in Peru since 1899 as decent and law-abiding citizens, rose up against their neighbors and burned their stores and shops.[20] While most Americans know nothing about the concealed internment of thousands of Latin American Japanese, which is different from the internment of the American Japanese, the story of Art Shibayama and others who, in March 1944, were taken from Peru and imprisoned at a Department of Justice camp in Crystal City, Texas, remains another of the sad chapters in American history.

In a similar display of violence against a discriminated group believed to have more power than they had, Germans rioted against Jewish shop owners of Berlin and went through the city, breaking windows and burning shops during the early days of World War II.[21] Six years before the broken and burned stores of Japanese lit up the night in Lima, Peru, ninety-one Jews in Berlin were murdered in a pogrom called the "night of the broken glass," or *Kristallnacht*. On that night, November 9-10, 1938, thirty thousand Jews were rounded up and deported to concentration camps. The world has seen such tremendous violence generated by racial, religious, and ethnic hatred that one would believe that whenever people are brutalized, castigated, condemned, exiled, demonized, or ignored because of their ethnic or racial origins, all of us would leap to our feet and cry, "No, not on our watch!" Alas, this has not been the case in other parts of the world, nor with the genocide of the Native people of this land, nor the mutilation and murder of Africans, nor the dispossession of Mexicans. Our American situation promises us something different from other countries because we have an ideal national creed that asserts our commitment to a higher system of values and the virtues of equality, justice, and fair play. Yet injustice, murder, and derogation of others are not special modes of ignorance reserved for the poor, downtrodden nations of Africa, Southeast Asia, or South America. Refusal to develop our own will toward harmony, peace, justice, and order is a rejection of genuine status and security. To be secure in our homes and in our persons we must be willing to respect the self-worth of others and to protect privilege for all human beings. If we cannot do this little, if we are unable to divest ourselves of entitlements that others do not possess, if we are unwilling to respect the ancestors of all of our citizens, then we will not be able to redress the evils of racism. I say this knowing that some will claim that they have no responsibility for racism, imperialism, or classism; they will assert that my arguments seek to portray all whites as perpetrators of hatred and purveyors of pain and discrimination. Their assertions will be invalid because that is not my argument. However, I am very clear that European imperialism and American racism have impacted the world and created enormous historical, psychological, social, and economic dislocations. My argument is that we all have an obligation to clean up the mess that has been caused by the betrayal of the best ideals of humanity.

# CHAPTER THREE
# THE MYTHIC CONDITION

The American past, with all of its racial discontent—of Native American dispossession; of the enslavement of Africans; of segregation based on culture and origin; of anti-Semitism, anti-Africanism, and discrimination—underlies every conceivable interpretation of the violent fury periodically seen in our larger cities. To say that we are victimized by history—that is, both by the cards dealt by history and by an ignorance of historical context—means that we are subject to misunderstanding the nature of the disillusionment, anger, and hopelessness that exists in our country. I am in agreement with Cornel West that there is hopelessness, but I do not see the complete, destructive form of nihilism that he speaks of in his book. Nihilism can mean different things to different people but I do not see the total disregard for institutions, anarchy, acceptance of nonexistence, and resignation to nothingness that West finds in the African American community.[1] Neither do I agree with him that most of the rage in the African American community is directed toward black women. This opinion borders on kitsch, created to achieve popular appeal. Most violent rage by black men is expressed against other black men; this is a statistical fact. Violence in the black community is directly related to the nature of American society. Thus, violence against other blacks is symptomatic of a larger national problem as well as the confusion derived from self-deprecation encouraged by white racial domination.

Of course, the mean streets of experience teach a sort of hopelessness about the will of white Americans to overcome the practice of racism. The social and cultural existence of African Americans itself is fragile, a cup of water balanced on the tip of a long narrow pole. Indeed, racism can create a depressing psychic condition that leads to alienation, destruction, and violence.

Colin Ferguson got on a Long Island train in New York in 1993 and, when the moment arrived, his bitter anger came through the barrel of a gun as he shot and killed six people, wounding more than a dozen others. He hated the life whites had created for themselves and for black people. So his indiscriminate shooting of whites was cause for alarm. One Asian was also caught in the gunfire. Ferguson's act was mirrored by the 1994 firebombing of a train by a white subway rider in New York City. Both acts seem to grow out of a racialized environment where privilege and prejudice coexist. The FBI recorded hundreds of incidents of racial harassment, intimidation, and insults between 1994 and 2002. The overwhelming majority of these racial incidents were directed toward African Americans. More than three-quarters of all racial incidents are directed toward the African American community.

Diametrically opposite responses to the verdict of not guilty in the O. J. Simpson case demonstrated the fundamental difference in visions that the majority of whites and the majority of blacks hold in this country. Even blacks who disliked Simpson more readily accepted the verdict. After so many years of working the vineyards of race, it seems, as Ted Koppel remarked to a dozen or so African Americans during a taping for *Nightline* on January 23, 1996, that the perception of racial polarization is as great as it has ever been.

Two powerful books by Andrew Hacker and Derrick Bell dramatically make the point that racism is the Achilles' heel of American society.[2] Both authors contend that the African American population has been the critical thermometer of social justice in American society. In fact, Hacker has proclaimed that there are essentially only two critical societies—separate, unequal, and hostile—in the United States. These two societies, one black and the other white, constitute the major axis around which all other questions of race and ethnicity revolve. Bell believes that racism, particularly as it is expressed against Africans, is a permanent feature in the American society. Both of these views recall the Kerner Commission Report, issued after the urban insurrections of the late 1960s. The Kerner Commission Report said that there were essentially two nations, one white and richer and the other black and poorer.[3] In the succeeding decades, little has changed in the economic positions of the two communities. Whether one analyzes salary or estate wealth, the African American community, on the whole, is far poorer than the white community.

Two separate national visions have created two societies, and only with deliberate attention to the state of race relations will the nation be able to mold a single cohesive vision, perhaps with the objective of forming a truly united society, that is, a more perfect union. Indeed, black and white have become more than races and colors; they represent metaphors of political difference, cultural distinctions, economic opportunities, legal commentaries, and social distance. These metaphors of distance may be seen in terms of people of the Wilderness and people of the Promise. The Wilderness and the Promise are integrally connected to our social, economic, and racial future.

A friend of mine, who drives a bus for a living in a large metropolitan center, tells me that he sees an endless variety of African people on his route. He swears that some of the African American people who board the bus think that they are a part of the American aristocracy. Some think they are yet enslaved. Others have warped notions of their own responsibilities toward the black community. He has noticed church leaders who feel that they are the true keepers of the religion of Christianity and who drug their members with too much out-of-this world rhetoric and little actual factual information about our conditions on earth. My friend claims that the people who get on and off of his bus are clearly a part of the American public, but are as far away from the Promise as anyone can imagine. They speak of America as a foreign country: "Americans will do such-and-such." "The United States government is in trouble." "Look at what they are doing to the South Americans." "The American foreign policy is anti-Africa." They speak with distance. Their words hold the nation at bay. It is rarely "our government" or "our policy," because the speakers do not participate in the same world as those who make the policy.

Black and white Americans have limited themselves to two powerful visions: the Promise and the Wilderness. While there are nuances, degrees of acceptance or rejection of one vision or the other, in the end it seems we are either living out the Wilderness or the Promise. One may find it impossible to live both visions simultaneously; however, a person may live them sequentially. Or, as we shall see, some people may live the illusion of the Promise while located in the Wilderness. They are the super-executives, the high-priced athletes, those who make sure that their secretaries do not show them negative information about race. These are persons who accept the idea of material acquisition as a gateway to the Promise, but who often see that their path to the top is blocked. Others may participate in questionable profit-making activities to achieve their objectives. Their perception of the Promise is an illusion because they are still psychologically bound to a Wilderness attitude.

When the Pilgrims landed on Plymouth Rock in 1620 they brought with them their vision of the Promise: religious, political, and social agendas that became embedded in the white American character. To these early European settlers, America, because of its indigenous population, was a dark, scary Wilderness. It was untamed, uncivilized, uncultivated, and, above all, godless. The ethic of hard work, discipline, religious piety, and self-sacrifice could surely make the land what the Puritans called the "city of God."

But, as we know, the land was neither unoccupied nor uncivilized, and the indigenous people who met the Europeans performed very civilized greeting ceremonies of hospitality and sharing. However, many of the initial meetings were cultural probings, familiarization sessions in which each group took note of the other's mannerisms, styles, tastes, and attributes. Yet few Europeans accepted the Native Americans' ideas as consistent with their own notion of a "new heaven and a new earth." The natives could not be accounted for in the social or religious construction of the "city of God," except perhaps as "sinners." Native Americans, decimated and isolated on reservations, would later be considered, alongside Africans, people of the Wilderness, outside of the Promise as understood by whites. The Native Americans were to be relegated to reservations in order to open the land to the children of the Promise who would occupy the land as if it were theirs from the beginning of time.

The decimation of the Native Americans went hand-in-hand with the Christian destruction of the Africans' pride, sense of religion, self-respect, and brutal subjection.[4] When the Trail of Tears of 1835 dried up and the thousands of Native Americans who were forced to march from the eastern United States arrived in what would become Oklahoma, space had been usurped for the European population and the Native Americans had become residents of one of the deepest parts of the metaphorical Wilderness. Even now, to most Americans, they are out of sight and out of mind.

When the first twenty indentured Africans in an English colony disembarked at Jamestown, Virginia, in 1619, the European settlers were already well on their way to carving out farming and trading niches in the North American continent. Native Americans had engaged in several skirmishes with the settlers, raided some settlements, and lost sections of their land. This was particularly true from Massachusetts to Virginia, where the population grew rapidly after the founding of the Plymouth community. With the arrival of Africans in

Virginia, however, there was additional labor to clear the land, plant crops, build houses, and police the colonial boundaries. Since they were indentured servants, the Africans assisted the colony in its work but were understood to be culturally different. Initially, those early Africans were able to assimilate into the political culture and were able to own property, intermarry with whites, and hire their own indentured servants.

The Judeo-Christian culture gave the early settlers a source for metaphors. These Europeans were the chosen few who had to fight to inherit the Promised Land. Like the Crusaders five hundred years earlier, they defined a mission, laid out their strategies, and began the struggle between the "good guys" and the "bad guys." In the minds of the early white settlers, the "truth" was incontestable: They had been given America by Providence. Nevertheless, the Promised Land was an emphatically materialist vision based on racial supremacy. Other myths would take their place alongside this idea of "the chosen" and catapult the white colonists into the modern world.

Slavery did not occur right away when Africans landed in the English colony of Virginia. Most early Africans, like many white indentured servants, worked for a few years until they had enough money to buy their own freedom. But in 1641 the Massachusetts Bay Colony introduced African slavery as a way of permanently holding Africans in servitude. By this time, Native Americans were already being enslaved in Massachusetts. Nine years later, in 1650, Connecticut established African slavery, and in 1661 Virginia passed a law that made Africans permanent slaves. These legislative acts laid the foundation for the racial condition confronting us now.

The Virginia law was actually enacted to deal with the many children of white men and black women. The law read in part: "Whereas some doubts have arisen whether children got by any Englishman upon a negro woman should be slave or free, be it enacted . . . : That all children borne in this country shall be held bond or free only according to the condition of the mother."[5] White women having children for black men was considered unthinkable.

Most Africans were not mixed, and since the child took the condition and the race of the mother, most were classified as Africans and as enslaved persons. Some Africans coming from the continent of Africa were immediately sold into bondage. A good example of this is Phillis Wheatley. She was born in Senegal, West Africa, around 1752, and brought to Boston at an early age and sold into slavery in the service of the John Wheatley family. She learned to write English around the age of ten or eleven and soon began to write poetry. In 1773 she published several poems and a book, *Poems on Various Subjects, Religious and Moral*, becoming the first African American woman and only the second woman to have a book published in America. But it was not easy, not simply because she was a woman, but because she was a woman *and* an African. A controversy ensued as to whether or not an African could write a book, and this had to be settled by white men.

A group of leading white men were assembled by Wheatley's owner to hear her read her words and then asked to sign an affidavit attesting to the fact that Phillis Wheatley could indeed read and write, and that the poems she claimed as her own were indeed hers. The first African to be published in English in America was off to a literary start confirmed by white men.

Here is the Wilderness in black and white. Almost innocently, the scenes were played out between blacks and whites in the early days of America, creating the patterns that would establish the racism and the stratification we know today. Whites dictated the activities and the behaviors of many blacks. Pleasing white people at one's own expense became the pattern with some blacks. Whites had their feelings of superiority reinforced by their ability to pass judgment on the acceptability of blacks. Our ancestors often took the abuse while hating it— as well as the perpetrators of their suffering. For generations the Wilderness abounds with growing anger. Whites feel betrayed because they have simply done what was required of them by the society that their ancestors created. In their words, "We didn't create the society, this is the way it is." And the African Americans say, "We ain't gon' take it no more." Communication breaks down around the two visions, two experiences, and two societies living in one geographical space. Almost everyone who enters American society at this point becomes a part of the Wilderness or a part of the Promised Land.

Let me explain what I mean by asking the reader to consider the American myth of immigration: People who come on their own to America and work very hard can overcome the social, economic, and lower-status positions of their past and achieve the Promise of happiness and economic security. They can also find a new identity. The fact that many European ethnic and nationality groups have entered the United States with such a vision and have apparently succeeded in fulfilling their ambitions underscores the idea that America represents the Promised Land.

But in all Promised Land myths there exists those for whom the dream, the Promise, is distant and often unreachable. They constitute the Wilderness dwellers, those whose distance from the dream of economic security, social justice, and the pursuit of happiness is maintained by stupendous walls of ignorance. They are the ones who exist in the margins, on the fringes, perhaps seeking an entry to the Promise, as those in waiting, or more likely are resigned to the inevitability of their own conditions. While most of the Wilderness dwellers are African Americans, there is an increasing number of Latinos and Native Americans who may also be defined as Wilderness dwellers. Yet neither the Wilderness dwellers nor the Promise dwellers have anything like a basic civic understanding of the origins of diversity in the American society.

Quite frankly, we are basically historically illiterate as a nation about the destructive nature of white supremacy as an ideology of dominance pervading every arena of American life. We have come to accept the abnormality as normal, the distortion of racial supremacy as the only American way of life. One of my Vietnamese students at Temple University recently said to me, "Professor Asante, America is a great country." I agreed that there were aspects of the country that were unsurpassed and asked, "Nguyen, do you know what Africans did to help make it great?" He did not know exactly what I was asking and I answered for him, "Africans were brought in large numbers to help lay the material bases of the nation. We worked from 'can't see in the morning till can't see in the evening' to build the buildings, to clear the forests, to harvest the crops, and to manufacture the goods for 244 years." I gave him a brief history of the African presence in North America. Nguyen did not know how to respond; he had never heard this information before and was visibly disturbed that no one had given him a proper orientation about the history of America. To Nguyen, as to many other Americans, the United States of America is a white country, though it has always been a nation of many cultures.

However, Nguyen is not alone in his ignorance of the intimate relationship Africans, Native Americans, and others have with this country. In fact, African Americans, victims of the same information system as others, often cannot give a factual account of African American history in the United States. Victimized by a lack of information about the past, we have little understanding of how we can transcend the present crises and racial quagmires of our society.

This is to be expected in a society where none of the popular reference works on cultural literacy have made knowledge of African American history or the sources of racial tension the central subjects of their works. Our ignorance of the contours of American history complicates every attempt to understand the depth of bitterness and frustration that lurks in the Wilderness. And unfortunately, few American leaders have fully understood the type of political and social leadership that is necessary to educate the general public about the abiding issue of racism. So politically explosive is this issue of historical and enduring racism that few presidential politicians have risked their chances for election or reelection by speaking honestly about the need to rid the society of racism and its effects.

Former President Bill Clinton's appointment of five African Americans and two Mexican Americans to his cabinet soon after his first election represented the most progressive step ever taken by an American president in government appointments. Perhaps the brutal truths of America are more poignantly imprinted on the minds of southerners than northerners. Of all the presidents during the last half of the twentieth century who have tried to grapple honestly with race in America, only Lyndon B. Johnson, Jimmy Carter, and Bill Clinton, all southerners, have shown a real will to confront the issue head-on. Indeed, Clinton's appointments can be seen as wise counterpoints to one of the lowest ebbs in race relations in more recent times. Neither former President Ronald Reagan nor former President George H. W. Bush sparked any hope in the Wilderness dwellers. In fact, Bush's appointment of Clarence Thomas to the Supreme Court was considered by the majority of African Americans to be a direct insult to our history of civil rights struggle, since Thomas did not fight for civil or human rights. Indeed, he was thought of as an anti-African, the counterpoint to our struggle.

In some ways, Clarence Thomas's nomination and appointment to the Supreme Court was the Bush administration's final slap in the face of African Americans, who knew that the only reason Thomas was nominated was his conservative political leanings, including a stance against affirmative action. The late and wise Judge Leon Higginbotham of Pennsylvania wrote perhaps the best statement on Thomas's situation. He understood, better than most, that Clarence Thomas was no Thurgood Marshall. Higginbotham, a respected jurist, wrote to Thomas in these words: "Candidly I and many other thoughtful Americans are very concerned about your appointment to the Supreme Court."[6] Higginbotham claimed that Thomas could not have enjoyed the social, political, or professional positions he held had there not been the struggle of the civil rights organizations and leaders Thomas criticized. Indeed, Thomas would be illegally married to his white wife, according to Higginbotham, had it not been for civil rights organizations that fought for the right of persons to be able to marry whomever they loved.[7] Higginbotham's letter will probably be viewed by history as one of the best critical statements ever given to a sitting Supreme Court judge.

The Thomas appointment to the Supreme Court, the California uprising after the first verdict in the Rodney King trial, and the O. J.

Simpson verdict wrenched the consciences of this nation as few events in the twentieth century. These situations were directly related to the atmosphere that had been created by elected political leaders. One might say that the elder Bush and others, steeped in a primitive view of Africans as incapable of knowing their best interest, made the Clarence Thomas appointment an anti–Thurgood Marshall act. This was psychological terror on our collective memory, given the fact that Marshall had been the lead attorney for the NAACP against discriminatory laws, and Thomas had argued against the civil rights leadership.

The April 29, 1992, acquittal in a California state court of four white policemen, Sgt. Stacey C. Koon and Officers Laurence M. Powell, Timothy E. Wind, and Theodore J. Briseno, on all but one count among the charges of assault and excessive force in the videotaped beating of Rodney King will be seen as one of the landmarks in racial relations in America. All four officers accused of the beating of King have publicly said they did not do anything wrong. Almost one year later two of the officers, Koon and Powell, were found guilty of violating Rodney King's civil rights in a federal court. Indeed the federal government felt strongly enough about the possibility of King's civil rights being denied that federal charges were immediately brought against the policemen after the not-guilty verdict in California. The case had all the vicious persistence of racial misunderstandings that have plagued America since the beginning of its history. This is a source of the Wilderness. In some strange way the later not-guilty verdict in the O. J. Simpson case was psychologically connected to the first Rodney King trial. It was as if those in the Wilderness were, to quote Terry McMillan, "waiting to exhale."

African Americans feel a tremendous sense of alienation from the authorities and the institutions of this nation, but it does not mean that African Americans are resigned to an onward march of inequality and injustice.[8] Perhaps the first sense of alienation resulted from the African enslavement and the creation of the so-called Atlantic Black— the disconnected, isolated African, called in previous times "the American Negro." The enslavement of Africans created psychological schisms that are yet to be overcome. In America the African was forced into a tight, shallow space. It was a space filled with numerous dangers, yet that tight and dangerous cultural space was the defining characteristic of the Wilderness. To be in danger or at risk psychologically and culturally is to be under the threat of nonexistence, and therein lies our fear.

One of the great Spirituals recalls, "I am a sojourner here," indicating that "this" is not really our home, "I am just passing through." While the poet may have been speaking of the earth, he could just as well have been referring to the American psychic space. A few years ago William Grier and Price Cobb wrote in their book *Black Rage* that "the viciousness of life in America for black men makes them remove themselves even further. If I establish first that I am a stranger in your land, I will at least avoid the shock of being attacked in my own home by kinfolk. We are strangers and I dwell for a while in your world—therefore, what you do to me cannot truly come as a surprise."[9]

However, the issue is now the surprise some whites feel hearing of the fury felt by many African Americans. They wonder why African Americans seem never to be satisfied. They act as if all debts have been paid and the scores settled. They have forgotten the recent history of the country, when we fought to throw off slavery, when we rejected forced ethnic cleansing, when we resisted the night riders in Alabama by sending our sons northward, when we campaigned against unfair labor practices, when we protested against peonage and restrictions on land ownership, when we petitioned to vote and even had our voting privileges taken away in the South. Whites may have forgotten, but we have not forgotten how Africans were not allowed to testify in courts, to serve on juries, to bear weapons, or to own the land that we toiled over and made productive. Furthermore, when we wanted to be educated, we found obstacles everywhere we turned. Is it enough to say that those elements of racism and white domination have disappeared? No, it is not enough, not when our disenfranchisement continued in the 2000 presidential election in Florida; not when racial profiling in the state of New Jersey conspires to rob us of our rights as citizen; and not when the subtleties of racism undermine our economic well-being in the discrimination that still exists in the banking and insurance industries.

We have not come to this place empty-handed. "Whites have rights, too," a twentysomething-year-old white student said in a heated discussion with African American students at Temple University. A black student shot back, "Indeed whites do, more than anybody else—and that is the problem." Other whites have voiced their concerns with comments like, "If blacks are not happy here, then let them go back to Africa." These angry whites tend to be males who feel, contrary to all facts, that they are losing economic control. In fact, Ellen Goodman reported in her column in 1994 that one white male said, "I have no civil or constitutional rights because every minority comes ahead of me and, yes dear, that includes women."[10] Goodman writes that it's really anxiety that these white males feel, but because anxiety is associated with weakness, they say they are angry. It is the difference between "admitting fear or making someone else afraid."[11]

In the past, urban unrest has had the potential of inducing social and economic anxiety. It will probably always have that power, since violence creates an atmosphere of uncertainty, even uncertainty about one's own life. Urban rebellions, social riots, and political uprisings are, in effect, acts of war. But war is not sustainable without resources, and consequently the periodic outbursts in America's urban centers are seen as revolts of the alienated. The conditions of internal colonialism produce predictable responses. Isolated and alienated from the Promise, the Wilderness dweller does not embrace the police in the same way the people of the Promise do. Actually, many people see the police as the enemy of the African American community.

Given the brutal encounters between the police and the people it is easy to see why African Americans continue to say that the police have become an occupying force with little organic relationship to the community. As an occupying force, the police often see blacks and Latinos as enemies, the *dark side* of their American experience. It is an oft-repeated pattern: The police do not live among the people, but they lord over them. They are rarely governed by civilian boards but are a law unto themselves and have become independent militias in many urban communities. It is easy for African Americans to believe that unless something as gross as the brutality perpetrated against Haitian American Abner Louima in a New York City police station in 1997 or the brutal police slaying of Guinean Amadou Diallo as he was trying to open the door to his apartment in 1998 occurs, our afflictions at the hands of the police go undetected and unannounced. Police appear not to study the culture, but they often taunt and provoke African American youth by disrespecting their culture. Indeed, many black youth believe that the police have become the prison guards of the colony and, much like prison guards throughout the nation, they view themselves mainly as controlling an increasingly black and brown population.

Thus, when the people acted to express their rage over the initial verdict in the police beating of Rodney King in Los Angeles, the police acted as soldiers against their erstwhile enemies. If the reaction of the Wilderness people seemed obscene, it was only because the not-guilty verdict in the case of the policemen who beat Rodney King was considered obscene. As defenders of the status quo in race relations, the police, more than any other sector of society, know precisely the fury and alienation of the African American community. And they know, too, that it cannot be controlled by force. What they seemed not to know was the cause of the anger, the history of the fury, or the reason for the alienation. Yet the police are often at the crux of the problem—whether one wants to examine history, attitudes, or behavior, they only have to investigate police culture for answers and solutions.

Understandably, as a response to brutal conditions, the young African American often learns that the best defense is a good offense; aggression is respected as power, and power allows you to do as you please. This is the lesson taught by American history. In fact, the *Dred Scott* decision in 1857 established the importance of power—that is, legal power—in the United States. Chief Justice Roger Brooke Taney said that the Constitution never contemplated Africans becoming citizens and that Africans "have no rights that any white man is bound to respect."[12] And now, at the simplest historical and intellectual levels, the Wilderness dwellers know that something is terribly wrong when the law of "might makes right" is invoked to the disadvantage of African Americans.

One might say that while the legal importance of the Simi Valley, California, state court verdict in the case of Rodney King was not as significant as the *Dred Scott* decision, the social declarations of the beating and the verdict itself were profoundly significant to the person in the street. In the nineteenth century the relationship of the Wilderness dwellers to the judicial system was dependent on judges who were slave owners. Although Judge Taney was a kind of minority himself, a Catholic in a Protestant society, he obviously wanted to show that he was just as committed to the white supremacist cause as Chief Justice John Marshall, also a slave owner, had been.

The United States was born with a political defect from which it may never recover.[13] The enslavement of Africans, while simultaneously expressing the value of liberty, created a duality in the American soul that is maintained in the split between the Wilderness and the Promise. Overcoming this aspect of the American passage from the Wilderness to the Promise may mean the end of civil duality. But this cannot be accomplished until there is a common store of information about the Africans' presence in this nation.

What is necessary from whites, it seems to me, is a political commitment to end racism, or at least to begin the process of attacking racial prejudice. So much racial prejudice against Africans has been built up because of the social, political, and economic structures of American society that many whites believe such prejudice is natural. "I thought we had ended racism years ago during Martin Luther King's time," said a well-dressed white woman who was asked what she thought about the racism against African Americans.

In fact, television talk shows and interview programs consistently demonstrate that there are *religious* Americans who teach religion to their children, who preach Christianity and other religions in their communities, yet who are bigots against African Americans and others. And these examples of blatant Skinhead or Ku Klux Klan–type arguments and statements are only the visible parts of the racism. Therefore, when politicians speak about controlling the anger and frustration of Africans they miss the point: Righteous anger is often seen as a measured response to the persistence of the doctrine of white supremacy, often operationalized as racism.

Racial anger with its outpouring of violence, as in the case in Los Angeles, may not be the response preferred by the perpetrators of racism, but it is a crucial response, and, as Frantz Fanon knew, whenever the oppressed respond to the conditions of disrespect, the response is a therapeutic action.[14] So whatever else we can say about the outbreak of urban violence in Los Angeles, it represented one of those small revolutions that Thomas Jefferson, the second president of the United States and a slave owner, once said was necessary from time to time.

"No other people would have taken what we have taken for as long as we have taken it," said psychologist Na'im Akbar of the Florida State University.[15] Akbar and others believe that people without our history of patience, spirituality, or suffering would have reacted far more violently and with much more determination than we have during our American sojourn. There have been ample reasons for our anger, and many of us have come to understand that our fury will be misunderstood by those who want to misunderstand. I remember how angry I was when some whites seemed angered by the Los Angeles insurrection. Their anger said to me that they had no appreciation of the conditions of the Wilderness. It is necessary from time to time to reeducate those who do not know how we got to this place about American history. Such reeducation, it seems to me, will prevent, or at least temper, the unreality that pronounces blackness as simply a political and ethical construct.

This is precisely why Afrocentrists have argued for the regaining and reassertion of a theoretical perspective that allows Africans to project a humanizing agency; otherwise, we continue to beg the real issue of race and racism in America. Blackness must be seen as a moral position, not a biological fact. Furthermore, one cannot pose the problem of race in America as a problem of the separation of black men from black women through years of oppression. We are all, male and female, victims of the same racism, even if not to the same manner or degree. Those who speak of gendered racism seek to claim that the enslaved male had it better than the enslaved female. We know, of course, that racial oppression occurred irrespective of gender.

The sight of armed policemen beating a prone Rodney King reopened a wound that did not heal quickly. Indeed, the image of black men being beaten on the streets of cities and towns is inexorably linked to black men being lynched in woods and back alleys. It is also connected to the sexual and cultural exploitation of black women. We are too close to the hellish memories that James Allen and Hilton Als illustrated in their powerful book *Without Sanctuary: Lynching Photography in America*, and that Ralph Ginzburg revealed in *100 Years of Lynching*, to forget the terrible history of lynching.[16]

Consider a brief sampling of the foundation of our anger from the pages of American newspapers. I have included the dates and the names of the newspapers to indicate both the extent and the range of the attacks on African Americans in the twentieth century. What appears below is just a small sample of lynchings I found in various newspapers across the country during the twentieth century, and do not include the numerous other forms of violence against Africans.

April 27, 1903: *New York Times*—Fifty-year-old Joe Shively was whipped with barbed wire and hit in the eye with brass knuckles by thirty-eight men in Bloomington, Indiana, on April 26th. Their motive appeared to be local objection to a colored man boarding with a white family. Two daughters of the family were also whipped.[17]

June 8, 1903: *New York Herald*—Belleville, Illinois, schoolteacher David Wyatt attempted to assassinate county superintendent C. Hertel, provoked by the latter's refusal to renew his teaching certificate. His jail cell, where he was subsequently confined, was broken into by two hundred men with sledgehammers. The men mashed his head before dragging him into the street by a rope they tied around his neck, whereupon they were joined by others who kicked and tore him to shreds with knives. His body was then hung and set aflame in the crowd's determination to "teach the Negroes a wholesome lesson."[18]

July 2, 1903: *Chicago Record-Herald*—A mob of fifty men shot and killed Ruben Elrod at his house in Columbia, South Carolina. Three women who lived in the house were warned to leave the county after being stripped and flogged. No reason was given for the attack.[19]

July 15 and July 27, 1903: *Chicago Record-Herald*—A man identified as Ed Claus was lynched near Eastman, Georgia. He had been captured by fifty farmers after an extensive chase and brought to Miss Susie Johnson, a schoolteacher who had been raped by Claus, for identification and sentencing. Despite his protestations that he was not Claus, the Negro was tied to a tree and fired at mercilessly by the mob as the rape victim looked on. Following this, on July 26, the real Ed Claus was located near Darien, Georgia, and secured by police.[20]

August 13, 1903: *Chicago Record-Herald*—Police officers cut down a still-conscious Negro from a mob tree-hanging in Whitesboro, Texas, on August 12. This incident was for an attempted attack on Mrs. Hart; the man was being held for identification when the mob took possession of him. The mob then turned on the town's colored residents, terrifying them into leaving at once.[21]

March 9, 1904: *New York Herald*—A race war in Springfield, Ohio, resulted from the murder of a white policeman and the subsequent lynching of Richard Dickerson, a Negro who had been confined in jail. Negroes were determined to avenge Dickerson's lynching by killing all the city's policemen, while whites announced they would burn the Negro district during the night. Militia were called in to help quell the mob. Dickerson's coroner reported his death by hanging by the neck to a street corner pole and bullet fire, but no one was held responsible for the lynching despite two thousand witnesses.[22]

August 1, 1910: *Montgomery (Ala.) Advertiser*—Fifteen to twenty Negroes were hunted down and killed by a mob of two or three hundred men near Palestine, Texas, "without any real cause at all," according to Sheriff Black.[23]

October 13, 1910: *Montgomery (Ala.) Advertiser*—A white woman named Mrs. Crow gave birth to a child of "doubtful color," and after months of denial declared that Grant Richardson was the child's father by assault of her. Richardson was lynched on his way to jail in Centreville, Alabama, after the deputy sheriff's custody of him was overpowered.[24]

⊠

November 13, 1911: *Birmingham (Ala.) News*—Gov. Cole L. Blease of South Carolina devoted considerable time in a gubernatorial address commending the recent lynching of a Negro at Honea Path by a mob led by Rep. Josh Ashley. He said he would sooner have resigned his office and led the mob himself rather than deterring white men from "punishing that nigger brute."[25]

⊠

January 23, 1912: *Montgomery Advertiser*—Norman Hadley, a farmer, was shot in his home, and four Negro tenants (Belle Hathaway, John Moore, Eugene Hamming, and "Dusty" Cruthfield) were arrested for the crime. A mob of one hundred men broke into Harris County jail, where the men were being held, overpowered the jailer, and hustled the four out at gunpoint. They were strung up on trees, protesting their innocence to the last, while the mob fired three hundred shots before dispersing.[26]

⊠

May 4, 1912: *Savannah (Ga.) Tribune*—The lynching of a Negro near Jackson, Georgia, was linked to his endeavors to recruit his own people to return to Africa. His apparent success threatened white farmers in the community who depended on slave labor.[27]

⊠

August 13, 1912: *Harrisburg (Pa.) Advocate*—Mayor Bennington, Sheriff Ellison, Judge Maynard, and Prosecuting Attorney J. O. Pendleton issued a statement that the lynching of Walter Johnston for allegedly attacking fourteen-year-old Nite White, was a case of mistaken identity.[28]

⊠

February 9, 1913: *Atlanta Constitution*—A mock trial of Mrs. J. C. Williams's alleged murderer was conducted by a mob of one thousand in the Houston, Texas, courthouse. David Rucker, aged thirty, was found guilty, chained, soaked with oil, and set ablaze. Andrew Williams, also Negro, had been hanged by a mob for the same crime earlier, and his innocence has since been established.[29]

⊠

August 5, 1913: *Memphis Commercial-Appeal*—"Lynching Bad For Business" editorial states, "the Negro is about the only dependable tiller of the soil . . . is also very useful as a distributor of money. About all he gets goes through his fingers. . . . Furthermore, the white man of courage can most always control the Negro without being compelled to resort to violence."[30]

⊠

September 23, 1913: *Birmingham (Ala.) News*—Henry Crosby frightened Mrs. J. C. Carroll, a white woman of Louisville, Kentucky, when he asked whether her husband was home. She ran to a nearby house with her infant, and Crosby's body was later found hanging from a tree.[31]

⊠

April 30, 1914: *New York Age*—Two half-drunk white men entered a black home near Wagner, Oklahoma, and raped and assaulted a seventeen-year-old colored girl, who screamed for her twenty-one-year-old brother's help. He shot one of the brutes in her defense, but the other got away. Local authorities came looking for him in vain that evening, and arrested her instead. A mob took her from jail at 4 A.M. and lynched her.[32]

⊠

January 3, 1916: *Philadelphia Inquirer*—Because of a remark that offended a white girl in Anderson County, South Carolina, two Negroes were lynched and a Negro woman badly beaten. The Negro woman asserts that all they said was "Hello."[33]

⊠

January 22, 1916: *New York Herald*—The bullet-riddled bodies of five Negroes (four from one family) found hanging from a tree near Starkville, Georgia, increased the total lynchings in that section to fourteen in five weeks. They were accused of having knowledge of Lee County Sheriff Moreland's killing.[34]

⊠

April 4, 1916: *Atlanta Constitution*—Oscar Martin's preliminary hearing in the attack of a thirteen-year-old girl in Idabel, Oklahoma, ended in a mob attack by five hundred men. They overpowered court attachés and hanged the Negro from the second-story balcony of the courthouse.[35]

⊠

May 16, 1916: *New York World*—Screaming for mercy, eighteen-year-old Jesse Washington was burned to death in front of fifteen thousand for killing Ms. Lucy Friar, a white woman, near Waco, Texas. He was dead one hour after the rendering of the jury's guilty verdict.[36]

⊠

August 27, 1916: *Philadelphia Inquirer*—Jess Hammet was removed from jail by a mob of one thousand at Vivian, Lousiana, and hanged from a telegraph pole for allegedly assaulting a white woman. The woman's parents pleaded with the mob on Hammet's behalf because some years before, when he was their servant, he had cared for the woman who now accused him.[37]

September 3, 1916: *Minneapolis Tribune*—Lynch leaders in Stuttgart, Arkansas, declared the method of their recent lynching of a Negro they took from DeWitt jail as "humane." Their correspondence to the town newspaper read that he "did not live nine seconds after his feet left the ground, as the bullet wounds on his body will prove. . . . The only request made by the criminal was that he be hanged or shot, and not tortured or burned.[38]

September 8, 1917: *Chicago Defender*—"Above is the head of Ell Persons, Negro, who was burned to death in Memphis, Tenn., on May 18th. This head was cut off the body and is seen here on the pavement of Beale Street (principal business street of the Negro section)." Persons's ears, lower lip, and nose were severed by souvenir hunters. Copies of the photograph were on sale in Memphis for a quarter.[39]

October 13, 1917: *Chicago Defender*—Eight hundred oil field workers—whites, Mexicans, Germans, and Italians—employed in a Houston, Texas, suburb, seized Bert Smith, had a ten-year-old white boy castrate him with a knife, brutally hung him to a tree, riddled his body with bullets, and horribly mutilated it with sledgehammers and butcher knives after cutting it down. Smith was a Negro cook who had complained to the camp head, within earshot of some whites, about indecent remarks made to his mother and sister when they visited. A week later, Smith's sister was attacked on her way to visit him by three whites, who raped her and left her blood-stained garments hung over her head on the limb of a tree, where she was later found. Smith's lynching followed his attack on the white messenger of his sister's fate.[40]

April 5, 1919: *Chicago Defender*—Private William Little, a Negro soldier returning to Blakely, Georgia, from the war, was harassed by whites for wearing his Army uniform. Since Little had no other clothing, he continued to wear his uniform over a few weeks and was advised through anonymous notes to leave town if he wished to "sport around in khaki." He was later found dead from a mob beating on the city outskirts.[41]

May 1, 1919: *Knoxville (Tenn.) News*—George Holden was shot to death in a third lynching attempt for allegedly writing an insulting note to Onlie Elliot, a white woman. Holden was on his way to Shreveport, Louisiana, for safekeeping following the first two attempts, when a mob held up the train he was on. Acquaintances of Holden said he could hardly write his own name.[42]

May 10, 1919: *Chicago Defender*—Luther Wilson (white) of Dade City, Florida, blackened his face and attacked a sixteen-year-old relative by marriage. Upon her recognition of him he said if she told about the incident he would swear his innocence and blame a black man. Wilson was reported and caught by a mob at a creek washing the black substance off his hands and face.[43]

May 15, 1919: *Vicksburg (Miss.) Herald*—Lloyd Clay, a twenty-four-year-old Negro laborer, was roasted to death and hung in Vicksburg, Mississippi, by a mob of up to one thousand who snatched him from the jail he was in on charges of entering nineteen-year-old Lulu Belle Bishop's bedroom and attempting to violate her. It was later revealed that the violator was the woman's secret white lover.[44]

September 6, 1919: *Chicago Defender*—The charred and bullet-riddled body of Eli Cooper, an aged farmer who sought to organize farm laborers, was found in the ashes of Ocmulgee African Church, one of four churches burned along with several lodges by a crowd of white men. Cooper allegedly said, "Negro has been run over for fifty years, but it must stop now, and pistols and shotguns are the only way to stop a mob." Another lynching had taken place near this scene in which sixty-five-year-old Berry Washington, who was jailed for defending his sixteen-year-old daughter from rape by a white man, was strung to a tree.[45]

October 4, 1919, *Atlanta Constitution*—Ernest Glenwood's body was found floating in Georgia's Flint River on October 2 after his disappearance on September 22, when he was taken into custody by three masked men. Glenwood had been charged with circulating incendiary propaganda among Negroes in Dooly County, for which he was bound and severely whipped.[46]

December 2, 1920: *Knoxville (Tenn.) News*—Miss Bessie Revere, daughter of prominent Quitman, Georgia, woman, gained consciousness in time to stop a lynch mob that formed to attack her rapist, who the press said was black. Miss Revere said her rapist was James Harvey, a prominent white man.[47]

⊠

January 27, 1921: *Memphis Press*—Henry Lowry retained consciousness for forty minutes as his body was roasted by inches from his legs up. As the flames reached his abdomen, he admitted his guilt to two questioners. He cried out only once before losing consciousness, having failed at attempts to pick up and swallow hot coals in order to hasten death. Lowry's wife and children witnessed.[48]

⊠

February 3, 1921: *Knoxville (Tenn.) News*—Jim Roland, a Negro farmer, was lynched near Camilla, Georgia, after shooting Jason I. Harvel, a white farmer, who had ordered the Negro to dance at gunpoint for the amusement of himself and his white friends. Roland, who was with his Negro friends, grabbed for the gun, which went off, killing Harvel. Roland was chased by a posse that riddled him with bullets after his refusal of their leader's command to dance.[49]

⊠

March 18, 1921: *Memphis Times-Scimitar*—A series of warnings by masked white men to Negro brakemen of the Yazoo and Mississippi Valley Railroad to quit their jobs culminated in the lynching of Howard Hurd of Memphis. His body was riddled with bullets and had a warning note "to all nigger railroadmen."[50]

⊠

August 19, 1921: *Baltimore Afro-American*—A mob of up to two thousand hanged and riddled Jerome Whitfield's body with a thousand bullets, on suspicion of assaulting the wife of a white farmer. He was tracked down by bloodhounds and brought to the woman, who expressed doubt that he was her assailant.[51]

November 25, 1921: *St. Louis Argus*—After it was hanged and cut down by one mob and before it was burned in a city hall bonfire by a second mob, the body of nineteen-year-old William Turner was hauled through the main streets of Helena, Arkansas, to provide a moving target for white men armed with pistols. The victim's father, August Turner, was summoned to the park to remove his son's charred remains after the celebrants had their fill.[52]

February 17, 1923: *Chicago Defender*—The only drug store in Milledgeville, Georgia, displayed a large bottle with fingers and ears of two lynched Negroes in alcohol. The inscription—"What's left of the niggers that shot a white man"—referred to the killing of Lindsay B. Gilmore following his pursuit of two Negroes who stole cheese and cash from his grocery store. Witnesses stated that Gilmore was shot by a local officer with a faulty aim.[53]

April 20, 1923: *New York World*—A mob that included many male and female University of Missouri students lynched James T. Scott, a Negro janitor at the university who had been charged with an attempt to assault the fourteen-year-old daughter of the head of the German Department. Scott swore his innocence and said he could prove it, but a young man dumped him over the side of the bridge where a five-hundred-member crowd had taken him. His noosed neck snapped audibly.[54]

⊠

June 15, 1923: *St. Louis Argus*—The bullet-ridden body of Henry Simmons, a native of the Bahama Islands, was found hanging from a tree on Palm Beach Island, Florida. Simmons had made enemies because of his outspokenness about the treatment of American Negroes by Southern whites.[55]

⊠

August 11, 1923: *Washington (D.C.) Eagle*—Ten thousand colored persons are said to have left Yazoo City following the burning at the stake of Willie Minnifield in a nearby swamp. He was accused of attacking a woman with an ax at a point twenty-six miles distant.[56]

⊠

October 10, 1924: *Chicago Tribune*—Two girls who had been accosted could not positively identify the Negro who was killed by a mob in the Jewish "ghetto" section of Chicago as the man who committed the crime. William Bell was kicked and beaten by a one-hundred-person mob composed principally of foreigners, and died from a blow to the head with a baseball bat. Racial tension had been running high in the ghetto since a number of Negro families moved in.[57]

⊠

March 12, 1927: *Chicago Defender*—Clarence Darrow, Chicago's internationally known criminal lawyer, champion of oppressed people, and free-speech advocate, was forced to leave a hall in which he spoke in Mobile, Alabama, under special police protection because he was menaced by a mob.[58]

May 10, 1930: *New York Sun*—After the burning of the Sherman courthouse in which alleged rapist George Hughes was killed, a mob seized Hughes's body from the ruins, dragged it to the Negro section by the rear of an automobile, strung it up to a tree, and set it afire. With clubs, bricks, bottles, and fists, the mob looted, wrecked, and burned a three-block section of the Negro district.[59]

October 4, 1930: *New York Negro World*—A mob of seventy-five men wrested Willie Kirkland from the sheriff's hands, hanged him to a tree, and, after riddling his body with bullets, toted it through Thomasville, Georgia, behind a truck and deposited it on the court-house lawn. Twenty-year-old Kirkland, who was serving out a term for horse stealing, was said to have been identified twice by a nine-year-old girl as the man who attempted to attack her. The camp warden verified Kirkland's presence in the camp on the day of the girl's alleged attack.[60]

March 4, 1933: *Indianapolis Recorder*—Nelson Nash, who was brutally lynched in Ringgold, Louisiana, for the murder of local white banker J. P. Batchelor, was the wrong man. Batchelor and his wife were forced out of their house by the murderer to open the bank safe, which Batchelor refused to do. Mrs. Batchelor would not identify the lynched man as the perpetrator, nor would she say whether her hus-band's assailant was black or, as was later suspected, white.[61]

March 27, 1933, *New York Herald-Tribune*—A Lowell, North Car-olina, physician, Dr. James W. Reid, saved a Negro from a lynch mob by hiding him in his cellar and then by driving him to Charlotte for safekeeping in the Mecklenberg County jail.[62]

⊠

July 23, 1933: *Knoxville Journal*—Reports on the lynching of a Negro in Caledonia, Mississippi, suggest he made an improper proposal to meet a white girl in a nearby cotton field and was instead met by a band of white men, who hanged him and riddled his body with bullets.[63]

⊠

October 19, 1933: *New York Times*—A frenzied mob of three thousand men, women, and children in Princess Anne, Maryland, sneering at guns and tear gas, overpowered fifty state troopers, removed twenty-four-year-old George Armwood (a Negro prisoner accused of attacking an aged white woman), and lynched him in front of the home of a judge who had tried to placate the mob. The mob then cut down the body, dragged it almost a mile through the main thorough-fares, and tossed it on a burning pyre.[64]

⊠

October 26, 1934: *Macon (Ga.) Telegraph*—"All white folks are invited to the party," said the announcement to citizens of Greenwood, Florida, as thousands prepared all day for the lynching of Claude Neal, twenty-three, who was seized by a mob from jail in connection with the murder of a white girl. A "Committee of Six" representing the mob announced a timetable for the lynching in the newspapers and over the radio.[65]

⊠

October 27, 1934: *Birmingham (Ala.) Post*—Claude Neal's bullet-riddled, seminude, mutilated body swung from a courthouse tree in Marianna, Florida. An eyewitness said Neal had been forced to eat his castrated penis and testicles and say he liked it before the mob sliced his sides and stomach and cut off his fingers with knives. He was burned with red-hot irons, choked with a rope around his neck, and dragged through the streets behind an automobile. A woman came out of the Cannidy home after the body was disconnected from the rear bumper and drove her knife into his heart. The crowd then kicked and drove their cars over him. Photographs of his remains were to go on sale later at 50 cents apiece, and Neal's mutilated fingers and toes were freely exhibited on street corners.[66]

March 13, 1935: *Atlanta Constitution*—A fifty-man mob hanged Ab Young from an oak tree near Slayden, Mississippi, for the shooting death of Hardy Mackie, forty-five, a state highway worker. Young met death with a hymn upon his lips as the car he was placed upon with a rope around his neck was driven out from under him.[67]

April 28, 1936: *Hickory (N.C.) Record*—Lint Shaw, a Negro farmer once saved from lynching through the pleadings of a judge, was tied to a pine tree and shot to death near Colbert, Georgia, by a mob of forty men eight hours before he was to have been tried on attempted criminal assault.[68]

April 14, 1937: *New York Times*—Two Negroes were tied to a tree, tortured, and lynched by a mob of more than one hundred white men near Duck Hill, Mississippi, less than two hours after they pleaded innocent in Montgomery County Circuit Court to a charge of murdering a white man. One of the men's eyes was gouged out with an ice pick and he was burnt with a blowtorch before he died, while the other was flogged with chains and a horsewhip before he was shot.[69]

December 15, 1938: *Philadelphia Tribune*—An NAACP investigation into the lynching of Wilder McGowan in Wiggins, Mississippi, on November 21 for allegedly attacking a white woman revealed his innocence. The woman described her attacker as "light-colored . . . with slick hair." McGowan, who was not in the crime vicinity, was dark. The NAACP characterized his lynching as the culmination of the "pent-up anger of whites against an innocent Negro who had refused on numerous occasions in the past to accommodate himself to the attempts of white ruffians to frighten colored citizens. . . ."[70]

August 26, 1944: *New York Amsterdam News*—A lynch-killing of sixty-six-year-old Rev. Isaac Simmons on March 26 in Amite County, Mississippi, because he hired a lawyer to safeguard his title to a 220-acre debt-free farm, was revealed in an affidavit sworn by his son. The trouble started when his land was thought to have oil, and whites started to muscle in to take away his property.[71]

September 1, 1955: *Washington Post-Times-Herald*—The body of fifteen-year-old Emmett Till of Chicago, who disappeared after he allegedly made "fresh" remarks to a white woman, was found floating in the Tallahatchie River, shot through the head. A 125-pound cotton gin blower had been tied to his neck to make the body sink, but Till's feet floated to the surface, leading to the discovery.[72]

March 8, 1960: *Birmingham (Ala.) News*—Four masked white youths hung a Negro man from a tree by his heels in Houston, Texas, and carved two series of "KKK"s into his chest and stomach after beating him with chains, allegedly in reprisal for recent sit-in demonstrations by Negro students at Texas Southern University. A group of students from the all-Negro university staged sit-ins at a supermarket lunch counter, drugstore, and another store.[73]

June 10, 1998: *New York Daily News*—Three white Texans were accused of chaining a black hitchhiker to the back of a pickup truck and dragging him by the ankles down a road until his body was torn to pieces.[74]

A selected litany of crimes against Africans is not meant to stir up guilt but to remind us of the distance we have come in this nation—and also of the distance we still have to go to correct the wrongs of the past. The reasons for fury are not groundless; they are based on historical experiences with white supremacist attitudes.

The horrible catalog of more than two hundred years of lynching (a word derived from the name of William Lynch of Pittsylvania, Virginia, who led a vigilante group in 1780) poisons most of what we think and believe about the possibilities of white people "treating us right." If Andrew Hacker is correct, the torments of our past are unforgettable and perhaps, as Derrick Bell has also suggested, impossible to overcome.[75] Certainly, every record of social and political struggle in the Wilderness shows the optimism and durability of those Africans who have spoken of hope and dreams in spite of the family of horrors that have been visited upon the dwellers of the Wilderness. Jesse Jackson's plaintive "keep hope alive" reverberates across the nation like a long, drawn-out solo without the participation of the nation at large.

"Can't we all get along?" is not merely a question of an individual

—Rodney King—but the collective query of an entire people. I believe that the simplicity of Rodney King's question might conceal the collective bafflement of African Americans. What has been the general white community's response to this King's question? So strong is the feeling of injustice in the Wilderness that many residents believe the justice system will not strike for them, but against them. Because the Wilderness is occupied territory, like other oppressed areas of the world, the police are often the targets of antipolice attitudes and behavior. After the uprising in Washington Heights in New York City during the summer of 1992, many Dominican residents said the police exhibited hatred toward the community. In their view, the death of Jose Garcia was just the most explicit example of the police shooting to death a young Dominican without justification. People who come to New York from the Dominican Republic are often looking for economic security and opportunity. However, like others in the Wilderness, these new immigrants are quickly embroiled in the daily battle to survive. Here, as they seek measures—perhaps illegal—to ensure their survival they are confronted by the police as enemies of the neighborhood. This deep-seated feeling about police hostility serves to fuel the fury in the urban trenches. This is the world of the urban poor, the lowest end of the Wilderness, the area most abused by lack of health care and other facilities: unemployment, disease, drug pushers and users, petty criminals, and political neglect. Here the people live on the edge of fantasy, seeing on television a world they know they can neither understand nor afford. It is both real and unreal, because they know that there *are* people who live in decent houses, have jobs, eat good food, and can buy clothes for their children, something these Wilderness dwellers cannot afford.

While it certainly is possible for the people of the Promise to understand the feelings of the Wilderness dwellers, their economic structure and activities usually insulate them from the world of the Wilderness dwellers. They often live in affluent neighborhoods in expensive houses removed from the Wilderness in physical space and psychological distance. Furthermore, people of the Promise may see the Wilderness dwellers on the streets but they have no real association with them. This is reminiscent of the bomber pilot who drops his payload of bombs on people thousands of feet below and then flies away, never to see the magnitude of destruction on the ground. Of course, one must distinguish those whites who are also victimized by the economic structure as well as identify those blacks who have little to do with the Wilderness.

One should not think, however, that the Wilderness is limited to the poor. Highly successful corporate executives experience all of the conditions of the Wilderness. African American businesspeople have often complained about the inequality of the playing field. William R. Spivey, a successful corporate leader, has written in his book *Corporate America in Black and White* that the African American faces enormous pressures and difficulties due to racism and discrimination. Overcoming racial hurdles has meant that blacks often have had to exceed whites in order to have a chance in the corporate world.[76]

Racism produces its own distortions in society. In fact, some have argued that in the minds of some Los Angeles citizens, what the rioters took from stores were liberated goods, contraband of war that could no longer be used to abuse the sensibilities, desires, and needs of people who could not afford them. The rioters struck at property, the heart of the system—the property of those they believed had exploited them. They found the rightness in what they did in the profanity of their own regime of poverty. What they knew is what all Wilderness dwellers in this country know: that each day African Americans and others face discrimination in the marketplace, that each day police assault and beat black men, that each day the fury grows when those men are arrested and do not come home, and that each day more victims are made and more hate stored for another season. In effect, the Wilderness is humiliated daily and only occasionally does someone catch the violence on video so that others may see. And it all builds to another mighty angry explosion in some urban Mount St. Wilderness.

# CHAPTER FOUR
# THE WILDERNESS OF RACIAL DISCONTENT

Africans have lived in this land longer than the nation has existed. We were here before George Washington was president, and when he sat down to eat dinner at the Morris House in Philadelphia, we cooked the meal and our hands served it. If you listen to us you will hear that we speak our own language, but we understand English. We wear the same name-brand jeans and dresses as the other inhabitants of the country. We are attuned to the same consumerism, generally practice versions of the same religions, and are educated in the same schools. We are distinguished from the rest of the inhabitants because of our color and, if you listen to our pathos, because of our previous condition of involuntary servitude. We were forced here against our will and we resent the fact that our culture was maimed, distorted, and crushed. We recognize that our history was stomped on and twisted into the ground.

*We are the people of the Wilderness.*

We bring an impatience to America. We are on the move and want it to be on the move. When we talk you will hear that we are warm, friendly, passionate, humorous, and spiritual. We respect grace and wisdom, both qualities that have taught us how to survive the Wilderness. Here in our America, the alter ego of the Promise, we spend our days counting the time when our rebellion will be over. Although we have tried to protect ourselves for nearly four hundred years from the winds of racism that blow over the Wilderness, we have still lost too many to the lashes of anomie and nihilism that drive people into drugs, degradation, and death.

We are often defined by our youth: their impulse, their swagger, the rhythm of the Wilderness, is definite, steady, and sometimes martial. They have had to be that way. Their music and dance have risen to defend the culture and to resurrect the history. There was a time when mothers taught their sons how to be in America. There was a time when fathers protected their daughters in America. It was a time when mothers and fathers of children of the Wilderness knew that the dangers confronting their offspring were the racists who roamed the American cities and hamlets harboring ill will toward black people. How do people survive in such a situation and be whole? The answer is that too many of our people do not survive and many are the walking wounded, the homeless, sometimes found pushing grocery carts in the colonial section of Philadelphia and near the Chicago Loop.

There has been personal and collective fury, and there will be fury so long as we do not deal with the primary issue of white racial domination that influences every aspect of this society. The African American community must inoculate itself against racism and racism's offspring in the form of justifications, explanations, and interpretations that seek to continue the historic social domination. Whites, on the other hand, must consider confronting the meaning of their privilege. Perhaps also whites will interrogate preference in order to create racial harmony. But this will require whites to get beyond the idea that they are being dispossessed because others are being treated fairly and justly. It is in the best interest of whites and blacks to have a society of harmonious race relations. Our lives and property will be more adequately protected in a society of racial peace than in one where the Wilderness and the Promise are in permanent antagonism.

But what is clear is that African Americans must act even if whites do not act. And our actions for harmony and racial peace cannot depend upon a change of heart in the white community. Yet whites have a grave national responsibility to work out their own prejudice and hatred. No African American, not even the black conservative, can do this for white Americans. And no African American, not even the black anti-African conservative, is safe in a racist society.

The great Los Angeles rebellion after the Rodney King verdict should be seen as a warning of a serious national condition that, if left unresponded to, will produce unnecessary racial tragedy after tragedy. How do we avoid racial confrontation and restore respect with a sense of urgency? This is the question that Afrocentric theorists have tried to answer with their critiques and analyses. They have understood the necessity for centeredness; that is, the acceptance of African Americans as subjects rather than objects on the fringe of white America's history. By turning to agency, action, and participation as opposed to passivity, victimization, and spectatorship, the African American assumes the kind of centrality that serves as a basis for national cohesion. This is the key to mature racial encounters and interactions. Pluralism without ranking becomes the platform for mutual respect and social survival of the American nation.

More than two hundred years after the founding of the United States there remains deep racial discontent in this country. Most African Americans feel that white racism is a national problem that is rarely given attention by the nation's white educators and political leaders. Whites grow weary of hearing about racism; this is particularly true with those immigrant whites who aspire to own "whiteness" as a property because it grants them privilege and status. An Afghan who migrated to the United States after the September 11 terrorist attacks had to deal soon after with the question of race. She was asked, "What race are you?" The woman was stunned by the very American question and initially could not decide if she were black or white, but was soon convinced that "it would seem more American" if she said she was white.[1] Clearly, there is a great price to pay for indicating on official forms that you are black. Thus, the system pulls into its great churning wheel of fortune all immigrants who may be unaware at the time of the social and historical consequences of these kinds of choices. Of course, this quest is usually inherent in a white racist society where the identification with whiteness gives access to privilege not open to blacks. In this way, the immigrant European, while not historically implicated in the enslavement of Africans, is economically and politically linked by the advantages awarded to whites because of what Professor Winston Van Horne of the University of Wisconsin–Milwaukee has called "abstract whiteness,"[2] a kind of reserved status bestowed upon those eastern and southern Europeans who choose northern European whiteness over their own national origins.

There have been other responses to the American racial classification system, however. A Detroit schoolteacher who was born in Egypt sued the government to have his status changed from white to black because he did not look white and had never identified himself as anything but African, Egyptian, or black. Whiteness, he contended, did not help him either socially or politically. Since the United States classifies all people born in North Africa as white, the schoolteacher was simply given a classification as white because he was born in Egypt. But North Africa is Africa, and Africa is basically a black continent except for those who have entered from Europe or Arabia.

Africans have resisted the marginality imposed by the privileging of whiteness over people of color. Indeed, the last quarter of the nineteenth century was a fateful time for African people engaged in a colossal political manifestation of self-conscious action. A meeting of the National Conference of Colored Men that drew 140 delegates from nineteen states was held in Nashville, Tennessee, in May 1879 to discuss emigration. In the same year, New Orleans's Committee of Five Hundred Women agitated for every right that the Constitution was said to have guaranteed. However, these activities on the part of

Africans to be self-actualizing did not go unheeded or uncontested. Southern whites who believed that the independence of Africans in liberated areas of Kansas and other states would be dangerous to the political economy of the South struck against the black migration movement. Bulldozers and intimidators were employed throughout the South to threaten and kill blacks who agitated for settlement and legitimate civil rights or resisted racism. African assertion of agency—freedom from white control, influence, economic exploitation, and harassment—was considered a blow to the status of whites over blacks. Nevertheless, many African Americans, led by Pap Singleton and other passionate emigrationists, left the South for Kansas and Oklahoma.

Each advance was a difficult advance, each step a hard step, each stride a stride against the odds, because the political and social system of the United States was designed to protect whites from losing privilege while exposing blacks to the vilest forms of prejudice. Viewed from the vantage point of any objective observer, the attitude of the United States—not simply the South—toward Africans in law and practice was cruel, abominable, and discriminatory. So African Americans say to each other, Yes, you have made it this far and we know how far you have made it! I have never seen an African American in a position of authority that I take for granted who is unapologetically African; I know how tough it has been for that person to keep sanity and position. It could be easy, but it is not, because the psychologically grotesque and socially anarchic feature of racism is that it seeks to destroy, absorb, or minimize African American autonomy and culture. White supremacy cannot allow mutuality; blackness must be insulted, controlled, assaulted, or obliterated.

On May 4, 1899, the *New York Tribune* reported that the National Afro-American Council had called upon the African American community to set aside June 2, 1899, as a day of fasting and prayer, and June 4, a Sunday, to be a day to implore "God, the Father of Mercies" that he may set "His own hands" to repay those who have persecuted

Africans because if "vengeance is to be meted out let God himself repay."[3] Every African knew that the conditions under which he or she lived would take a major effort to overcome, yet all were confident that victory would eventually come.

Their words would resound through the decades:

> We pay out millions of dollars yearly to ride in "jim crow" cars, some of them scarcely fit for cattle, yet we are compelled to pay as much as those who have every accommodation and convenience. Indians, Chinamen and every other race can travel as they please. Such unjust laws make the railroad highway robbers. In some sections of the country we may ride for thousands of miles and are denied a cup of tea or coffee because no provision is made, or allowed to be made, to accommodate us with something to eat, while we are ready to pay for it. Waiving hundreds of inconveniences, we are practically outlawed by many States, and also by the general Government in its endorsement of silence and indifference.[4]

At the beginning of the twenty-first century, as at the beginning of the twentieth century, we recognize patterns of discrimination and racism that create a most powerful fury in the Wilderness dweller. What we see today in terms of the prisons and jails, in terms of the criminalization of black men and women, and in terms of physical abuse has a long history. W. E. B. Du Bois predicted in 1903 that the problem of the twentieth century would be the problem of the color line.[5] He did not come to that conclusion without attention to what had happened in the nineteenth century. Indeed, DuBois knew intimately the details of the proclamation of the National Afro-American Council, declared in these words:

> We are dragged before the courts by thousands and sentenced to every form of punishment, and even executed, without the privilege of having a jury composed in whole or in part of members of our own race while simple justice should guarantee us judges and juries who could adjudicate our cases free from the bias, caste and prejudice incident to the same in this country.[6]

While there has been change, the fundamental white supremacist position of society has never been relinquished. The proclamation of that early civil rights organization also spoke to the treatment of Africans in jails and prisons when it said:

> In many sections we are arrested and lodged in jails on the most frivolous suspicion of being the perpetrators of most hideous and revolting crimes, and regardless of established guilt, mobs are formed of ignorant, vicious, whiskey-besotted men, at whose approach the keys of these jails and prisons are surrendered and the suspicioned party is ruthlessly forced from the custody of the law and tortured, hanged, shot, butchered, dismembered and burned in the most fiendish manner.[7]

The African American population has known more irrational violence, more studied attempts at harassment, and more racial killing than any other community in America, with the possible exception of its aboriginal people. Those who wrote the above appeal knew the facts but could not predict that just a mere twenty years later, on July 27, 1919, there would be a race riot in Chicago that would rage virtually uncontrolled for four days, with white toughs beating isolated blacks and blacks beating white peddlers and vendors in an orgy of race madness. As rumors circulated of atrocities, members of each group sought more and more revenge. When the wave of violence was over, the toll was 38 dead, including 23 blacks and 18 whites, and 537 injured, including 342 blacks and 195 whites.[8]

The origin of the Chicago Race Riot of 1919 was in the gut-level hatred born of a racist society in which white workers on the killing floors of the stockyards and living in all-white neighborhoods felt threatened by blacks moving into the area, and fought to maintain a lily-white existence in jobs, residence, and recreation.

The summer of 1919 was called the Red Summer because of the violence against blacks across the country. A monstrous lynching occurred in Mississippi in June, in which a lynch mob severely wounded an accused rapist but feared that he might die before they had a chance to have a public lynching. Fearing that the accused, John Hartsfield, might expire, the mob asked a doctor to try to prolong his life. Thousands of whites flocked to Ellisville, Mississippi, to see the black man lynched with the sanction of the governor, Theodore G. Bilbo. Asked if he would try to prevent the lynching, Bilbo responded, "I am utterly powerless." The mob argued over the best way to kill Hartsfield. Some wanted him hanged; others wanted him burned. They hanged and burned him, and then riddled his body with bullets.[9]

The fury in the Wilderness has a historical underpinning. It is not unrelated to the fact that in Chicago the *Whip*, an intensely race-conscious black newspaper committed to defending the dignity of the black community, could write in 1919, after the blighted hopes of the war period and the increase of violence against blacks, "We are not pacifists, therefore we believe in war, but only when all orderly civil procedure has been exhausted and the points in question are justifiable. . . . The bombers will be bombed."[10]

But the experience is as contemporary as it is historical. The Hispanic uprising in the Washington Heights section of New York City on July 6, 7, and 8, 1992, a little over a month after the Los Angeles conflagration, was instructive. Washington Heights residents, largely Dominican, angered by the death of Jose Garcia at the hands of the police, went on rampage through the streets of New York. They said, "The glass is now full and it has begun to spill." Jesus Rodriguez put it this way: "We're in the United States but we are marginalized."[11] The words could have been those of African Americans: Those seeking to find respect often found disrespect, those seeking to find commonality often found marginality.

The time is ripe for the full blossoming of an American response to race and ethnicity that is based upon historical realities, economic conditions, and social relations. Why should Dominicans have to feel like outsiders in their adopted country? Why must African Americans fight the battle of place, that is, the battle of citizenship, which is ultimately the question of respect in this nation sanctified with our blood, sweat, and tears? Who is to say, other than Native Americans, that they have a more legitimate right to this land than we have? But in the end it is not an issue of competing places, but rather the ingredients for making a truly human nation.

To characterize the struggle of the Wilderness dwellers as the "politics of complaints," as done by some conservative writers, may make good copy somewhere, but the problems of white racial domination in American society are real. They exist because they have not been dealt with in a straightforward manner, and no amount of the "politics of denial" will make the problems go away. What is necessary is the moral will to transform the economic, social, and cultural grounds that separate the Promise from the Wilderness. Examining history is one approach to establishing the basis for a collective national will.

The 1960s did not start off as a good decade for race relations. Both the North and the South had their share of racial incidents. This was the era of Birmingham, called "Bombingham" by some of us because of the many bomb attacks on African Americans by whites. It was the time of the reign of the cattle prods and the bombing of a church where four young girls died. Cleveland, Ohio, saw its communities wrestle with the bitter aftermath of the death of a white minister, protesting segregation, who was accidentally killed by a bulldozer, and violence erupted when the police with weapons drawn dispersed African American youths. In New York City, African American children on their way to summer school found themselves in conflict with a white superintendent. The Progressive Labor Party entered the conflict with charges of brutality against the police. Fires and gunshots resulted and another incident in the violent 1960s was recorded for history. Three civil rights workers, James Chaney, Andrew Goodman, and Michael Schwerner, were abducted and murdered in Philadelphia, Mississippi, a city of brotherly love. The indictment named law enforcement officials of the community. An African American lieutenant colonel in the US Army was shot and killed by a Klansman as he was driving through Georgia. In Philadelphia, Pennsylvania, two policemen attempted to push an automobile with two individuals inside. There was an argument between the police and the wife of the car's owner. Bystanders thought the police acted abusively and mishandled the case. Subsequently, two nights of unrest occurred.

During the 1960s the emotions of this nation were rent with scars of bitterness and we hung out our personal and collective ethnic identities to be tested by the winds of political events. What the nation discovered during periods of unrest was that the leadership necessary to overcome this ordeal had to come from the deepest wells of ethical character, otherwise we were on a dangerous road.

Like Los Angeles in 1992, Selma, Alabama, in 1965 was the symbol of American racial discontent. Civil rights marchers started on their trek from Selma to Montgomery in a classic nonviolent posture, only to be interrupted by state troopers, officers of the law, as they settled into their march. Here, as in some other cases, rather than protecting marchers and demonstrators the troopers saw themselves as the protectors of the status quo. The state troopers operated from the system of racial preference and white supremacy that had been the standard of the old South. In their acceptance of the system, the troopers struck against the demonstrators for justice in a blind and ill-fated attempt to turn back the clock of progress. Whites who supported equal rights for blacks were attacked alongside them. In the aftermath of protests and demonstrations, a white clergyman and a white housewife were killed. They, like other whites of goodwill, had been at the forefront of the nonviolent protest. Soon the Deacons for Defense were organized in Bogalusa, Louisiana, with the express aim of supporting the inadequately protected demonstrators. Malcolm was dead. Vietnamese body counts came into living rooms on the television screen every evening. It is within this context that the Watts rebellion of 1965 occurred.

Before the Los Angeles uprising of 1992, the Watts rebellion of 1965 had been called the watershed insurrection. It lasted for a period of five days; 34 people were killed, 4,000 were injured, and $40 million worth of property was damaged.

Thomas Bradley became the first African American to serve as mayor of the city soon after the Watts rebellion. However, he was never widely popular among the black community because he was seen, perhaps unfairly, as soft on the issues of racism and discrimination. Bradley's style, a sort of slow-man's waltz, often seemed out of step with the fast-paced rhetoric of change in the African American community. The Watts rebellion was the prelude to his tenure as mayor.

Bradley's relationship with the African American community was never passionate. It goes without saying that the white community was not passionate about him, either. He was, after the Watts rebellion, a sort of humdrum, nonthreatening politician who kept the lid on the smoldering black community for several years. But he could not stop the Mexicans, already growing in numbers, from expressing their frustrations. So just five years after Watts, in 1970 and 1971, Bradley had the misfortune of cleaning up after yet another Los Angeles uprising. The Mexican American community rose up against the police. There were four deaths and more than $1 million in damages. Los Angeles was fast assuming the unenviable role as the most volatile and unstable American metropolis.

The Chicano community—politically conscious Mexican Americans born in the United States—had increasingly felt the same kind of hostility that the African American community felt from the police. And their resentment probably ran stronger than that of the African Americans because they viewed California as a historical part of the Mexican nation. A land-hungry white population conquered and annexed Mexican lands under an 1848 treaty that ended the Mexican-American War, which had been provoked by the United States in 1846. When it was over Mexico had lost half of its territory, a mass of land the size of Germany and France combined, including California, New Mexico, Utah, Nevada, Arizona, half of Colorado, and the part of Texas that had not been annexed earlier. For Mexican Americans this remains a psycho-historical fact that does not register often with many white policemen recently hired from southern states such as Louisiana and Arkansas. Mexicans were defined as Wilderness people, though some identified with a white status, emphasizing "Spaniard" over "Indian," in order to attain privilege in a system that favored whiteness. However, the darker Mexicans, the ones with thick Native American ancestry and perhaps no Spanish ancestry, recognized that they, like African Americans, were separated by a wall of racist ignorance from the fruits of the Promise.

The Los Angeles Police Department was beginning to have a reputation as one of the most violence-prone in the nation. The violence meted out by the police force was not limited to Africans and Chicanos, although those two communities were heaviest hit. Whites also complained about the mistreatment and rough handling of young white males by the police. In effect, the police force in Los Angeles had become a community unto itself, detached and disconnected from any organic relationship with its city.

You avoided the police if you could. "They's some sick psychos," an African American man in his thirties told a group of winos hanging around a grocery store on Vermont Avenue in September 1964. I had arrived in Los Angeles from Oklahoma in the summer of 1964 to get married, attend graduate school, and become a writer. My first book of poetry had just been published and I was eager and ready for the turbulence of a literary career with a manuscript of a novel in hand. A number of events blocked my early literary ambitions. I did not get married and that was a good thing, because my novel did not sell and I would have had a difficult time sharing in the support of a family. And then Watts erupted in a hailstorm of violence.

I personally saw Watts as a prophetic prelude to other revolts against the police and the white establishment in the Wilderness. By the summer of 1965 I was a student in Los Angeles and spent the entire period of the Watts uprising in the midst of the turmoil.

When the smoke literally cleared and I could return to my classes at Pepperdine College, I began washing dishes at a local restaurant and writing and reading poetry against the Vietnam War at venues along Venice Beach to pay my rent on West Fifty-fourth Street, just off Hoover. I had found this boarding house operated by Annie Miller, a motherly woman with a ready smile, within my budget of two hundred dollars a month. There were six other men living in the apartments she had constructed on the property behind her house. Because of the lure of the big city I immediately struck out to acquaint myself with the surrounding areas. Soon I was an authority on the area, from Santa Barbara to Imperial, from Crenshaw to Central.

This was my neighborhood, I owned it psychologically, and even though I would go to Pepperdine and finish my doctorate at UCLA and direct the Center for African American Studies there, I would never leave the South Central mentality: the Wilderness, the struggle against disrespect and meanness. I knew what it meant to be trapped, caged in a neighborhood; to have armored patrol cars and light military tanks rumbling down the streets. It had never been the reality of whites as far as I knew, but it was my reality.

Los Angeles in 1965 was my community and that reality was a defining one for my relationship with the rest of the country. Bus trips to Mississippi for voter registration were still popular among college students, and discrimination against African Americans in Los Angeles in housing and employment was common. I could not escape the Wilderness even if I tried. This same Wilderness attitude is found in people who experience discrimination and prejudice in employment, access, property, and opportunity, and who self-consciously understand the meaning of being treated differently and unequally.

My Georgia and Tennessee childhood had introduced me to the activism of the civil rights movement, which I had been a part of since my high school days in Nashville, when Fisk University student Diane Nash was the queen of demonstrations. Living in Los Angeles, with its urban mask—that is, pretty lawns, neat bungalows, and relatively clean streets concealing the terrible poverty and human suffering—prepared me for the larger Wilderness struggle. Nothing we did to raise the standard of living and ease the pain of poverty in the self-help organizations of South Central or the block grant programs on

Central, Vermont, and Western could ever turn back the terrible face of urban racism. We could not, as we often thought we could at the time, make ourselves acceptable to whites. This was the wrong avenue. It led to a cul-de-sac in our thinking. It intensified the Wilderness emotion. It supported the idea of white supremacy.

The Wilderness is a metaphor for the feeling of economic, social, political, and professional abandonment that is often found in the inner cities, but can be found anywhere and everywhere bigotry creates the death of hope. The conditions of the Wilderness—denial of opportunity, anti-African hostility, abandoned houses and stores, religious and racial prejudice—are factors that lead to resistance action. Thus, wherever Africans speak up and out against the ideology of white supremacy, they are fighting the supporting structure for the Wilderness. On an individual basis this means that lawsuits might be brought against racist employers or institutions. On a collective level it may mean demonstrations, petitions, and violent explosions against the elements of pain and persecution.

As Wilderness dwellers, some of us live in the deep inner recesses of the Wilderness from which it is almost impossible to escape. Others of us are on the shallow fringes where we are able to see quite well the workings of the system but know that at any moment we could slip back into the depths. The truth is that nearly 90 percent of African Americans who are now considered successful have compelling rags-to-riches stories. Jackie Joyner-Kersee's East St. Louis upbringing is not dissimilar from Bill Cosby's North Philadelphia childhood or Jesse Jackson's North Carolina road to glory. They, like thousands of others, left the abandoned houses and stores of the deep Wilderness and found some answers to the enigma of America. But even more, they had to overcome or push back the internal realization of the Wilderness. This is the most difficult part of being victimized in America, because it stresses you out without anyone knowing. A sense of being lost, abandoned, with no way out often affects the mind of the Wilderness dweller for as long as he or she lives. Fast cars, investment portfolios, yachts, houses in Dakar and Paris, acceptance at a country club, and even a seat on the Supreme Court cannot completely eradicate this sense of Wilderness. Everything tells you: You cannot escape the Wilderness.

The outward signs of the Wilderness can be managed somewhat, even personally. That is, I can buy clothes, if I have a job, and I can get an apartment or a house to change the condition of my life. I can even work in the public sphere to change the nature of the community in which I live. These things we do and have done.

I will never forget that in the aftermath of the 1965 Watts rebellion, a number of community organizations were created as self-help agencies. Euphoria gripped a number of groups. Some of them did not last until the end of the decade; others are still around. Among the most important was the Brotherhood Crusade, which had a series of impressive leaders, including the legendary Walter Bremond, who helped to organize the charitable monies of the Los Angeles African American community. But by far the most significant group to emerge from the Watts rebellion was the Kawaida Organization under the leadership of the brilliant philosopher Maulana Karenga, a young man who had studied political science, history, literature, and languages with the intent to raise the consciousness of the African American population.

Karenga had prepared himself very early for intellectual leadership. An impressive debater and orator, Karenga studied political science and spent a considerable amount of time analyzing the condition of Africans in America. Believing that a cultural crisis was the root cause of most problems in the African American community, Karenga applied his developing political theory to the organization of the community. US, a cultural and political organization, served as his base for the teaching of Kawaida philosophy. Among the tenets of his philosophy were cultural nationalist themes such as the need for Africans to speak an African language, and the recognition of the seven principles of nation building: *umoja*, unity; *kugichagulia*, self-deterimination; *ujima*, cooperative economics; *ujamaa*, collective work and responsibility; *nia*, purpose; *kuumba*, creativity; and *imani*, faith.[12] But it is probably the founding of Kwanzaa in 1966 that was Karenga's most important contribution to the cultural life of African Americans. It is a self-determined holiday, celebrated by millions of people to honor the historic deeds and first fruits of the ancestors of African Americans.

Yet despite the gains that came from this period of racial and social turbulence, we were not out of the frigid steppes of prejudice and racism. Events occurred that propelled the nation once more, in other places, toward new relationships between the Wilderness and the Promise visions.

In the summer of 1966, the Chicago police arrested an African American male for turning on a fire hydrant. Firebombing, window smashing, and rock throwing were the immediate responses of the community. The National Guard came into Chicago to reinforce the police and put down the disorder. Five hundred fifty-three people were arrested and three were killed.

The next two years saw more than one hundred cities in the United States involved in some type of urban unrest. The most violent outburst during this period was the Detroit uprising, which was precipitated by two incidents. The Detroit police raided the Five Blind Pigs, an after-hours drinking and gambling establishment, and arrested eighty-two people. In addition to the anger caused by these arrests, the earlier killing of an African American by a white street gang added bitterness to African American emotions. When the figures were counted and the situation assessed, the Detroit rebellion had caused $22 million in damage, 7,200 arrests, and 43 deaths. Although the media tried to downplay the uprising, it was one of the most severe domestic outbreaks of violence in American history.

We did not know it then, but with a little forethought, we might have been able to tell someone that it would happen again in Los Angeles. The vital statistics of the African American condition only got worse over the years. If the Wilderness increased in its viciousness, how were we to escape 1992? Of course, statistics cannot measure the human suffering that goes on in the Wilderness. What has happened in many cases is that the wills of Wilderness dwellers have been broken and they become tired of fighting discrimination and abuse. They then strike at those authorities they hold responsible for their personal fates.

After the Los Angeles uprising of 1992, some whites and a few blacks came up with the radical idea that the African American community needed to be more congruent to the white community. This was actually the deficit model being extended to corrective social and political policies. The theory was that if blacks could be made more acceptable to whites—more agreeable to whites, more like whites, and maybe even whites—then there would not be such a great gulf between whites and blacks, and blacks would be more easily accepted as "true Americans." What was overlooked was the fact that few blacks *want* to be white; indeed, most people simply want to be left alone to do what they need to do. The problem in the United States has never been how blacks *are* but rather how whites have seen blacks.

Some white officials in Los Angeles now seem to be looking for ways to make the African American community more acceptable to whites. But there is nothing inherently *wrong* with blacks. We would not need federal intervention in the housing, education, and economics sectors if whites were not racist. We are not denied jobs, loans, or admissions because something is wrong with our blackness; we are denied because many whites are racist. Perhaps a massive training program, funded by the foundations and the government, could deal with the question of white racism. Granting monies to researchers to explore the origin, development, and provenance of racism among whites might be revolutionary. At the present time, if money is given for the study of race it is usually given to white academics to justify the provenance of racism or to study the impact of race on blacks. What may really be necessary at this juncture in social and human sciences is the examination of the nature of white children's orientation to race and, of course, the nature of white racism itself.

How does a child learn to see African Americans as inferior? What mechanisms of training, value orientation, ethics, and socialization might be useful in combating the insidious racism that begins very early to destroy the possibility of a genuinely human community? Answers to these questions are at the heart of Martin Luther King Jr.'s dream. He was not asking merely for tolerance, but for the elimination of racism, the erasing of racism in American society.

# CHAPTER FIVE
# THE DISORIENTATION

A white man from the tree-lined and rock-manicured streets of Simi Valley made his way in the late evening toward a section of the American Wilderness in South Central Los Angeles soon after the 1992 uprising. Smoke still lingered in the air, broken glass was everywhere, the bombed-out buildings were the skeletal remains of the rage of Los Angeles. In a land where so many platitudes replace real communication, where single issues occupy entire groups of people for long periods of time, where beautiful words without real substance provide profiles in courage, and where escapism is the principal adventure, this Simi Valley Samaritan was struck dumb by the intensity of the collective fury of the people.

"Why?" he asked, half muttering to himself as he walked toward a knot of people who were already helping with the cleanup effort. "Why?" he repeated, almost in disbelief. He walked resolutely, as he mentally prepared himself to assist in the rebuilding of the community and do anything he could to create a climate of goodwill.

The perplexed Samaritan from Simi Valley was genuine in his earnestness, but he did not know very much about the bewildering conditions that caused the fury in the American Wilderness. Like the others who repeatedly emerged from various areas of Southern California to say that they were shocked by the extent of the rage in Los Angeles, the Samaritan was a victim of the same denial of realities that led to the brutalization of Rodney King, the first not-guilty verdict, and the uprising. This man, with his Simi Valley consciousness, was like so many other whites—and some African Americans who exist on the fringes of the American Wilderness. They seem to lose the ability to comprehend the extent and analyze the reasons for the fury within the African American community. To them, the Wilderness represents strangeness, distance, mystery, and alienation like they have never known. And yet they are able to live in America and know something of its history and the intimate involvement of Africans, enslaved and free, in the construction of the American nation; they are aware of neither the depth nor the reason for our fury. Their daily encounters with Wilderness dwellers in this large metropolis, most often seen as the epitome of the American melting pot, yield no real understanding of life in the Wilderness. Nothing in their experiences prepares them for understanding the wishes, desires, hopes, disappointments, and brutalities experienced by the Wilderness dwellers.

Deep in his thought, the Simi Valley Samaritan jumped back, startled, as he heard a voice. He looked into the shadows, past the broken glass of the bombed-out furniture store. To the left he could make out the faint outline of a black man, who looked to be in his mid-thirties, in baggy clothing with an object in his hand.

"Excuse me," he said, swallowing hard to hide his panic.

"It ain't about having things, it is about having everything," the voice said.

The Samaritan was perplexed. He didn't know whether to run or respond to the voice, which seemed to be moving closer.

"I heard you," the voice said. "I heard you asking, 'Why?' "

Now the voice was a handshake away from the Samaritan. It

belonged to a tall, dark, muscular young man who held the scorched remains of a cellular phone in his hand.

"This is my store," he said, motioning to the wreck of a building behind him.

"I'm David," the Samaritan held out his hand before dropping it limply at his side.

"Come on in, David." The store owner motioned for him to enter the wrecked store. David was about to get intimately acquainted with life in the Wilderness.

He still wanted a straightforward answer to his question— Why?—but he was afraid to ask it again.

The owner said to him, "I'm Kofi. I have owned this store for six years. I never expected to be wiped out like this, but I understand the anger. Everything is gone. They've looted everything."

"You say you understand?" David volunteered, hoping to elicit more understanding himself.

"You know, David, you see African Americans and Chicanos, but you don't really *know* us. There is a grinding pain and hurt here, not just for the televisions and radios. It ain't about material possessions only. It is about a spirit," Kofi explained.

"Why the rage to destroy their own community?" David asked sheepishly.

"But they don't see this as their community."

"You owned a business here, and you're black."

"But they know that my getting this business was different from all of these other businesses," Kofi said, walking toward the front of the building and pointing down both ends of the street. "They know what an African American has to put up with to get a loan; they know that it is not our community the way you make it seem. I know that."

"Every group of people who come to America makes it on their own," David said. "Why can't blacks do the same thing?"

"Man, you're taking my time. You want a lesson, I'll give you a lesson in American history. Our ancestors worked in hot fields and along cold, damp riverbanks with no shoes. They picked cotton till the tips of their fingers bled and went home to their shacks to find that their children had died of dehydration or starvation. When it snowed they wore burlap to protect their scarred and bleeding feet while building up this country for other people. No, it is not the same. We've worked as hard and longer than anyone, but let me try to get $50,000 or $100,000 to start my business from your bank. Racial prejudice and discrimination are ingrained in the way whites respond to African Americans."

"What do you mean?"

"I mean even the police treat us differently: rudely, almost with hatred," Kofi argued.

"This is America; are you serious?" David said in disbelief.

"Let me tell you something. In the most affluent white suburbs, we're the ones the police follow the most, the ones who must always give an accounting of our presence, the ones who are stalked like prey in department stores, and the ones who are refused entry to elite jewelry stores—when, in fact, white thugs are robbing them crazy."

"Well, I want to help. What should I do?" David exasperatedly asked.

"Damn, David, you've got to start in your own neighborhood by getting your friends and neighbors to discuss their own prejudices against African Americans. Ask them where those prejudices stem from? Debate them openly. Ask them whether their biases are reflected in their jobs, their responses to African Americans, and so forth. Hell, I don't know what kind of therapy whites need. Anyway, I've got to think about rebuilding my store. Have fun." Kofi turned and walked toward a parked car a half a block away.

David, the Simi Valley Samaritan, still pondered the question, Why? And so it is between the Wilderness and the Promise, the well-intentioned whites, safely ensconced in lush neighborhoods all over America, having been able to secure their jobs and mortgages, not because they are more intelligent, or more ambitious, or more talented, or more deserving than African Americans, but because they are white, and they feign ignorance of the reasons for social unrest and the lack of

African American advancement. They have only to look at themselves and they will see the reasons for the anger and the hostility.

Remember the facts: Rodney King was hauled out of his car in Los Angeles in 1992 and pummeled with nightsticks by police more than fifty times as he lay writhing on the ground. Four of the police officers were initially brought to trial and found not guilty. They were retried by the federal court and two were found guilty in the beating. But after the first verdict, the city of Los Angeles exploded in an orgy of violence. The Los Angeles insurrection was the most costly in the nation's history. Fifty-eight people were killed, more than a billion dollars in damage was done, and the uprising caused a considerable amount of personal suffering, with 13,212 arrested and 2,382 injured. It was multicultural, transracial, and transclass in nature. Hispanics outnumbered African Americans in arrests for looting, but at least seventy-two whites were arrested for the same crime, in addition to about twenty Asians.[1] A withering storm of fire made ashes of the relationships that had already been strained anyway. Public officials—from Mayor Tom Bradley to the county commissioners—hoped aloud that upon the heap of burned buildings and bruised feelings the city would build new relationships.

Cities with large gaps between the rich and poor—among them Atlanta, Seattle, San Francisco, and Las Vegas—reacted to the verdict in the Rodney King case with disturbances that included deaths and fires. But many other cities felt the rumble just under the surface, because the reasons for the uprising were not simply the verdict to free the police officers who beat Rodney King, though that was the trigger.

Every large city in America has a record of alleged police brutality against Africans. Wilderness dwellers are the victims of white fear and police diligence in support of that fear. We imagine that when many whites see a police officer stopping a black motorist they feel a sense of safety that "their man" is on the job or just "better someone else." On the other hand, when *we* see the same man being stopped by police, we know that the interaction is likely to be tense between the officer and the African American. Indeed, if the police officer has taken an aggressive position against the motorist some African Americans, out of habit and experience, slow their cars to let the police officer know he or she is being watched. This is a pattern of behavior practiced in the Wilderness in the hope that the tide of brutality can be stemmed. One feels the need to do something to report police abuse against any motorist—especially a black motorist, who usually will not have the support of the white community.

Most African males over thirty years of age have been stopped aggressively by white police and we know the scenario. I have personally been stopped three times and treated quite harshly each time. Never mind that I have a Ph.D. degree from UCLA; I felt that because the police were acting on their fears and prejudices they felt they had to demonstrate their control.

In one incident, in Philadelphia, I had parked my car in a legitimate space in order to rush into my son's school for five minutes to get him and return to the car. When I returned to my car, a policeman was standing beside it, waiting for me. He asked me if I didn't know that he had declared it a no-parking zone. I told him that there was no indication that it was, and anyway, since there was no other place to park I would still have risked getting a parking ticket in order to be able to pick up my son. He said he had spoken to me on another occasion about parking on the street and running into the building to retrieve my child and that was enough. I told him I had no other choice but to park there and he could give me a ticket. My offer to pay the ticket upset him. He grew very angry. I said to him, "Please give me a ticket if you believe that I have done something illegal." He cursed, spat on the ground, and grew quite livid, even shaking as he talked to me at the top of his voice. I knew enough to remain silent, not to move, and to express my regrets that I had parked in the "zone." He turned away without giving me a ticket, but I knew that I had been very close to being hurt. I felt what all African Americans have felt in the presence of ignorance and arrogance.

Those who live the Promise cannot even dream of the daily insults in the Wilderness. Los Angeles—like Philadelphia, New York, and Chicago—insulates the two communities and there is a world of difference in the way the police treat whites and blacks.

The fact that Philadelphia, Chicago, and New York remained relatively quiet during the Los Angeles uprising of 1992 does not prove anything about the police forces in those cities or the race relations between African Americans and whites. We would all like to think that our relations are better than those in another city, but the fact of the matter is that they cannot be any better because the conditions are the same.

The social meltdown in Los Angeles is evidence enough that cultures brought together in American society do not necessarily meld into a new culture. While this may have worked in the case of northern Europeans who came to this country, most other groups—the Japanese, the Koreans, the Greeks, the Albanians, and so on—have remained connected to their historical roots. Africans, of course, never melted in the pot in the first place, and have been caught in a suspended state because we have neither permitted ourselves to be truly Africans nor been treated fairly as Americans.[2]

Rodney King said the shooting and looting were not right: "We are all stuck here for a while, let's try to work it out. Can't we all get along?" His lonesome voice, broken because of the many blows to his body, could only haltingly call for peace amid the thunderous voices of the multitudes who kept saying, "No justice, no peace."

These words, spoken by the vast majority of Wilderness dwellers, were created out of the logic and circumstances of their lives. People who do not have electricity today or water tomorrow have the inexorable arguments of reality. They know that sooner or later society will respond to their action and the electricity and the water will return.

But others ask, Why is this so? Why is it that only when we rise up to crash the glassy facade hanging over the Wilderness and see it shatter in a thousand small hurts does the government understand that it must do something? Why is it that the Republicans and the

Democrats have competed with each other to see who could be quickest to take the urban communities off of the agenda? Why is it that this nation has never followed through on an urban policy to save the cities, to bring life back to the historic centers? Model Cities and the Great Society were two government programs that ran out of steam because there was not enough political will in the nation. Why is it that the real issue is always pushed aside to make room for the expedient discussion? The real issue is, How do we end white supremacy, the doctrine of mistreating Africans *because* we are Africans?

Peace works only where you have justice or at least the perception of justice. Many African Americans believe justice may be impossible under a regime where white privilege and white power are the rule of thumb. How do we change the perception? What can be done to create a new basis for a social contract, a public order? The first thing that can be done is to recognize that whether people fall into the Promised Land or the Wilderness, we are all part of the same country, despite our historical circumstances. This puts the question of identity at the base of the new perception. Whites can no longer think of themselves as the quintessential Americans. An American can have Native, Asian, African, Latino, or European background. Finding arenas for propagating the idea of an American citizenship that takes into consideration all creeds of American culture is the task that must be undertaken by a committed cadre of new revolutionaries.

Urban America is the most volatile Wilderness community. Here, the sense of abandonment is greatest. Here, hope is severely bruised. Here, the resentment begins early, in the child who wonders why he should be so much poorer than his peers in the suburbs.

Life in the Wilderness is the ultimate social demonstration, the showplace extraordinaire. So in Los Angeles, the show capital of America, we are our most ritualistic selves. A mixture of the real and unreal, the substance and the shadow, the pain and the symptoms bring us to the point of perpetual combustion. To stand in awe of the Los Angeles conflagration is to stand in all of the depth of our degradation in the Wilderness. To blame the Los Angeles uprising on the Wilderness dwellers is to miss the point of nearly four hundred years of economic, social, and political discrimination against Africans.

Of course, there are cases of individual madness and reactions to crowd psychology that frighten all of us, as when someone terrorizes individuals or groups because of race, religion, gender, or place of origin. Furthermore, our consciences are stung by the immorality of wanton abuse and attacks. Nevertheless, it would be a mistake to let the circumstance of Los Angeles overshadow the underlying problems in the Wilderness, because until we assess and resolve them, there will inevitably be more furious passages in the Wilderness.

The conditions in Los Angeles are found in other urban centers, with their sense of no fair play, alienation, unemployed and idle youths, broken and dilapidated schools, abandoned buildings, dashed creativity, mountains of resentment, and cultural disorientation because of dreams obliterated. To the young, fixed in this disorientation from a promising future, escape seems almost impossible. As journalists, two Chicago teenagers gave readers an account of how they saw the projects, where a five-year-old child was dropped to his death from a high-rise apartment because he would not steal candy. The young reporters wanted out, but felt trapped.[3] In spite of all of this, there is yet a stubborn flicker of vitality in the Wilderness that refuses to be snuffed out. I have seen it in the most depressed neighborhoods in this country, where families hardly have enough food to eat and where no jobs exist. The oral traditions, spiritual fervor, gregarious nature, and love of the physical competition that appear in much of African American culture can inspire creative responses to anomie, alienation, and cultural oppression.

Kobe Bryant, Shaquille O'Neal, Allen Iverson, Venus and Serena Williams, and Tiger Woods are symbols of physical prowess and power that are respected highly in the Wilderness. There is an understanding that is implicit in recognizing the talent of these individuals.

Achievement in a racist society does not come without some personal price. Each of these individuals—and many others in education, science, business, and the professions—have arrived at some personal satisfaction because they have overcome the odds. Most realize also that their own stories of conquest create hope, drama, and optimism.

Take the case of Jeff, a twenty-year-old rapper from a North Philadelphia neighborhood where it seems everyone is a poet, a rapper, a talker with the rhythm of the hip-hop culture. Jeff became a local hero because he went to the talent show in the park and demonstrated his artistic and musical prowess. When questioned about his future, Jeff quickly said, "If Shaq could come from where he came from and do what he does, I know that I can achieve anything I want to achieve." Statements like this may be overstatements, but what they suggest is that there is a well of optimism in the most desolate, distant corners of the Wilderness. Thus, the option exists; the potential for good is always present. But the stark conditions in the Wilderness can create a volatile combustion that erupts when social and political events collide. If we are to make the nation work, then moral credibility, social responsibility, and intellectual integrity *must* be placed in the service of reconciliation of the Wilderness and the Promise.

An adequate understanding of Watts in 1965 might have noted that the vitality and hopefulness of the Los Angeles Wilderness had been drained, and that in the face of personal and social failures South Central Los Angeles might revolt again. The people of Watts were Wilderness dwellers on the outskirts of the Promised Land. I believe most experts using the "blow your stack" analogy felt that tensions had been released in the 1965 Watts uprising and that there was no longer any real serious problem of confrontation. They were wrong. Mount St. Wilderness will explode every time fury builds because the rage is inescapable where people believe they have been and are still being mistreated.

What was missed in various analyses of the Watts uprising of 1965 was the fact that the destruction of the will and the decentering of the people's identities were at the heart of the indignation. Tormented by alienation, poverty, and prejudice, many of the people were drained of their vitality and their will. Living in depressed neighborhoods with depressed economies, they became depressed people. But the lessons of 1965 and 1992 must not be lost for another generation.

In fact, the five days of burning in 1992 were nothing compared to the years of smoldering flames under the breaths of the residents of South Central Los Angeles. They could sense long before the fire at the corner of Florence and Nomandie that something was going to happen. They knew this soon after the 1965 uprising. There were voices always speaking about the distance between the reality and the illusion, between the said and the unsaid. Tension had existed too long between the ideal and the real in terms of the propaganda of the Promise and the actuality of the Wilderness. Street preachers, rap artists, scholar-activists, and itinerant hustlers had called for a "referendum" at the corner of Central and 103rd, at Figueroa and Florence, at Slauson and Vermont, and the people voted with their own anger.

The street speakers knew that the conditions in the community were classic prerevolutionary conditions, and that they were prophets of doom. But they were not prophets without honor, they were prophets who were heard on the streets by young people who said that they could not be disrespected anymore. They were the ones who vowed to end racism without understanding the insidious nature of white supremacy. Yet the voice of those prophets, whether as New York's "Last Poets" or as Los Angeles's "Watts Prophets," told the truth as they saw it at the time.

A new generation of poets has arisen. They are the spoken-word artists who electrify the crowds at the Pearl of Africa on South Street, or the Soul Café on Forty-second, or the Café Future in Inglewood. For those who cannot hear these new words, or heed their warnings, these visionary *djelis* are saying that buildings and programs without attitudinal change will only delay a greater outburst. Los Angeles, like the American nation, will be poorer in human relations if we do not deal face-to-face with the fundamentally anti-African ideas, language, and behaviors found in this society. Indeed, more than attempting to deal with racial tensions, we must confront racism itself. By the same token, and equally important, must be the re-creation and reconstruction of cultural values based on progressive democratic ideals. But contrary to the opinion of conservatives, the necessary values are not *white* values but *human* values, rooted in our own orientation to environment and place. From this vantage point we have rejected elevated harmony in keeping with the African ideals.

Ethics and morality are grounded in the manifold ways Africans have responded to historical experiences in this land. But it is a mistake to assume, as conservatives do, that the problem is a lack of "white values." Indeed, it may be that certain so-called white values—such as individualism, the profit motive, and selfishness—are the reasons for the dysfunctional relationships in this society. Contrary to popular opinion, most Wilderness people seek to provide positive environments for their children. They want to explore the fullness of their limited lives. They love their neighbors. They believe in cleanliness, loyalty, and decency. They are not Enron or WorldCom executives. They often, however, live around petty drug pushers who prey upon the community. They cheat no one and they do not steal; they are just poor.

Criminals ought to be locked up. No one in the Wilderness who cares about the conditions of life in the community would support anything less. While we know that the social and economic situations of people often drive them to extremes in their values and morals, we also know that the African American people have always had a positive response to higher values.

Criminals ought to be rehabilitated, if possible. Criminals are people who have made a habit of being antisocial, anticommunity, and antifamily. They are small, selfish individuals who must be rehabilitated before they are returned to the community. A proper intervention has to include methods for inspiration and transformation. Without inspiring and transforming the attitudes in the community, intervention techniques are useless, because they do not reinforce the community's need for humanizing itself through culture, art, science, history, literature, and beauty.

Given the opportunity to truly practice the values of collective protection of the individual, which is a noble obligation, alongside the profit motive, an enlightened America might yet enthrone a new holistic relationship between people that depends more on mutuality than platitudes. In such a regime, politicians might be encouraged to demonstrate their support for the rights of all Americans to liberty, freedom, justice, equality, and security. This is more difficult than it seems because it requires not rhetoric, but a genuine commitment to overthrow white supremacy in every sector of society. Can it be done?

Not to examine the political impotence of local and even national leaders in regard to the race issue is to miss the point of our national disaster. Politicians debate issues of war and peace, of ways and means, and yet have been unable to address the issues posed by the Wilderness dwellers. This is because they refuse to address the beast of racism that provokes most of the responses in the Wilderness in its own lair. Banks that will not make loans to African Americans for businesses, insurance companies that overcharge persons who live in African American communities, committees that discriminate in promoting African Americans, and companies that refuse to hire even African Americans who have more than the skills necessary—these are the culprits that must be prevented from creating the havoc of hatred. These are the institutions that must be challenged at the first hint of discrimination in order to assure the social survival of the American nation.

The response cannot be merely housing or jobs. This defeats the entrepreneurial interests and abilities that exist within the African American community. The correct response is one that demands fairness from business and civic leadership that does not yet exist in this country.

The slow rebuilding of South Central Los Angeles, on top of the slow rebuilding of the Los Angeles community of Watts, indicates that only continued political pressure on the government and private sectors can truly bring about economic and political change. It is fitting, in some ways, that Los Angeles becomes the test case for the extent to which the nation is willing to travel toward bringing Wilderness dwellers into the Promised Land. With numerous new ethnic groups, mainly from Asia, added to the large numbers of Chicanos and the established African communities, Los Angeles is set for the future progress of this nation—or for imminent danger, if we can't have one nation made of many people. Success will be achieved when the predominant white population understands the nature of living together with others without the notion that whites must dominate.

A few years ago in New York City, a relatively well-to-do white man was kidnapped and held against his will for several days in a hole in the ground. The authorities searched numerous places for him, hoping to find him before a ransom was paid. When they finally found the man, he looked rather "wild" and his demeanor suggested disorientation. He had been held by several Spanish-speaking kidnappers who had slipped him scraps of food every day but kept him essentially in the dark. When asked what was the most difficult part of his experience, the man answered in words similar to these: "I thought I was losing my mind. I felt helpless. People were speaking in a language that I could not understand, but I knew they were speaking of me. It angered me that I had been caught in this situation. The worst thing was the possibility that I would actually lose my mind and never be found."

It is an awesome achievement that in nearly four hundred years of Wilderness living, most African Americans have remained sane. In spite of the disabilities connected with dislocation, displacement, and detachment from historical and cultural roots, some Wilderness dwellers have dared to reconnect with those roots. The need for reconnection exists because of the tragic tearing away of the very fiber of the African's soul in the process of enslavement, discrimination, and racism. Keeping their sanity has been a losing battle for too many residents of the Wilderness.

Since it was our different origin, our peculiar condition, that launched us on this unique journey in the Wilderness, it should not seem strange that we have wrestled Lucifer to maintain our sanity. When the ships of the souls came and we were torn away from familiar places and spaces and brought across the ocean to the Americas, we experienced a mental, psychological dislocation. We were no longer oriented, and our disorientation became the first order of our lives. In the Wilderness, our physical liberation would be achieved before our mental liberation.

Stripped of the names of our ancestors—Obafemi, Omowale, Niang, Keita, Owusu, Agara, Mutombo, Birago, Emeka, Essien, and Adekunle—and given the names of Europeans—Smith, Williams, Loury, Thomas, West, Gates, Washington, Sowell, Jefferson, Jackson, Connerly, and Gillespie—we lost our way in the Wilderness. Some of us would become masters at denying the reality of our sickness, claiming that we were really never "Mutombo" but always "Johnson," and that our ancestors were never Africans but always Europeans. So complete would be the process of denial and disorientation that some African Americans would despise the color of their skin, the curliness of their hair, and would derogate anyone who reminded them of their African origins. These are the people who seek reinforcement from the white community in their disorientation. When the whites would say, "You're not an African. You're an American, just like me," the dislocated African would repeat the comment without considering the various levels of complexity of such an easy statement. For example, to accept one's continent of origin is not to deny one's citizenship. Every white person knows that. When a white person claims to be American, she is often claiming more than citizenship; she is claiming to have metamorphosed into a "new person" in which her European heritage, collectively taken, has helped to define the reality of who she is. On the other hand, the African person has often been forced to relinquish his or her culture and origin.

African Americans are often confronted with the question, "Are you African or American?" But we are both African *and* American inasmuch as one represents our historical origin and the other, our national citizenship. This choice is not to be confused with the oft-repeated notion of "double consciousness" attributed to Du Bois. This great scholar offered that he felt in his body the strivings of "two warring ideals in one dark body."[4] I believe that most African Americans do not experience such doubleness as defined and expressed by intellectuals in universities. Wilderness dwellers who are comfortably African have no desire to be white, nor are they confused about their citizenship. Charshee McIntyre has argued that the "two struggle streams" have always been present in African history in the United States: cultural perpetuation or cultural abnegation. Both are open to the African person.[5] By choosing the first course, the African brings something of value to the human table; by electing the second, the African declares that he has nothing of value to share with others. With this last choice the person abnegates, surrenders, reasoning that since white supremacy—even when it is interpreted as the mainstream—is so strong that it is best to declare not so much whiteness, which whites will not accept, but that he is not black or is only black by accident and nothing else. This form of behavior has been labeled by African American psychologists as a particular mental illness called *extreme misorientation.*[6]

Extreme misorientation may be found among many Wilderness dwellers who have accepted white cultural values, such as materialism and individualism, as superior to their own traditions of humanism and collectivity. These are the persons who have tried all their lives to distance themselves from other Africans. Often they attended schools where they excelled in every aspect of European culture and society, at times being considered more "white" in behavior and attitudes than whites by their colleagues. They attempt to imitate the white person in every way, even trying to talk like whites or to disclaim any interest in African American or soul food in order to be declared "white" enough. Contrary to popular opinion, these blacks are not ridiculed for "acting white" simply because they are studious, enjoy school, or read books. The vast majority of brilliant black students are not criticized as "acting white." This term is reserved for those African Americans who reject their own culture and believe that by adopting the gestures, mannerisms, and culture of whites, they will gain privilege in society. Often they are correct, because in a white racist society, the tendency is to seek the status of whiteness, where privilege resides.

Years of negative propaganda about Africans has conspired to create in some African Americans such serious cases of self-hatred that they will claim descent from *any* white ethnic group rather than identify with Africa. Because of the amount of miscegenation that occurred during the enslavement period, many African Americans do in fact have a mixture of European ancestry.[7] However, inasmuch as race has been defined in the American social context in a political way, the self-hating African seeks to claim a European heritage to guard against the stigma of Africanness. In other words, such a person buys into the system of white supremacy.

Some African Americans believe that we can achieve only by becoming white in our attitudes, behaviors, and customs—even if we remain black in color. There are many ways to do this in the Wilderness. One might take a white spouse; write books in support of white conservative positions, especially books attacking other blacks; contribute millions to institutions with a history of discrimination; or master the European classics and claim to have little or no knowledge of Africa or of African American culture.

Opting to do this can mean choosing to seek acceptance by evading one's historical origin and culture, likely believing in the inferiority of one's own culture and hoping to be seen by whites as "cultured" in the European sense. In the Wilderness, those who choose to take that path are considered "sellouts" or abnegators because they seek to distance themselves from what they perceive to be the inferiority of other Wilderness dwellers. Their idea, meant for white audiences, is: I'm not like them. Of course, the average Wilderness dweller with no airs and no interest in giving up her identity agrees that the abnegator is not like the rest of the African American community.

In the Wilderness, Africans who harbor self-hatred often become the conservative voices: the anti-African blacks, the token blacks, the critics of civil rights, and the surrogate spokespersons for the system to which they aspire. They are usually despised by the Wilderness dwellers for their cultural weakness, their lack of historical depth, their willingness to sell their political souls to the highest bidder, and their lack of moral integrity.

Fortunately, many African Americans in the Wilderness have chosen to follow another course. Relocation or reconnection has been a pursuit of Africans in every period of our history. They have chosen to perpetuate their culture by reconnecting with the traditions, customs, and foods of their African culture. This is the explanation for what some writers have called the Africans' fascination with the nationalist movement almost from the beginning of their presence in this nation. Most frequently, a *black nationalist* is defined as a person who believes in self-determination, self-definition, and the cultural reconstruction of African Americans. According to many scholars, this remains the most popular philosophical statement among African Americans.

From the earliest moments, when the slave ships landed in Massachusetts, Virginia, North Carolina, and Georgia, many captive Africans refused to submit to the process of Europeanization forced upon them. Those who did not escape to live with the Native Americans but remained enslaved often used their time to salvage as much as they could of African culture—music, dance, art, poetry, and word games. Since the oral form of communication was the chief avenue open to us during the long years of enslavement, we developed, using our African cultural base, a complex verbal and dramatic style. It was infinitely important to those early plantation societies for some African person, man or woman, to maintain a connection to the ancestors. However, the racist ideology of white superiority has been the biggest barrier to ancestral reconnection.

Inasmuch as the ideology of white superiority is not limited to a particular socioeconomic segment of the white population, it serves as an instrument of controlling the Wilderness dwellers and retaining white privilege. Certain mental defenses are developed in the Wilderness against such an aggressive ideology. One of the key defenses among African Americans has been the establishment of space as a psychological protection. A second is a countering strategy of black nationalism to blunt the effects of racism.

Very early in the African experience in this nation, Africans were forced to establish religious, social, and economic space as psychological protection against racism. Nevertheless, the inability of Wilderness dwellers to control their space is well known. It is, almost by definition, impossible for victims to retain control over their spaces. Often our churches were infiltrated; our social and commercial organizations compromised by money, influence, or promises; our land stolen by crooked speculators, and our jobs eliminated for new immigrants.

After the Civil War, the schools that African Americans established were based on a curriculum of white supremacy that denied our own intellectual agency as a central force in our historical experiences.[8] Reading and writing rather than curriculum development were the principal objectives of the early educators. It would take time and reflection for African Americans to see that the lessons in the *McGuffey Readers* and other schoolbooks were supportive of white supremacy while simultaneously poking fun at African Americans.

Black nationalism, which inspired African Americans to control and cultivate the institutions in their own communities, emerged as a political, cultural, and economic response in the Wilderness communities. Whether in its revolutionary nationalist or its cultural nationalist manifestation, black nationalism became a strategy of choice dictated by the reality of white racism. The revolutionary nationalist seeks to transform society by demanding to change the nature of economic, political, and cultural power. On the other hand, the cultural nationalist critiques the capitalist and socialist philosophies as essentially the same: Both philosophies are seen as bastions of white supremacy. In its mature, modern form, black nationalism is hardly any different from the manifestations of Chinese nationalism as expressed in the Chinatowns of North America or the many other ethnic and national bases for economic and cultural improvement—whether they are Greek, Ukrainian, Italian, Jewish, or Cuban.

Nevertheless, the ultimate political interpreters of the Wilderness, the systematic nationalists, remain the most stimulating and energizing voices within the Wilderness. They are appealing, particularly to the youth in the Wilderness, because they are neither afraid nor ashamed of being African and they have access to and are capable of interpreting and disseminating shared historical information. They do not try to conceal the profound transgenerational, multiclass sense of fury within the community. Thus, the Wilderness dwellers have always understood and continue to honor systematic nationalists such as Malcolm X, Bobby Seale, Na'im Akbar, Frances Cress Welsing, Wade Nobles, Marimba Ani, Maulana Karenga, Elijah Muhammad, Sweet Honey in the Rock, and John Henrik Clarke. When the American slave system abrogated all the rights of Africans as human beings in an attempt to create a people without hope, it was the nationalist voices that kept our sanity. After the Civil War and during the gloomy days of the Compromise Period from 1877 to 1916, the nationalist voices kept rising, unafraid and unapologetically African. The paradox, then, is that although they are criticized by white and black, Left and Right, they alone have been the true heroes among the masses in the Wilderness. Indeed, neither the black Marxists nor the black conservatives command the audience accorded the nationalist elements because, while they may have a sense of fury, neither the Marxists nor the conservatives demonstrate cultural fearlessness, empathetic understanding of the daily struggle, or liberating historical knowledge. Both Marxist and conservative African Americans are often victims of the white intellectual elite who lead their philosophies and therefore are perceived as being unable to speak independently on the issues that confront African Americans. Even the Black Radical Con-

gress resurrects essentially the class arguments of the Soviet-era the-
oreticians without any genuine analysis of the fall of the Soviet Union.

According to an article in the *Atlanta Journal and Constitution*,
"Black college students are following a new kind of hero: the men and
women of academe."[9] But who are these men and women that college
students see as heroes? The article highlights the positive impact of
Afrocentric scholars on college students. Students are eager to hear
and read the works of these intellectuals who explain history, sociology, anthropology, politics, and science in the context of the African
American experience. They empower the masses with radically new
historical information and revolutionary critical analysis. This has
fueled the magnetic attraction to these new intellectual heroes who
have become travelling *djelis* of this new generation. A powerful group
of scholars centered around Temple University graduates such as
Adisa Alkebulan of San Diego State University, Miriam Ma'at-Ka-Re
Monges of California State University–Chico, James Conyers of the
University of Houston, Patricia Dixon of Georgia State University,
Reiland Rabaka of California State University–Long Beach, Troy
Allen of Southern University, Kwame Botwe-Asamoah of the Univer-
sity of Pittsburgh, Niyi Coker of the University of Alabama,
Katherine Kemi Bankole of West Virginia University, Geoffrey
Jahwara Giddings of Antioch College, Daryl Zizwe Poe of Lincoln
University, and many others have become known as new *djelis* for
truth and justice. Using African cultural idioms and the ancient
Egyptian language to express their sentiments, they hark back to the
community intellectual tradition of earlier organic African American
scholars such as Edward Wilmot Blyden, Martin Delany, Anna Julia
Cooper, and Alexander Crummell. The torch of the older generation
has been passed to them. Their heroes are not athletes or entertainers
but scholar-activists committed to making the world better. Indeed,
they are the premier examples of people who have risen from the
Wilderness to demonstrate what is possible and necessary. This core
of scholars is not the ordinary group of imitative thinkers one is accus-
tomed to seeing and hearing, but the most on-point, direct, conscious

individuals writing and speaking on issues of culture. The legacy is rich, overflowing in its abundance of examples.

There is the story of Arthur Schomburg, a Puerto Rican of African ancestry, who vowed in his youth that he would collect every book, article, and pamphlet written about the African race in order to disprove the lies that had been told about Africans. The Schomburg Collection in New York City forms the core of the Schomburg Center for Black Research.

There is the story of Anna Julia Cooper, who received a Ph.D. from the Sorbonne in Paris at sixty-six years of age. So committed she was to knowledge and to the dissemination of knowledge that she returned to the United States to teach for another thirty years.

Two late-twentieth-century giants of the same school are John Henrik Clarke and Yosef ben Jochannan. The walking encyclopedia John Henrik Clarke was a legend in his own time. Every African American teacher worthy of the title is acquainted with Clarke's works and talents. He was a short, intense man, gifted both with the pen and with the tongue. He could speak on any subject in African or African American history and make sense and meaning of it. His irascible nature often created sparks between him and others, but his over-riding concern was the proper presentation of the history of African Americans. Yosef ben Jochannan—Egyptologist, professor, and fighter for the rights of African people in Africa and the Americas—is the father of the modern African American interest in ancient Egypt. Often attacked for his views and writings he has become a household name among African American writers and students interested in ancient Africa.

Another reason, however, that these intellectuals are now so pop-ular in the African American community has to do with the expression of their fury. The first thing that captured me as a student at UCLA was that while some African intellectuals enamored by Europe were hesitant about African culture and history, the nationalists had no fear of anti-African authors and lecturers. These heroes exist because the African American community sees them as champions—intellectual champions of the contest for the definition of African people's life chances. They influence the rap artists, the filmmakers, the playwrights, and the choreographers in ways that escape the other intellectuals. The words of the scholar-activists become, through the mediation of the artists, the words of the poor and distressed, and vice versa. These nationalist speakers can come into a community and attract hundreds of people who will travel miles to hear their latest analysis of the contemporary or historical situation confronting the African world.

At present, in every part of the Wilderness—indeed, in each major community—there are study groups, forums, and creative movements, initiated by intellectual activists and preserved by a level of anger that invigorates productive action. In cities such as Los Angeles, Philadelphia, Chicago, Minneapolis, Atlanta, and Detroit, the initiative is manifest in the development of Afrocentric Academies; in Washington it is seen in the rites of passage programs; and in Atlanta and Philadelphia it is demonstrated by the founding of Afrocentric fraternities such as Mesu Netcheru at Temple University and KMT at Morehouse College.

The Wilderness is a place, a state of mind, and a contested territory. Power in the Wilderness is divisible among several archetypal characters. Regardless of whether it is power over human beings or power to control one's neighborhood or one's block through verbal or physical persuasion, power in the Wilderness is not a solitary quality. It is always shared with a host of individuals or groups. The main characters operating in the Wilderness, in addition to the ritualists with adolescent rites of passage programs and study group leaders, are antiauthoritarian philosophers, gun enthusiasts, warriors, rappers, and junior Malcolm Xs. Although most of those who define the nature of the Wilderness tend to be male, there are enough women in the leadership cadre that it is impossible to say the Wilderness power is male.

It is both male and female. This is particularly true in the cases of the dissemblers, rappers, little Malcolms, and warriors. Sometimes these characters overlap, each of them professing some affinity to the culture of the Wilderness.

Take the group of word merchants I call "dissemblers"; they use words as commodities. They live at the edge of the Wilderness, but do not participate in the life of the Wilderness. They will sell anything for money. Indeed, of all the character types, the dissemblers are the only ones who profess cultural abnegation. The rest of the characters, to some degree, express solidarity with African culture. Dissemblers are included in this characterization of types, however, because they affect the image of the Wilderness dwellers. Whites, and some conservative blacks, are very likely to believe the characterization of the Wilderness by the dissemblers because they tend to be expert at understanding the psychology of whites and of those who are outside the Wilderness. Given the nature of the Wilderness and the opposition faced by its inhabitants, there are few cultural abnegators whose voices can command the interest of the Wilderness dwellers. They are creations of the margins, of the outside, having almost no presence in the Wilderness. They have often been cast by the white press as interpreters of the Wilderness, but they have no visible organic relationship to the social, political, and economic bases of the Wilderness. In fact, most of the cultural abnegators would not seek to appeal to the masses of African American Wilderness dwellers. Their audiences remain essentially the white opinion makers rather than African Americans or any other Wilderness peoples. Consequently, the archetypes I will concentrate on are those who have become, by virtue of their presence in the Wilderness, male and female forces with significant bases of power within their respective communities.

The sociologist Elijah Anderson's "old heads" is a generic term that might be used to describe the person who carries the Wilderness experience up front, on his sleeve, ready to speak on his experiences with society at the spur of the moment.[10] In many ways this is an old head, one who might be young in age but who possesses Wilderness badges—such as literacy; attention to the news, both national and international; observations of neighborhood changes; sporadic employment; and the gift of eloquence—that others may not have to the same degree. There have been thousands of such old heads—philosophers—in the Wilderness, and each one has his own peculiar story to tell about the structure of the Wilderness.

John Vincent Leaphart of Philadelphia was a Wilderness dweller who brought insight into the madness that rained terror on the mental shelters, protecting the fragile human ecology of the Wilderness. He was a typical old head, celebrated on the streets of Powelton Village and respected by students at the University of Pennsylvania and Drexel as a storehouse of knowledge.

The Vietnam War had ignited the consciousness of many Americans and depleted the emotional reserves of an entire generation. King had been dead for four years and his dream was quickly vanishing; chemical irritants and additives had been indicted as manmade agents of death. The year was 1972 and MOVE was born as a *coup de resistance.*

Leaphart, a homeless African American, and Donald Glassey, a white student, galvanized their ideas about interracial peace, antipollution, antimaterialism, and communalism to create MOVE. In creating MOVE, they attempted to capture the antiauthoritarian nature of the Wilderness resistance. Leaphart and Glassey declared an end to paying all utility bills, since electricity, water, and gas were natural resources. They sought to create a commune that would look to the natural environment—rivers, streams, forests, and grasslands—for what they needed to live. Leaphart particularly denounced the chemicals in food. MOVE appealed to others to abandon the political system.

Unlike most leaders in the Wilderness, Leaphart did not burst upon the radical scene as a charismatic orator or an eloquent speaker. He had none of the fire of Malcolm X or Bobby Seale, nor was he in the lineage of Martin Luther King Jr., Jesse Jackson, Al Sharpton, Maulana Karenga, or Louis Farrakhan. Leaphart was a quiet, gentle, and philosophical man, with a temperament more like an Elijah Muhammad than anyone else in the public eye. A small, slight, cashew-complexioned man, he had the same gait and the same powerful eyes as Muhammad.

When he spoke people listened, but it was not because of the power of his delivery or of the quickness of his mind. He was reflective, at times almost retiring. But there was an authority that presented itself in the gentleness of his philosophy, a gentleness that was to be misunderstood many times before his tragic death in the MOVE bombing. He was like a lone ranger.

At the time of the May 13, 1985, bombing of the MOVE house by Philadelphia police, Leaphart was fifty-two years old and had propagated a strongly antitechnology doctrine based on respect for natural things. He was no flaming revolutionary bent on killing those with whom he disagreed. Those who claimed that he was a violent and militant revolutionary did so because of their own ends rather than because of anything said or done by Leaphart.

He wasn't even a black nationalist; that is, he did not believe in the preservation of African American culture and traditions.

He wasn't a communist and had no social ideas that could reasonably be called Marxist.

He wasn't a revolutionary seeking the violent overthrow of the United States.

He was a middle-aged philosopher, a street vendor/teacher who opposed the destruction of the natural environment. This is what got him into trouble with his neighbors and with the government. Leaphart's followers took his message to the extreme ends of the political action spectrum, often interrupting events to shout their "truths" about polluted food and air or corrupt political institutions.

No Black Power thinking crossed his mind, either. He had dropped out of school in the third grade and, as one of nine children, he had learned how to survive in an urban environment.

Leaphart's gentleness became legend. He walked his dog up and down the streets of Powelton Village in West Philadelphia, becoming something of a street corner sage, a man so in tune with his surroundings, so comfortable with life in the raw, that his very existence threatened those whose lives were controlled by technology. Leaphart was the great opposition to the calling cards of the industrial society: efficiency, convenience, and progress.

Leaphart was an original homeless man. He was not on the streets, however, because of some mental illness or because he was forced to live outside of the normal environment. He was on the streets because there he found the true essence of living without suffering the indignities of the Wilderness. There he could converse with anyone who would listen, eat with friends when he ate, and sleep wherever he could find an extra place. But all of this changed somewhat in 1970 when he met Donald Glassey, a white Michigan State University graduate who also earned a master's degree from the University of Pennsylvania. Glassey was influenced by Leaphart's philosophy and became increasingly convinced that Leaphart's approach to life was natural, livable, and gentle.

In Glassey's view, Leaphart did not rape the land, pillage families, or pollute the environment. As far as can be determined, it was Glassey who announced Leaphart to be John Africa. But neither Glassey nor Leaphart knew enough about Africa to claim the pristine environment for the continent that they did. Nevertheless, because of his philosophy and his gentleness, Leaphart was to have a new name.

Here was not a John Doe or a Vincent Leaphart; here was a *John Africa*. He was an old head, like so many old heads in New York, Los Angeles, Cleveland, Baltimore, Detroit, and other, smaller communities. The Wilderness atmosphere allows for the growth of old heads. They sit on the park benches, stand on the street corners, hang out at Mr. Max's store or the barbershop. Normally these old heads are men. They can be any age, but normally they are more than twenty-five years old. Women get together at corner churches or African braiding shops, but they rarely just sit and talk about beauty without bringing in politics. In some urban communities women have taken leadership roles as old heads who define priorities and act in the interest of the Wilderness.

When the bomb fell on the little row house in Philadelphia and John Africa was killed, an old head was gone. Ramona Africa, the only adult to survive the attack, became, in her time, an old head as well. A respected philosopher of the Wilderness experience, she presented the case of her family with eloquence and passion, in the memory of John Africa.

A different spirit from the philosopher is the gun enthusiast. The gun enthusiast is usually a young male who has lived in the Wilderness all of his life. He has been the victim of violence, either parental or societal, and feels that in order to survive he has to be tougher than the next person. The gun is his instrument of power.

Whose gun is the biggest—a phallic interpretation, a phallic imagination, and a phallic fantasy—is the baddest game in the Wilderness. In my mind, the idea of the gun is a metaphor for violence of all kinds against another human being. At one time the struggle between the Crips and the Bloods had to do with who was the baddest or who could show the most muscle or firepower: that is, who could outduel the other. Los Angeles in 1992 changed a lot of the conflict, but it did not change the relationship the gang members had to guns and to male identity. They were not ready to be unarmed—as long as the police kept bringing in more guns and bigger guns. In fact, their guns meant power, control, aggression, and freedom. This was a patriarchical game rooted in the environment of the white capitalist patriarchy.

The John Wayne, Clint Eastwood, and Arnold Schwarzenegger phenomenon has impacted on everyone in America. But undoubtedly, young black males, lacking proper male guidance, disaffected by the school system, and confused by a fantastic sense of reality, believed disproportionately in the gun as a means for solving their problems.

The gun defined honor and respect in the Wilderness and thereby made violence inescapable. Within one decade, 1980 to 1990, the use of the gun in violent crimes rose almost 150 percent among young black males ages ten to seventeen, as compared with nearly 50 percent among young white males. Neither Wayne, nor Eastwood, nor Schwarzenegger is black. However, they represent the quintessential American strongman: quick with a gun, appealing to women, tough talking, and dominating. There is no equivalent black mythical figure in either movies or television in America. In the late 1980s the television program *Hawk*, with the charismatic Avery Brooks, briefly presented the image of a strong black male defender of the law who did not hesitate to shoot criminals with his big gun. The show was almost universally applauded by black viewers but could not maintain high ratings among whites—possibly because of the combination of a black man with a gun who feared no one and regularly killed black and white crooks. But Hawk may well have had a positive effect on young black males because of his culturally sensitive approach to his duties and responsibilities. On the other hand, the actor Wesley Snipes may soon emerge as a film figure of mythical proportions because of his skill at subduing the bad guys.

Whenever it occurred within the Wilderness, the ascendancy of the gun cult, or more correctly, the acceptance of the gun as a weapon of male identity, was surely to surpass in reality anything John Wayne, Clint Eastwood, Arnold Schwarzenegger, Wesley Snipes, or Avery Brooks did on film. It would be the beginning of a ruthless reign of terror in the most desolate Wildernesses of America. The gun enthusiasts would lead a devastating toll of murders, robberies, and thefts as the accessibility of the gun made their criminal encounters more effective and, hence, more fearful. In many ways, the gun, which has been used to dominate women during rape alongside other heinous crimes, became in its elevation as a weapon of choice during the drug era, an equalizer of fear. Who was packing and who was not? No one knew how to determine the relative degree to which the community was armed or unarmed.

To be sure, there have been other uses of the gun in our history. Robert F. Williams, a charismatic leader, wrote a book called *Negroes with Guns* in 1962, demonstrating that with guns Africans could demand more freedom and respect.[11] Williams had chosen to fight off white vigilantes who came to harass him in his North Carolina home. He was charged with kidnapping and then fled the country for Cuba. Some called him a saint-Satan type of leader because he showed that he was self-confident and that he would shoot white people. Williams died on March 23, 1973, as a heroic figure in African American history. But he was more interested in fighting for civil rights and decency than he was sticking up someone over drug money or in killing children in the streets. In fact, the toughness that we felt with Robert F. Williams was not an insane terror but a quiet resolve to take care of business if necessary. But the cult of the gun now found in the Wilderness has little to do with Williams's mission; rather than defense, it is often aggression that motivates the young Wilderness dweller.

Wilderness youth enamored with the gun are frequently fond of the control they feel with that symbol of power: the look, the walk, and most of all the gun itself. This is the media-influenced crowd. There is a dangerous splendor in the manner of one's stride when he knows that he is packing something. Like the victory walk, a relic of the chained marches during slavery but now an indication of physical prowess, the stride with the gun is a definite statement: "I'm bad; don't mess with me." All too often these youth are "messed with," and wasted before they reach their twentieth birthday. This orgy of madness will not end until there is a concerted attack on the source of the disorientation. Otherwise, I see no solution to the continuation of young death, fighting, as it were, to occupy space on a corner or a block, for someone else.

These young men hold the occult, the hidden secrets of the warrior tradition, in their hearts. The gun is the source of their mystery—and often their death. Despite their bravado they are always afraid; this is the fear of the bigger gun. I have been in the prisons of this country and talked to the young brothers who are spending their youth behind bars; I have many letters from them and they all say the same thing: They were unaware of what they were doing because they did not have a sense of themselves as persons. In many instances the gun gave them their identities—and, of course, took their identities.

The gun is a mixed symbol. Huey Newton, minister of defense for the Black Panthers, was a sex symbol. Huey Newton was a hard man. Huey Newton was an antiracist. He honored the gun as a part of the American creed. He believed that the gun was the best defense against those who disrespected you. He accepted the logic of the bigger gun. He died violently at the end of a gun. This seemed to be the logic of the revolutionary who believed that the American idea of freedom meant that you had to fight violence with violence in order to establish peace.

But it was Huey Newton, Bobby Seale, and the Black Panthers more than any other contemporary group that symbolized the possibility of a polarized America in which blacks with guns would challenge whites with guns in order to bring about justice. This symbol was a nightmare because it reflected the end of hope and the beginning of despair. Few wanted to see armed camps in the black or white neighborhoods. African Americans had responded to the growing numbers of paramilitary organizations in the white community by setting up their own militant organizations, but these remained a far cry from the hundreds of anti-African and anti-Semitic groups that had formed on the fringes of American society. Efforts to bring reason, racial harmony, and religion to the various white supremacist groups had been made by intellectuals, social activists, leftists, and preachers.

And all across the country, white groups—paramilitary organizations—were created with the purpose of training whites to fight with guns. Off in the mountains of Arkansas, Georgia, and Idaho, white power groups of the 1980s and 1990s practiced living in rural expanses and prepared to either assault or defend against those they saw as enemies. By 2000 it was estimated that there were more than seven hundred white hate groups in the United States. Some we read about in the press; others we seldom hear of. The urban Crips and the

Bloods were regular fare on the evening news or in the newspapers, yet neither the Crips nor the Bloods created the kind of interracial havoc stirred up by the white hate groups such as the Freemen, the Skinheads, and others, with their verbal and physical attacks on various communities of Jews, African Americans, Hispanics, and Asians. Some members had even infiltrated American military forces and would attack African Americans on sight. This was no longer the Ku Klux Klan with its Greek- and Anglo-derived name, but organizations called rather straightforwardly the White Aryan Nation, the Aryan Brotherhood, and so on. They are different from the Wilderness street gangs who are concerned about turf and territorial imperative within the Wilderness, not about killing whites because they are considered "nonhuman," "scum," or other epithets hurled toward blacks and Jews. While both types of gangs must be roundly condemned for their disregard for human life, there is a substantial difference in the politics and the resources of the groups. It should be understood that neither the white supremacist groups nor the black gangs represent significant proportions of the population.

Yet it is a fact that white groups are more organized, better armed, more political, and have more support systems than the urban street gangs of the Wilderness. They are serious about racial supremacy and do not operate without material, political, and social support in many regions of the country. They own property, have training institutes, and even promote their ideology of hate through computer networks and with newsletters that are distributed throughout the world. But regardless of the group, the presence of the gun is itself the threat of deadly violence.

These white groups have yielded their own teenage gun toters who enter schools or homes and shoot their peers or parents. The culture of the gun has become such a part of the white community's youth that it is difficult to say if the genie can ever be put back in the bottle. To claim, as the pundits often do, that the provenance of the gun is greatest in the African American community is to create a distortion. Black people are disproportionately armed, but it makes no sense to have gun buyback programs in African American communities without the same buyback programs in white communities. Michael Moore has demonstrated in his Oscar-winning documentary *Bowling for Columbine* and his book *Stupid White Men*[12] that America's gun problem is a white problem in terms of actual violence.

Crack and cocaine are the enemies of the law-abiding citizens of the Wilderness. They cannot go out at night, sit on the porch, or take their children to the park because some gun-carrying person seeking to "control" his own turf and to prevent other drug-carrying thugs from taking over his "territory" feed on the community. Thus, drive-by shootings, killings on the streets, and the mutilation of young black males are, 90 percent of the time, drug related. The Wilderness community itself is not violent, yet there are violent individuals on the street corners and in the community. In most urban areas the largest number of drug overdoses occur in the white communities, while the largest number of murders occur in the black communities. The irony is that both of these tragedies happen because of drugs.

The old Bloods and Crips gangs are not obvious racists and do not have the kind of reach that the racist organizations have in this country and around the world. Why, then, would the news media make the Bloods and the Crips the center of their reporting on gangs? Is it their proximity to news organizations? Who could create more terror in this nation than the white power groups, racist organizations that have decades of experience and layers of organizational depth? The gun has become an instrument of terror in a visible and terrifying way in the hands of young white males who hold antisocial beliefs. Indeed, the Bloods and the Crips are like Sunday school children in comparison with the hundreds of white hate groups, who I believe have inspired so many of the individual school-age gunners. Although it is true that many of the school-age killers who shoot their suburban peers are whites, the truth of the matter is that they learn the love of the gun from many of those white supremacist groups and the National Rifle Association (NRA). This is not the same path taken by the young gang members in the urban communities, many of whom have never even heard of the NRA.

In many ways the fear that is created among the Wilderness dwellers by the Bloods and the Crips, and their imitators, is a fear of randomness. Drive-by shootings, cross fire battles, and petty crimes aggravated by the drug traffic constitute instability in the Wilderness. They make life dangerous on a daily basis and this disruption of the normal routine of community threatens the fabric of the society itself. However, this is a different kind of terror and a different type of threat than the threat to annihilate people because of the color of their skin, the type of religion that they practice, or the country of their origin. Both are destabilizing and represent the decay of values and ideals, but the scale of possible turmoil is different.

The Wilderness creates its own special values and develops its own characters who are then able to fulfill the emotions and images that constitute those values. Young men and women often believe that power and reproduction are the keys to heaven, and they seek those two ends energetically. Those who are capable of demonstrating that they have either or both are the heroes or "sheroes" of the community. Others look upon them as having achieved a degree of distinction, or notoriety, if not fame, because of the weapons they carry or the number of children they have.

However, in the Wilderness, as in any male-dominated society, women are often abused and treated with disrespect. Gun enthusiasts, sometimes no more than hoodlums, sexually assault young women or turn them out to prostitute for drugs. Perhaps overwhelmed by the strength of women, these street toughs seek to control, colonize, and dominate them. The gun allows young men to engage in a sort of neurosis of the personality, a phallocratic madness, wreaking devastation on anyone standing in the way.

Women who dwell in the Wilderness are often afraid for their safety. The madness created by the cauldron of terror affects everyone and everything, and women, the anchor in so many homes in the Wilderness, are usually its first victims. Yet as much as the gun is feared, many women in the Wilderness see the gun enthusiast as a champion.

Patricia Gaines-Carter wrote in the *Washington Post* that she visited a jail one summer and remembered how attractive the young black men who carried guns seemed to her.[13] In her mind, they were the perfect examples of freedom and seemed to exude a strong confidence. Gaines-Carter speaks to the sexual attractiveness of the gun found among young people in the Wilderness. They see its potency and its potential for liberation from weakness. Many young men see their penises in the same way and believe that by making babies they can escape the stifling environment that makes them like all other men, only to learn, often too late, that they are just like most of the men who live in their Wilderness. The gun and the penis, carried like lightning rods or spoken of with the reverence that the medieval Zulu held for their favorite stabbing spears, are symbols of male identity. How do you know one man from another if not by the size of his gun or the potency of his penis? Youth in the Wilderness can usually rank the members of the social and political hierarchy by the number of shootings and the number of children—that is, who did the shooting and who had the children.

Guns are more certain than penises. They deliver faster and with greater accuracy and, consequently, have become glamorized more among the criminal element in the Wilderness. So now, instead of or in addition to impregnating women, gun enthusiasts use the gun to establish their prowess.

This has not always been the case. In fact, the gun first gained acceptance and power in the imagination of the Wilderness dweller because of the need to protect the community from white vigilantes in the South. More than in the northern cities, the small southern towns were the centers of the gun in our earlier history. We believed, as black southerners, that we had the right to hunt and as a result, African Americans had hunting guns that also saved many lives from white vigilantes and outlaws. My great-grandfather, Plenty Smith, had several guns and believed that it was necessary to defend himself from white rabble-rousers in central Georgia. He had to scare off only one group of trespassing whites who entered his farm looking for a fugitive to establish his reputation. I have often thought that had the whites of Dooly County wanted to get Plenty Smith, they could have gotten him. However, his reputation grew because of his stand with his gun on his land.

Whites have always had more guns in their communities than African Americans have. The percentage of whites with guns is more than four times the percentage among African Americans. Even though the press cites the crimes with guns in the Wilderness, blacks do not have the same access to guns as whites. Few large caches of guns have ever been found in blacks' homes or on farms owned by blacks, yet the stealing or collecting of guns by whites is a big business, and occasionally law enforcement uncovers a hidden cache of hundreds of guns and ammunition. There is nothing like this in African American history. In fact, even after the 1965 uprising, the run on guns by whites exceeded anything that had ever happened before in Los Angeles. Fear and terror occupied the imagination of many whites, who viewed the destructive power of the Watts uprising as a presage of what was possible. Indeed even though no attacks were made on white neighborhoods, the resultant fear in the white communities created a white backlash resulting in a rise to power of conservative politicians who fed on this fear. A cycle of declining trust was established that would eventually lead to a bigger insurrection. African Americans became convinced that with the rising tide of white hate groups, especially among white youth, the white population was up in arms against the legitimate aims of the black community. Thus, some individuals within the Wilderness felt they should arm themselves. I personally know people who went out and bought guns for the first time in their lives when they saw scenes on television of whites beating, heckling, and threatening blacks. Whites who see blacks with guns respond in the same manner, and therein lies the cycle of insanity made possible in a violence-oriented society.

In some senses, the Republican administration of Ronald Reagan was a scary time for African Americans. Even in the projects, among people who have little money for anything other than food, people bought guns to protect themselves from whites in the far-off suburbs and from the black hoodlums in their own communities. In May 1991 the Chicago City Council blasted the NRA for taking issue with the housing authority's ban on guns in the public housing projects. The NRA filed suit against the ban on guns in the projects because, according to the NRA, guns do not kill, people kill. The city council argued that this view perpetuates violence among the young. In 1990 the NRA had contended in a similar case in Richmond, Virginia, that the ban on handguns in public housing constituted racial discrimination against blacks. The argument was that such a policy keeps the urban poor from protecting themselves from criminals. Indeed, some argued that the NRA was not interested in blacks protecting themselves but in blacks killing themselves.

The National Organization of Black Law Enforcement Executives (NOBLEE) has taken a firm stand against assault guns and is in favor of a seven-day waiting period on the purchase of handguns. In its lonely stand, the NOBLEE has reaffirmed its commitment to the lives of black youth. As Gregory Freeman asserted in a commentary in the *St. Louis Post-Dispatch*, the community seeks restraint on guns to curb the rising tide of random shootings and homicides.[14] It is no secret that the black community as a whole takes a strong stand against guns. However, the overwhelmingly white NRA has consistently promoted the idea of full availability of guns. Many nations in Europe, Asia, and Africa have outlawed the gun for citizens and believe that it is not an individual's right to own a handgun, but in the United States a strong lobby for the gun industry has been able to prevent legislators from taking a stand against the gun. The gun industry is able to target any legislator who says that she supports a ban on handguns and cause her serious reelection problems. A considerable amount of money is spent in lobbying Congress to insure that the gun lobby's stand is successful. Black youths are the victims of this easy access to the handgun. In most cities it is easier to get a gun than to get a driver's license. So we see twelve-, thirteen-, and fourteen-year-olds with their own pistols, even though they are too young to obtain a license to drive. While most Americans think this is ridiculous and, indeed, even ludicrous, we have not yet found the will or the mechanism within government to change this situation. We have had too many political leaders without the courage to confront the issue head-on. As president, Ronald Reagan, himself a shooting victim and a pro-gun enthusiast, contributed to the bad feelings existing between people of the Promise and those of the Wilderness.

Reagan's image as a cowboy did not make us feel any better and, since the African American community had sensed in his rhetoric a virulent anti-African position, we could only expect the worst from him. His appeal to the scared, conservative white public was electric. They believed in him almost as a messiah. Reagan was going to put blacks in their place; to right what these frightened whites saw as wrongs, particularly the perception that blacks had gained too much and that whites had lost ground. Based on this illusion, Reagan and the Republican Right built a political machine that sustained an ideology of white against black, hostility of opposites, and neglect of the poor and disenfranchised. Once again, the gun-toting, gun-wielding hero rode into town and separated the good and the evil, the white and the black, and he rode into the sunset with the right wing firmly entrenched.

What seemed like an outlaw mentality at the top spread quickly among the Wilderness dwellers. In fact, historian Mark Naison says that the prevalence of firearms in the African American community is directly related to Reagan's policies in the 1980s. He cites social conditions and trends during the Reagan regime that contributed to the rise of an outlaw mentality in some black neighborhoods, where unemployment, poverty, and broken promises contributed to criminal activities.[15] So the terrorism of the gun is not a terror just in the African American community, but one that is felt in the white community via television news. In the white community it is essentially a fear of blackness, not merely the fear of the gun, that is felt by some whites. The gun is more pronounced as a weapon in the white community than it is in the black community, but the use of the gun on the urban streets is increasingly related to drug wars, armed robbery, and theft. However, the fact that the outlaw mentality exists in the first place means that we have become victims of a transformation in which some young males believe that the gun creates power. No one can escape this fierce rhetoric of aggression, not even those who practice it par excellence.

There are too many examples of the tough ones being killed by those who, in their own turn, become the tough ones. Our young males live in the valley of desolation, where violence seems generalized and there is no longer a separation between the good guys and the bad guys. This ripping of the moral fabric into so many shredded fragments produces a collective sense of being terrorized by the gun.

This is true, although we know that the entire black community has not gone to pieces and we know that only a minority of individuals is engaged in the threats of violence and degeneracy. In *Streetwise: Race, Class, and Change in an Urban Community*, the sociologist Elijah Anderson provides a penetrating account of life in the Wilderness. His study is about a shared territory, mixed between those of the Promise and those of the Wilderness. However, it is the Wilderness life that brings his account into focus for the reader, because he demonstrates that all people in the Wilderness are not engaged in social degeneration. In fact, the old heads are at their wits' end over the drug culture and the lack of respect in the Wilderness. For example, Anderson says that "in the traditional black community older men and women had such legitimacy that they could chastise unknown boys and girls and expect the parents' support."[16]

Anderson sees many young males as being considered predators by the larger community because of their demeanor and appearance, whereas older males earn greater trust through their demeanor and appearance.[17]

Since 1829, when David Walker wrote *Appeal to the Colored Citizens of the World*, African Americans have been pointing out the difference between the Promise and the Wilderness. Because the social, economic, and political conditions have been different for blacks at both the race and class levels, the gulf between the Promise and Wilderness is as wide as that of democracy and hypocrisy, or faith and despair. The young males of the Wilderness have internalized this discontent, and their displeasure has become the reality of Walker's warning that blacks would one day rebel against oppression.

It is not my intention to leave the impression that these young men—eager to use the gun if they have to, quick on their feet, and motivated by a quest for self-identity—are lazy. Just the contrary, they are very smart and enthusiastic about their work. Furthermore, most people, regardless of social classes, tend to have a negative stereotype of manual labor. What is necessary is redirecting the energies of these young men toward a more communal spirit. There has to be a change in the nature of what constitutes manhood, a refinement that is going on everyday in the Wilderness under the direction of many African American men who came out of the Million Man March process. The idea for a Million Man March was initiated by Louis Farrakhan, but the implementation of the march, including the writing of its charter, drafted by Maulana Karenga, was the result of the effort of numerous organizations and institutions. Those who participated in this process grabbed the tiger by the tail and are now in the throes of making a difference that will be felt in the years to come.

Los Angeles, with its explosive uprising, became the biggest threat to the national peace but also the greatest threat to a viable sense of manhood. We recognize the fact that the uprising was only the outward manifestation of the deep-seated fury and crisis in the Wilderness. Yet this was no transparent event; we were all affected by the Los Angeles situation. And we all know that nothing except a revolution in thinking at the highest corridors of power can provide the young, urban, African American male with a substitute for the gun as a symbol of manhood.

But manhood is a complex set of values and attitudes. In the Wilderness the examples may be thin, but they do exist. Men are defined by how they handle relationships rather than by what material achievements they have made. Relationships with women, other men, and even spiritual relationships are the defining characteristics of maleness in the Wilderness. Since the male demonstrates inner strength in the face of crisis, examples of African American males who are able to exercise intelligence, wit, and wisdom in challenging situations are role models. This is the uncle, the father, the guardian, the preacher, the teacher, the unemployed tradesperson, the police officer, who acts out of a sincerity that attracts respect. In these cases the establishment of manhood is dependent upon how we act with others. *Men* always respect others. Those who do not have jobs but who respect women are considered men. Those who defend their friends are considered men. Those who protect the weak, who listen to the children and the elders are considered men. Those who will not back down from confrontation are considered men. And those who are able to interpret the history of African American people despite the distortions and lies that have been perpetrated on the Wilderness dwellers are considered men. Manhood is discretion and discipline, laughter and authenticity. Manhood, like womanhood, must be based on knowledge and emotion. This is a long way from the period of the enslavement, when manhood and womanhood were based on the number of children one could have.

The late nineteenth century contained the seeds of the twentieth-century explosions in the Wilderness, not so much because of the concept of manhood or womanhood but rather in the continuation of the reign of white terror. In fact, the rise of an unrepentant and segregated South hindered the national drive for justice that had begun with the earliest abolitionists. The "southern mentality" quickly spread throughout the nation, and the fact that leading twentieth-century politicians were often southerners who had managed to maintain long tenures in Congress meant that their ideology insinuated itself into the national consciousness. To be an African man or woman in the context of this ideology meant suppressing the urge to protest in order to live. Atlanta journalist Henry Grady's "New South" was the Old South writ in color and adapted to the new legal situation of the masses of Africans. Thus, the enshrining in the national character of second-class status for Africans was white people's work. Of course, they occasionally found, as has been true in every era, some Africans who willingly participated in their own oppression, giving up both their manhood and their right to be considered human.

The very terror of racial domination has a psychic effect that causes African Americans to deny our own humanity. By this I mean we are willing to grant an anguished denial that we are African *and* American, not in any Du Boisian double consciousness sense, but in the real sense of our identity as of African origin and heritage and of American citizenship and nationality. Even more, the tragic feeling of being demoralized and demobilized—indeed, *clarencised*, as in the example of Clarence Thomas—by the effects of racial domination creates anger that cannot be satisfied by the wish for freedom. We can only find real peace in the freedom that is found in overcoming terror. The uprising in Los Angeles must be seen as an attempt to overcome the terror of domination.

It is passé to speak of violence in the Wilderness. Some areas of the Wilderness are synonymous with violence. Few Wilderness dwellers escape the devastation of violence. In fact, the statistics given for every type of crime are worse for African American males than for any other segment of the nation. We are victimizers and victims in both society and our communities. Homicides in Washington, D.C., reached 483 in 1990, and 82 percent of the victims were black males. Nearly 50 percent of African American males aged fifteen to nineteen who died in 1988 were killed with guns. By 1994 the number had risen to nearly 60 percent.

The monstrous system of oppression, which stalks our lives in political, social, economic, and psychological ways in a daily hunt for black flesh in the Wilderness, turns our children upon themselves. And we become victims, trapped in the quagmire of social and cultural disaster. We are surprised by our survival and emboldened by the hardness of our peers. We are the Wilderness dwellers.

Too often we create other victims, and we create them in more vicious and painful ways. We model our behavior after the system itself, and the coldness with which we engage in the process of pain is reminiscent of the clinical way in which the nation itself crushes our ambitions and our hopes. The too-easy compulsion to inflict violence on our peers is a cruel calculus of the killing inflicted on us in the killing of our dreams, our hopes, our trust, our respect, and our dignity. And where the dreams are killed, wild bushes of fury abundantly grow.

The use of the gun as a mediator of dispute, the domination of others by the threat of force, and, finally, our own participation as observers who do not intercede on behalf of others all contribute to the death of dreams and the killing of the possible. While this may seem simple-minded to those who enjoy much more complicated interpretations of the situation in the urban community, we can only change the situation in this nation with radical proposals that speak to cultural and economic transformation. Our families, teachers, spiritual leaders, and public officials must have an understanding that the road to masculinity does not have to go by way of the gun.

The violence in large urban areas is hyped, but we find the same madness in smaller cities. The *Jackson Sun* reported in 1992 that in that Tennessee city there was "a tidal wave of gunfire."[18] The acceptance of violence among the young has become a common complaint of parents. Some blame television; others blame cocaine. The answer is probably found in a combination of factors. Certainly one factor is the rise in the use of crack. Since the appearance of crack in the 1970s, there has been a steady increase in the number of African Americans killed by gunfire. In the Wilderness crack and guns go together like lovers: Where you find crack, you will find guns. Eliminate crack and we eliminate 50 percent of the homicides by guns. Since crack suppliers and crack users are in a cycle of need greater than the need to respect the law, they create a law unto themselves. They care about protecting their drugs at all costs—even the cost of taking the lives of their neighbors.

Drug wars cost the most in human lives and have made the

deepest inroads into our community consciousness. The worst part is the recruitment of thirteen- and fourteen-year-olds for the battle of the guns. While the image of gun-toting black youth that is often imagined by whites (and some blacks) is overstated, enough incidents have occurred and enough young men *do* have guns that we must view many of the very young as future statistics. These are the premurderers whose moral development is arrested at an early age because they possess the power of life and death without understanding the consequences of either. They have seen death on television and they view it as a fantasy. In the Wilderness they are boy-men who become boys again when faced with the consequences of their crimes.

Guns are everywhere in the Wilderness. It is most disturbing to see them showing up in schools. Students often believe the authorities are unable to protect them. This creates another dangerous situation, since with more guns there is greater potential for accidents and incidents. So furious is the rush for guns that some rap stars have consistently called for an end to the arming of black youth. Pulitzer Prize–winning playwright Charles Fuller, speaking to several hundred people at a banquet, appealed for nonviolence among African Americans. Subsequently he and his son rented billboards in North Philadelphia, a representative Wilderness community, and asked the community to "stop killing each other."

Our youth know too well the game of death because their elders often have not taught them the game of life. They have adopted the stance, the posture, the language, and the weapons of warriors. This is the worst fear of the American nation; it is our fear as African Americans. Haunting signs and symbols of aggression, the most important, perhaps, being the black skin itself, are everywhere in the urban areas. What white America fears is that we are as terrible as they are. What they believe is that our interest and aim is to destroy them. This is why there is such great apprehension about fairness. What if they were fair to us? Would we succeed in every other capacity as we have in basketball? Could we really do it in swimming and investment banking, or in engineering and computers? Of course, we know the answer to those questions—every African American would answer in the affirmative. It is being done in all these areas, every day, by many African Americans who have insisted on being involved in every sector of the economy. However, we recognize the difficulties often placed in the way of success. Those males who have struggled and won limited victories have done so not because the system is just, but rather in spite of the system.

It was the radicalized version of male identity that evolved in the era of Black Power that really captured us. We were no longer shufflers, we were no longer emasculated images of men; we were virile, lithe, dangerous, articulate, and brave examples of ancient warriors. A sort of frustration had set in for nearly one hundred years after the Civil War, when we saw our identity trampled and our manhood taken by the political system of white supremacy. Our rage was our salvation in the 1960s, but in the twenty-first century we are expressing a different kind of fury than before. We now know what the problems are, and we are furious that the nation does not have the moral will to confront racism among whites head-on. But then, we are asking whites to do it to themselves—and few Africans place much trust in the ability or the willingness of whites to examine racism among themselves. When Sen. Robert Byrd of West Virginia can speak of "white niggers," as he did on television in 2001, we ask, "How many times has he spoken of niggers in other contexts, without the television cameras?" So when we express ourselves emotionally we are called hypermasculine, hyperaggressive, and perhaps hypersexual. Indeed, some young males equate the absence of accountability with freedom—with being a man. However, this conception is caused by the environment of despair and is probably as associated with class as it is with race.

Too many of these young men see themselves as male because of their ability to own and hold a gun. In fact, in some communities if you do not have a gun, you are suspect as a man. Now, this is not just a black male problem. Actually the percentage of gun ownership to population among whites is more than seven times that of the black ratio. The NRA is 98 percent white. There is no comparable gun club among African Americans, although there is an increasing number of groups that believe that guns for defense is a morally correct position.

The logic of the gun is its long, black, slender barrel and its shiny exterior. Its design is therefore masculine, aggressive, linear. A small snub-nosed gun is not considered a "real" gun, although it is just as effective as a big gun in killing a person. A double-barreled gun is the best and the baddest. A gun that can shoot with rapid speed without reloading is a *very* bad gun. Police departments keep asking for bigger and badder guns, in order to compete, they say, with the criminals whose guns are the very baddest. The Cold War has moved to the urban communities, where the two sides try to outdo each other in the ability to deliver firepower.

A proliferation of drive-by shootings in the 1980s attested to the anonymous nature of the new violence in the Wilderness. Where African American history has been a history of violence with passion—not the sterile, uninvolved, distant, detached violence of the contemporary era—it has now become insane and random. When I was a child in Valdosta, Georgia, a neighbor was killed by another man because he had stepped on the man's shoes. The attack was a personal one, where the men knew each other and saw each other up close. Of course, our neighbor was just as dead as he would have been if a shot had been fired anonymously. It was a type of insanity, a product of the madness of limited life chances and self-hatred. Drive-by shootings, on the other hand, are outgrowths of the technological age, but with the same self-hatred and insanity. We view them with suspicion because they are random, distant, obscene, and without passion. The gun is such a vile weapon in the hands of the young men who know no truth but the voice of their peers.

The gun has changed the character of our behavior in the Wilderness because it has disengaged us from each other. Homicides with guns remain the most prevalent form of murder in our community. While it is usually the case that most murders occur among acquaintances, there is a dangerous pattern of random violence brought on by those looking for money for drugs and those involved in drug wars. There is no long tradition of psychopathic serial killers in the African American community; instead, we have tended to shoot those who offend our sense of dignity. Yet the numbers of murders in the deep Wilderness reflect a change in the pattern of behavior among even the most criminal element. While it is true that drugs have played a major role in redefining the nature of relationships, it is also a fact that the weakening of the social and cultural institutions have resulted from the commodification of power and the growth of consumer materialism, a society in which everything can be bought or sold. Secular humanists and progressive Afrocentrists have called for an ethical transformation.

By replacing the reign of the knife among those in the deep Wilderness in the African American community, the gun brought a different kind of relationship to society. The knife, whether the pin knife, the ice pick, or the switchblade, could not distance the wielder from the victim. One had to engage the other in order to do harm. Despite the fact that a considerable amount of death dealing has been done with knives, the gun brings a tireless and colorless anonymity to human death. It mirrors the masculinity of so much of contemporary society and rapes the community of its innocence. As a despoiler of innocence, a bringer of the naked, hard logic of our mortality, the gun has become a far-too-common solver of problems in the African American community. Like those who have pushed penis power, those who use gun power to dictate their will and satisfy their desire for control are reacting to a deep sense of inferiority. Indeed, violence is often glorified in the Wilderness by those who neither live in the community nor care what happens to the children of the community.

The battleground is everywhere. Since the police force in most large cities is viewed as an alien force, the war against it is relentless, constant, and steady. But what other response does the Wilderness dweller have? Doubt—the perennial African American problem, more persistent than our percussions, our sacred poets and prophets, our remembrances of ancestors—stations itself in the middle of the battleground in the Wilderness whenever the police are around. What we doubt is not so much ourselves but the capability of the larger society and its values to protect us from the possible police riots. Neither children wilding nor police wilding represents a sane society or the best we can be.

The Wilderness warriors are young. Each one is a general in his own right, having been born to the struggle, matured by conditions around him, and made fearless by the battle stories of his mother and father. The anger of the warrior is not aimless; it is profoundly directed toward those institutions and those people that are perceived as anti-African. One makes a mistake to assume that the Los Angeles insurrection was a mere outbreak of anarchy. To assume that is to miss what it means to live in the Wilderness or in this nation as an African.

Racism is not a problem of black people; that is, it does not originate in the black population. It is, at this moment in history, a profoundly white problem deeply imbedded in what whites consider "normal" thought, attitudes, and behaviors, when it is in actuality a form of pathology. Since it is thought to be normal, whites do not see the need to confront it. If one commits a criminal act, then one is called a criminal. Should not the person who commits a racist act be called a racist? Unfortunately, too many Americans consider racist jokes, racist acts, and racist remarks normal. Such attitudes encourage the warrior to prepare herself—in terms of personality, temperament, and edginess—for insults. If a Wilderness dweller forgets to prepare herself, she may be stunned by its unexpected infliction.

Thus, the warrior brings to the theater of war all of the skills and courage from a previous generation of children of warriors. This accumulation of resources and talents is used to assault the enemy. The enemy comes in many forms and there are many political trans-formations and social levels of the enemy. White racial hierarchy is the enemy. It kills the soul, it maims the spirit, it stifles intellectual growth, it mocks ethics, it crushes truth, and it turns respect into hatred. To fight the enemy, African Americans try all kinds of approaches. We have been known to confront racism, a manifestation of white racial hierarchy, directly; to appeal to allies for advice; and to work on our own defenses.

Our fury explodes unpredictably. It is detailed in a Johns Hopkins University study that suggests the higher rates of high blood pressure found in African Americans may be due more to living with racial discrimination than to genes.[19] Or it comes from knowing what the *Journal of the American Medical Association* reported in 1991: that the health status of African Americans has actually declined while the health status of the general population has increased.[20]

It comes when a young person goes to the Marines, gets a good discharge, and cannot find a job as a police officer or a security guard because of his race. It sneaks up on you when you walk into a store and the guard follows you around as if you are a rogue. It has no humor because it takes no prisoners and gives neither mercy nor any benefit of the doubt. And so to answer the charges against us, we must take up the weapon of truth and write and speak for ourselves. But the white political scientist Andrew Hacker is so right when he says that the nation allows the African American to be neither an American nor an African.[21] In either case we are victims of the legacy of enslavement, because some white Americans do not see us as "real" Americans and some African Americans do not see themselves as "real" Africans. It is this confusion that compromises the language spoken by those of the Wilderness and those of the Promise.

Take the case of the statement by the rap artist Sista Souljah on the senselessness of the violence in the African American community during the 1992 presidential campaign. Sista Souljah was quoted by the *Washington Post* as saying at Jesse Jackson's Rainbow Coalition Convention that "if black people kill black people every day, why not have a week and kill white people."[22] Bill Clinton, while campaigning before the same convention, said that it was unwise for Jackson's group to have invited Sista Souljah to sit on a panel at the convention because she is a racist. Jackson later called it a sneak attack by Clinton

—an effort to curry favor with white voters in much the same way George H. W. Bush used the Willie Horton case against Michael Dukakis during the 1988 presidential campaign.

Clinton probably sought to maximize his white vote by demonstrating that he could criticize a black person in the most liberal political forum. The result was that, although blacks supported Clinton for the presidency because he was the best possible choice— he left doubts in the minds of many blacks who saw his statement as blatantly political. Jackson called it a "Machiaevellian maneuver," meaning essentially that it had been calculated to demonstrate that Clinton was not in Jackson's pocket. But to many African Americans it showed the worst sort of discourtesy because Clinton misunderstood Sista Souljah's point. Meanwhile, Sista Souljah became more popular than ever, making the rounds of the major television talk shows as well as significant college bookings.

Apart from the fact that Sista Souljah said Clinton took her ideas out of context, the statement, even if it had been correct as quoted by the *Washington Post*, had meaning for most African Americans. This was a classic case of people speaking two languages and thinking they were speaking the same language. To African Americans the idea was not to "kill whites" but rather to stop killing each other. Sista Souljah's comments reached back into the psychological history of Africans in the United States and touched a fundamental chord in the song of our oppression. During the period of the Great Enslavement, Africans knew that an attack on whites meant certain death for the perpetrator and for anyone connected with him. Similarly, after the Civil War and up until the end of Jim Crow, attack on whites was off-limits to the African. We made a habit of attacking those closest to us—our family and our acquaintances—and there grew in our cultural mythology this great fear of attacking whites. Even the baddest man in town would seldom attack the vilest white man. When that happened, and it did occasionally happen, the man would have to leave town or defend his life from a white posse. For Sista Souljah to say what she is reported to have said is for her to engage in the most powerful rhetoric of nonviolence. The challenge is, if you are so tough, go and demonstrate it in the white community. Thus, it was the Eurocentric nature of this plea for nonviolence that is the problem with what Sista Souljah said. Most blacks understood it, but Bill Clinton, like many whites, did not understand it. Whites are the subjects; blacks are the subthemes. This is a Eurocentric formulation of the problem of violence, but it strikes a chord with all of us who have experienced the long night of terror in this country. Bill Clinton did not know what he was stepping into when he attacked this alleged statement on its surface value. He came off as lacking historical and cultural sensitivity to the psychological, moral, physical, and spiritual devastation that has befallen the Wilderness. Where he could only see race, Sista Souljah could see a lack of courage on the part of the warriors, a loss of meaning, and hypocrisy of the basest kind.

Perhaps the most challenging aspect of this warrior attitude is the cavalier conception of death. In many ways it is not an emphasis on one's own death, which is seen as possible but unlikely in the Wilderness, if one can be harder and more resourceful than his foes or his circumstances. The aim of the warrior is survival, but in the Wilderness it becomes survival by cannibalizing others. The lives of others become the energy for one's own life. As with historic cannibalism, it is either a matter of one's life or death or of the placation of the gods in a ritual sacrifice. The Wilderness prompts both responses: The warrior's contest on the battleground of respect releases the jackals of competition while the ritual of conquest is in the killing action itself. The acclamation one seeks to hear from the *djelis*, praise singers, and one's peers is, "He's bad"—meaning the opposite of what the hard "bad" normally means on the street. This "bad" is like Shine's bad, or Muhammad Ali's bad, or Stagolee's bad; it is the real bad. In actuality, in the Ebonics language, it is "good"; hence, the "baddest" becomes the best.

To avoid being misunderstood, it is necessary to affect a more than respectful attitude toward others. This is the primary rule of survival in some Wilderness communities. A friend of mine, an educator, tells a story of how she was walking down the street and was accidentally bumped by a young woman, who began almost immediately to apologize profusely for having brushed against her. In another case, a young man was running through the streets and stepped on the shoes of an African American taxi cab driver and almost instantaneously began to apologize as if he believed his life was in danger for having violated the driver's space. Both incidents demonstrate the Wilderness knowledge that respect is important, basic, and elementary. However, we must be willing to give respect in order to avoid any serious misunderstanding that might lead to conflicts.

The motifs of the warrior, the new equipment—not a boom box and knife anymore, but hip hop in the ear, rapidly changing, loose clothing styles to evade the enemy and keep him guessing, words and games to confuse, telephones for communication, and guns bought to protect himself and often to make war on enemies—are the physical and psychological accoutrements of war. In the struggles of inner-city life and in the battles for turf, for control over neighborhoods, and for drugs, the motifs of the warrior are evident.

But there is often internal anger in the Wilderness. We have turned upon each other because of the use of our own people to promote anti-African attitudes. These are the ones who, as the late writer Louis Lomax used to say, fool the white people and in so doing confuse some Africans. Their methods are simple. They despise their own people and seek refuge in the belief that they are special; perhaps chosen to be special because of their personal achievements. They wallow in the misconceptions of our own history and have a poor sense of the nature of the African's experience in this society. There have always been highly exceptional and creative Africans in this country and few of us can claim uniqueness of ability or creativity. Circumstances did not permit some others to demonstrate the full measure of their abilities. The foolers of white folks speak for themselves as individuals, but their aim is to be thought of as speaking for the Wilderness dwellers. A series of such personalities came into prominence with the conservative administrations of Presidents Reagan and Bush. Supported by the conservative think tanks such as the Manhattan Institute and the Hoover Institute, they sought to portray themselves as on the cutting edge of the political and social issues confronting the African American community. None of them had any real credibility with the majority of African Americans. Ward Connerly, Thomas Sowell, Glenn Loury, and Walter Williams were hardly names heard in the African American community, yet they were paraded before the media as voices of reason coming out of the African American community when in fact they were well-supported black fronts for white conservative politics.

The reasons for their isolation from the community are found in the nature of the anger in the Wilderness. It is an anger that stems from being tired of whites dictating to us who we should listen to and on what occasion. It smells like the system of enslavement that we have resisted from the very beginning. So we resent those who enjoy their privileges because of the struggles and agitations of those whom they criticize. For example, the condemnation of cultural nationalism by professors of Black Studies at some universities is the height of irony, since it was the cultural nationalist movement that created their jobs. Neither those who espouse conservative views nor those who espouse Marxist sentiments can take credit for their positions in Black Studies, whether at Cornell, Wisconsin, Harvard, Ohio State, Berkeley, or Temple. Our departments and programs have been made possible by those who felt that the study and preservation of African American culture and history were worthwhile—the so-called black nationalists. The reason for this is that the black nationalists have always believed in self-determination and self-definition. These people included the pioneers of African American Studies, such as Nathan Hare and Jimmy Garrett at San Francisco State, Ewart Guinier at Harvard, James Turner at Cornell, William Nelson at Ohio State, Leonard Jeffries at San Jose State, and others committed to the idea that African people should be viewed as agents, capable of speaking for themselves. Those who believe in the possibility of society based on human solidarity are angered by the players of white folk, who do not adhere to the principles of decency and goodwill for whites or blacks. The word in the Wilderness is that they would sell their souls to the highest bidders.

I believe that many of the black conservative white-folk players, manipulators, are critics and commentators who play on the sidelines of the Wilderness but whose purpose is to massage the egos of whites by telling them that their values and behaviors should be adopted by the black masses. Thus, we have books like *Losing the Race* by John McWhorter and *Out of America* by Keith Richburg as part of a complicated pathology that blames the victim for his own problems. Others seek to manipulate white racist sentiments for their own personal advantage. Many black conservatives believe that they can advance professionally in society by attacking blacks, but they add nothing to the discourse on racism. During the Reagan-Bush era, many blacks believed that the only way to advance in politics, education, or economics was to join the conservative movement. The argument made by those blacks was that they could join the conservative movement, talk the language, and become a significant minority in the movement—giving speeches, being featured on programs that were critical of the civil rights establishment, and writing essays against collective solutions to racism. Those who succeeded in convincing the white conservatives that they were "just like them" made a habit of explaining us to white audiences for money. The young people call them the authentic "shuckers" and "jivers"—the true hustlers—because they have no organic relation to the Wilderness, either as activists or as community political or social volunteers. Within the African American community, the representatives of the masses have always been those who were connected to the struggles of the people as activists in civil, social, or political arenas. These white-folk foolers, to gain acceptance among whites, are often shown attacking the civil rights organizations—the very organizations that made possible the environment for their avenues of achievement.

This new group, including both conservatives and some who claim a leftist orientation, screams in every possible way to whites, "Please validate me!" And the whites who succumb to this weakness often demonstrate in their response their own racism in its most virulent, paternalistic form. These are the trappers and the trapped, the ones who seek to ingratiate themselves with the white power brokers and whose artificiality and superficiality often expose them. It is a game. The conservative blacks are the trappers, the manipulators, and the whites are the trapped, the manipulated, in a complex relationship of white supremacy. The trapped ones who play the game believe that the trappers are actually honest, earnest, and well meaning. The whites, in a turnabout, are victims, entrapped and entangled in the most snarled political relationships because of their racial proclivity. They give their pats on the head, bless the black trappers, and believe that all is well. However, one cannot escape the Wilderness by assuming that blackness does not exist and by agreeing with those blacks who seek white approval at the expense of their dignity and the interests of their communities. They become individuals par excellence, but they neither interpret nor speak for anyone. Neither the trappers nor the trapped can be at peace; they neither trust nor respect one another.

I once invited Chuck D of Public Enemy to speak to the undergraduate and graduate students in the Department of African American Studies at Temple University. When he finished speaking about an Afrocentric vision, I asked him to respond to the idea of the media as a means to convey cultural values. Chuck D was in pure form. He said the media is a vehicle for social and cultural warfare because it has served as a channel for the dislocation of African American culture. He said that the "conscious rappers" understood that the airwaves are instruments for instruction and information. The question is, Who are the conscious rappers? Since to be conscious is to be in tune with the social, historical, and political interests of the African American community, are *any* of the major rappers smart enough or intelligent enough to see that their raps are pyramids that reach into the skies of our minds? Can we get a hearing from KRS-One, Common, Dead Prez, Mos Def, The Roots, and Talib Kweli? Or must we examine other rhythms to find the answer to the warrior's cry? What flags are being flown, what symbols are being used, what music is being played, what attitudes are being taught, and what weapons are being issued? Are we tuned in to the new spoken-word artists such as Tehut-Nine, Sara Jones, Saul Williams, Molefi Asante Jr., or Jessica Care Moore?

And the white authorities who control the auditoriums and theaters in the Wilderness where rap artists sing are quick to put the wrap on rap when they believe the music incites violence. In almost no cases have rap lyrics caused audiences to turn violent. When there has been violence it has been created either before the performances or after the rap artists have ended their shows. Of course there have been cases where audiences have gotten out of control because of the antics of some of the performers, such as a performer stalking off of the stage before the show is over. But even when the performer Tim Smooth walked off of a stage in New Orleans because of the censorship on profanity, security guards had to calm the audience but no one was injured and there was no violence. Nevertheless, the directors of the St. John Theatre in New Orleans placed a prohibition on rap music at the Reserve Auditorium, which they control. They argued that the music was profanity laced, lawsuit inspiring, and riot inciting.[23] None of these terms apply to all of the music, since most of the rappers do not lace their lyrics with profanity or inspire either lawsuits or riots.

I believe, as do many African Americans, that the whites who would like to shut down the auditoriums actually would like to shut down the music. Rap is an "in your face" type of music. When it is political music, its aggressive stance awakens the listeners. The so-called snakes of rap are the "dead heads" who write misogynistic and homophobic lyrics to cater to the baser elements in society. However, one must distinguish between rap artists who are purely commercial and those who are conscious. Rap artists are like everyone else: Some are interested in improving the conditions in the Wilderness and some are not. Our best tradition has been the socially aware artist whose connection to the streets of the Wilderness, whether psychically or physically, has enriched the music. So the attack on the rap artists is really an attack on the message of this fighting music. But rap is not giving up easily, because the percussive rhythms carry the lyrics into new venues and new avenues everyday. Rap does seem to be moving to a new address though; it is being upstaged by the power of the Spoken Word. Artists are springing up in the same community places, evening joints, book-shops, and small cafés that gave rap its initial energy. The hip-hop culture is becoming, as it should, a more mature and conscious community of poets, philosophers, rappers, and teachers.

When Yoruba, Congo, Wolof, Asante, Fante, Ibo, Ibibio, Mandinka, Baule, and hundreds of other ethnic groups were brought from Africa to the Americas, drums were often outlawed. Yes, it is true: We were robbed of our drums, distanced from that element of our culture that contained the traditions, rituals, and nuances of many of the various African cultures. Given the power of the drums to talk—that is, to communicate the historical and ritual messages of unity, joy, and victory—the European slave owners did not like to hear the drums playing late at night. They saw this "beating" of the drums as dan-gerous. It was a fearful, frightful sound. Whereas I am drawn to the drums like being pulled by my ancestral voices, several white friends are still made uneasy by the polyrhythms of African drums. Is it the belief that the drums represent the lack of civilization, while the piano, for example, represents civilization? Is not this the same irra-tional basis for arguing racial superiority of Europeans?

Fortunately, the drums as institutions were preserved, in limited ways, in the percussive memory of the masses. When we hear the rap-pers, we are hearing the *bongas*, *ketes*, *tom-toms*, *atumpans*, *congas*, *djembes*, *fontonfroms*—and the basic Africanity of the Wilderness. The drum, once so distant, is heard in every African American community.

It is the one constant in the music, dance, rhythms of conversation, and memory. There is nothing as magnetic as the re-creation of the ritual energy of the drums. Groups such as Universal African Dance Ensemble, Baba Olatunji's ensemble, Baba Chuck Davis's dancers and drummers, and many others have inherited the mantle that was hidden during the worst times of physical and cultural oppression. To say that the drum is back is not quite correct; rather, we must say that the drum has never left.

Hip-hop is the key to understanding the new Wilderness culture. What is the meaning of the song "Pigs" or "In Fear of a Black P!anet"? The young people in the Wilderness see a new form of poetry taking shape. The rhetoric of the raps becomes the most authentic representation of the rhythms of some of the most creative poets of this age. Like other new music, rap is the creation of the youth. It is preeminently the music of young warrrior-rappers. The weapons of the warfare are powerful lyrics song-spoken in a staccato voice imitative of the metallic and siliconic sounds of the urban centers. The X-Clan captures the name, iconography, rhetoric, and rap of the imagination by appropriating Malcolm X—El Hajj Malik Shabazz—in their name and in their arsenal of raps. Like Malcolm's stacatto rhythms, the rappers produce an urgent message.

In the Wilderness Malcolm X is the super-icon of resistance. This is not just in the visible symbols and images of Malcolm, but the profound visceral feeling that Malcolm X was the embodiment of courage and thus he became a fixture in the iconography of the resistance. The female counterpart used to be Angela Davis, but Assata Shakur has replaced her as the symbol of resistance in the youth pantheon. There has been a gradual but constant "bigging up" of the Assata myth through song, poetry, biography, and autobiography. Overall, however, Malcolm remains the symbolic standard for men and women in struggle.

Some see the Malcolm X phenomenon as a symbol of collective emotion, a return of passion and the eternal quality of resistance to evil. Malcolm X is the patron saint of the Los Angeles uprising, and in the years since 1965—the year of Watts and the year of his death—

Crispus Attucks, the first man to die in the Boston Massacre, March 1770. *(Courtesy Temple University Archives)*

John Henrik Clarke and Yosef ben Jochannon, popular historians who worked to correct African history in the last half of the twentieth century. *(Photo courtesy Molefi Kete Asante)*

Winnie Mandela campaigning to end racism. *(Photo courtesy Molefi Kete Asante)*

Two young African Americans on a pilgrimage to Egypt meet an Egyptian at Edfu Temple. Connecting to Africa became a major instrument for self-improvement in the 1980s. *(Photo courtesy Molefi Kete Asante)*

Africans participating in the making of a king ceremony in Philadelphia, 1993. *(Photo courtesy Molefi Kete Asante)*

Joe Louis and Duke Ellington succeeded in their professions despite racism. (Photo courtesy Temple University Archives)

Lerone Bennett, the most widely read historian of his generation, has written about the strategies needed to overcome racism. (Photo courtesy Molefi Kete Asante)

Lorraine Hansberry defined the struggle against racism with her play *A Raisin in the Sun*. (Photo courtesy Temple University Archives)

W. E. B. Du Bois wrote *The Souls of Black Folk* in 1903. (Photo courtesy Temple University Archives)

Elijah Muhammad, leader and founder of the Nation of Islam, sought to teach blacks to love themselves in order to overcome the effects of racism. (Photo courtesy Temple University Archives)

Martin Luther King Jr. and Ralph Abernathy. (Photo courtesy Temple University Archives)

Jackie Robinson broke the color line in major league baseball. (Photo courtesy Temple University Archives)

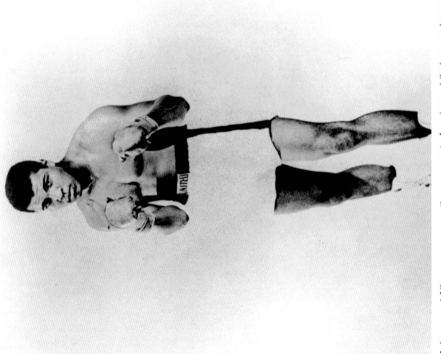

Muhammad Ali was an energetic opponent of racism while he was heavy-weight champion. (Photo courtesy Temple University Archives)

Thurgood Marshall was the first black Supreme Court justice. He was an accomplished civil rights lawyer prior to his appointment to the federal bench. *(Photo courtesy Temple University Archives)*

he has been canonized in the minds of young African Americans. Spike Lee's movie *Malcolm X* made him a priest and we have become witnesses to his warrior quality. "By any means necessary" is almost as common in the Wilderness as "I have a dream." Thus, Malcolm has become—as much as and maybe more than Martin Luther King Jr.— a folk hero of the young men and women of the Wilderness.

What is the source of this fascination with Malcolm X? It is Malcolm's interaction with his community to create a more revolutionary response to cultural domination. Since culture is a product of historical processes, Malcolm X as the great opposition to domination represents the epitome of self-conscious recognition of culture. He was a cultured individual in the best sense of the African American activist tradition.

Culture is fundamental to a people's self-assertion. African Americans are a people with a distinct historical relationship to this nation. Our history, if anything, has always been one in which men and women who have been deeply committed to equality have borne witness to an intensely collective concept of culture. Malcolm was such a person. He was, most importantly, a cultural spokesperson, an analyst and theorist of culture, a revolutionary cultural scientist. Thus, when he is examined within the context of our fury and within the framework of the African American situation, he emerges as a concrete example of the cultural hero.

Malcolm's identity as an intellectual and as an organizer must be seen in the light of his emphasis on transforming those who lived in the Wilderness. He wanted to see Africans in America transformed, changed, and perfected in their resistance to oppression. He expressed this in his concept of the radically different African person by saying, "He is the new, he is the new type. He is the type that the white man seldom ever comes in contact with. And when you do come in contact with him, you're shocked, because you didn't know that this type of black man existed."[24] This new type of African American is no Uncle Tom, no Aunt Jemima, but a twenty-first-century individual who dislikes disrespect and who truly believes in the idea of equality.

The ability to assemble behaviors, symbols, customs, motifs, moods, and icons into a single, comprehensive, affirming presence is a strong representation of the concept of culture. It is Malcolm's posture toward self-hatred; culturicide, the killing of African culture; and menticide, the destruction of the African mind, that governs his cultural ideology. In fact, Malcolm believed that this "new type of African" rejects the white man's religion and sees it as a racist religion of domination. Although the church brought a sense of cohesion—that is, community—to the black experience, it nevertheless was based on a wrong idea as far as Malcolm was concerned. He recognizes the real enemy: "That Uncle Tom can't see his enemy. He thinks his friend is his enemy and his enemy is his friend. And he usually ends up loving his enemy, turning his other cheek to his enemy. But this new type, he doesn't turn the other cheek to anybody."[25] I am certain that had Malcolm reflected at length, he would have seen the need for the African to reject the Arab's (Islamic) religion in the same way and for the same reasons that he rejected the white's (Christian) religion: the culpability of both religions in the degradation, enslavement, and humiliation of African culture. But his view was the preamble to the age of hip-hop, the spirit of rap, the idea that the African American or African cannot accept disrespect and be considered human, no matter who brings the disrespect.

Generations are often the engines of cultural and technological innovations. The end of the Second Major European War marked the beginning of a new generation of Africans. Malcolm X, born in 1925, reached the greatest heights of his cultural and social power in the early 1960s. However, it is perhaps correct to say that the Age of Malcolm began with his conversion in prison to the Nation of Islam.

Louis Farrakhan, often considered a rival of Malcolm's, has emerged as one of the figures most legitimate in the minds of the political hip-hoppers. There is in Farrakhan the same type of "in your face" rhetoric that Malcolm encouraged and that the rappers have captured in their lyrics. The fact that Farrakhan can attract more African Americans to a public lecture than any contemporary speaker, congressperson, or preacher has to do with the rhetoric of respect for the African that he embraces. An entire group of African Americans are outside the editorials in the *New York Times* and *Wall Street Journal*, white newspapers that seem to often deliberately misread the political sentiments of the African American community. Despite the attacks on him by the press, Louis Farrakhan, leader of the Nation of Islam, has a following within the black community precisely *because* he has challenged the standard interpretations of the American social situation. What gives Farrakhan currency is neither Islam nor a perceived anti-Semitism; rather, it is his consistent stand against the inordinate projection and assertion of white power that galvanizes his audiences.

There is no white monopoly on political, social, or economic policy ideas. Numerous black social scientists write and speak on every topic discussed in the media. Yet you would not know that these individuals, trained at the best schools and loaded with experience, ever existed because of the silence of the major media about these community intellectuals. Some of these names may be unknown to the wider community, yet they are household names among the most politically conscious Wilderness dwellers. I am thinking of Ronald Walters, Hanes Walton, Wade Nobles, Robert Smith, Gayle Tate, and Regina Jennings, among others. Whatever others may think of their ideas, they hold currency among a new generation of black students. They are our intellectuals. In their understanding of the Wilderness dwellers, they are in the tradition of Malcolm X, who was the epitome of what the warrior seeks. Spike Lee's film *Malcolm X* is a contract with history, written and sealed with the blood and the emotions of ten thousand Malcolms in the Los Angeleses of this nation. And make no argument against it: Every big city is a Los Angeles.

With the Age of Malcolm a new epoch began in the conception of a national culture or cultural nationalism, causing a far-reaching revolution in the traditional views held by members of African American institutions. Malcolm was not merely "our manhood," as Ossie Davis nobly put it at Malcolm's funeral, but the keeper of the ancestral flames of a proactive response to the human condition. His life represented the rebirth of the extensive African American commitments to cultural reconstruction that are not yet concluded. Despite the various political and social contours of the past twenty years, we have not yet succeeded in wholly realizing the fundamental cultural vision of Malcolm X. This is not to say that we have been asleep, because the revolutionary social and cultural ideas of many people are directly related to the Malcolmian vision of a conscious, awake, and dynamic African American culture. And by "culture" Malcolm did not mean simply singing and dancing, but the entire manner in which a people transmits its best values and behaviors. This involves economics, education, politics, social groups, family relationships, and communication systems.

The young warriors believe that what is necessary is the consistent and persistent dissemination of the ideas Malcolm espoused with regard to culture, essentially a "pattern or the habit of seeing for ourselves, hearing for ourselves, thinking for ourselves, and then we can come to an intelligent judgment for ourselves."[26] This is one of the most Afrocentric statements in Malcolm's corpus because it defines the moments of our realization that we are on our own. Warriors of the hip-hop generation take Malcolm's speeches and autobiography with great seriousness. They realize that Malcolm's intention to put the issue of the African American on the agenda of the United Nations was a bold move.

Malcolm X saw that the adaptation of the social and cultural imperatives of African people through ideas, attitudes, language, and history that was essential for changing the conditions of the African people first meant political and cultural requirements for a comprehensive transformation. There could be no other interface with our historical destiny; we had to center ourselves in our African reality. We were not, as some whites and "some Negroes" had maintained, "made in America Negroes, but Africans." But he also understood that we had not been paid for the enslavement and the segregation that set us back many decades vis-à-vis white America. His intelligence was his knowledge of the conservative reaction to our advancement. Furthermore, he never got tired of telling his audiences that America came to its greatness on the backs of black people. Payment would be one mode of squaring up the debt.

A long list of precursors contributed to Malcolm's pattern of growth. The doctrines of Elijah Muhammad had an early impact upon his thinking. Later, his mind grew with the richly textured worlds of Paul Robeson and Marcus Garvey. Perhaps it was his father's work with the Garvey Movement that prepared him for the more personal and concrete teachings of Elijah Muhammad. What do you tell a people who have been discriminated, abused, brutalized, and disrespected in every sector of American society? Muhammad told African Americans that the white man was the devil because only a devil could treat people the way whites had treated us. Malcolm was his principal preacher. Although Malcolm develvoped a new line of thinking in terms of the humanity of whites, he never conceded his belief that American whites were the most hypocritical people in the world.

African culture, already present in the thinking of the cultural nationalists, gained respectability with Malcolm's pronouncement that we were African people despite all the claims to the contrary by the African American establishment. He knew that the word "African" had come to have a negative meaning to most African Americans, so he explained the situation as one of cultural misorientation. He said, "The word 'African' was used in this country in a derogatory way. But now, since African nations have gained some independence and there are so many independent African states, the image of the African has changed from negative to positive."[27]

The concept of cultural reconstruction in Malcolm X's rhetoric was pregnant with possibilities that could be translated into a strong political movement. Others before Malcolm had recognized the power of cultural consciousness, but never with so much force as presented by Malcolm. Here was an African American who understood the implications of cultural revolution. Marcus Garvey, Edward Wilmot Blyden, Martin Delaney, and Paul Robeson were the progenitors who influenced Malcolm's mature understanding of the significance of African culture. For the first time since Garvey and the expressed symbol of Africa as a powerful instrument in cultural awakening, the African cultural attitude was revived through Malcolm's rhetoric. Here it came as a torrent, breaking the shackles of a genuflected people and announcing a new, more aggressive approach to cultural reconstruction. As we heard him and sat at his feet, it was inevitable that his faith would be reflected in numerous attempts to restructure our response to America. Thousands of urban Africans reached toward Malcolm's vision and when it was comprehended, they preached in Shangoan voices the truth that they had seen.

Furthermore, with Malcolm's challenge—that we were Africans—it became clearer that the term "Negro" was dead. In the struggle of ideas where cultural considerations were seen as primary or fundamental, the old Negro order, hailed in its day by Alain Locke and others as the "New Negro," was permanently laid to rest by Malcolm.[28] No one could be taken seriously without a response to the Chakan posture of his discourse. Malcolm fostered discontent within the camp of the old order, creating by the power of his logic schisms in the conservative body politic of African Americans. It is easy to understand the preeminent position of Malcolm as a cultural figure when, in addition to all I have said, we consider the intense reaction of the white American establishment to his call for black cultural nationalism. Malcolm was considered an extremist and a militant by most of the white press. Of course, the African American press, itself often tied to the white corporate structure, hardly treated him any better.

The cultural epoch of Malcolm wears a multifaceted umbrella under which walk a new woman and a new man, born of cultural struggle, who understand Karenga's notion of "history as the struggle and record of humans in the process of humanizing the world, i.e., shaping it in their own image and interests."[29] Even now, the legacies we have inherited from Malcolm are the most dominant motifs of our approach to humanity. In choosing to do a movie based on some aspects of Malcolm's life, as complex as that life was, Spike Lee understood the essence of our manner of movement. To capture some part of Malcolm is better than capturing none of him. Since culture involved struggle and struggle developed culture, Malcolm understood the necessity for African Americans to recognize the value in our traditions.

Malcolm marked an end to the apologia of the "Negro" and declared that we would "be free by any means necessary."[30] While we often understand Malcolm to include self-defense in his corpus, we know from his teachings that he was committed to changing the way we thought about ourselves and about Africa. Planting the seed of an affirming African presence, his cultural project was the root from which we grew strong and vital African sentiments and attitudes. Malcolm's vision provided the impetus for the cultural nationalism that exists always just below the emotional surface of most African Americans. Along with this impetus to cultural nationalism, Malcolm's rhetoric encouraged the ethical value of Afrocentric institutions. Thus, the cultural epoch initiated by Malcolm developed very quickly into a thousand parallel universes of freedom that stood against the sacrifice of Africanity and the abstract concept of integration. What Malcolm X strove for was the dispelling of illusions, because phantoms were not based on our reality. Africanity represents all of those things that Africans do as Africans. Culture, to be meaningful for him, could not be merely imitative. It had to be Afrocentric; that is, it had to reflect African people as subjects and not merely as marginal · players in the European experience.

Reconstructive culture, as understood by Malcolm, was fostered by a social responsibility based on the understanding of history. Such responsibility in the context of the African American community could only exist on the basis of cultural solidarity. What Malcolm understood was the need for a collective appreciation of Africanity as the first level of overcoming oppression rooted in physical or mental brutality. The appreciation of Africanity is the same as self-acceptance. When this prerequisite is absent, there is the possibility of serious cultural disorientation.

At the fundamental level, Malcolm was a cultural worker. His aim was always to collect the people into a community of solidarity so that new cultural energies would arise for the common purpose. In the creation of community solidarity, he wanted to establish a national consciousness that would render the old Negro order ineffective. His language characterizing that order is well known. Malcolm said,

> Also this type of so-called Negro, by being intoxicated over the white man, he never sees beyond the white man. He never sees beyond America. He never looks at himself or where he fits into things on the world stage. . . . And it puts him in the role of a beggar—cowardly, humble, Uncle Tomming beggar on anything that he says is—that should be his by right.[31]

Malcolm's view of culture was concentrated principally on an Afrocentric foundation. He did not assert and would never assert the development of the national culture as a result of economic necessity. He neither tried to prove nor would he have been inclined to prove that historical events were always caused by economic necessity. In reality, Malcolm was an astute observer of the historical conditions of African Americans. In the serious reconstruction of African culture, he saw that the struggle for power and the ability to create categories that are accepted by others frequently played a much more important role than economic necessity. Beyond this, however, was his insistence on African cultural autonomy, by which he meant all things considered cosmological, axiological, epistemological, and aesthetic.[32] In this regard, he was interested in the role African legends, stories of the universe and history, played in the interface with the cosmos. Race, culture, class, and gender are all in the category of cosmology because they constitute ways of dealing with the human cosmos as interpreted in relationships. Malcolm did not bother with the occult or astrology; his work was with the concrete experiences of African American people. But he was concerned about how language, dance, music, art, and myth operate in the realm of truth. At the axiological level, these are issues of proof and truth. Malcolm's approach to the question of value explains his axiological interests, which were always manifest as right conduct and good actions. Finally, he saw the unity of texture, rhythm, dimension as being dedicated to aesthetic appreciation in the African American tradition.

Given such autonomy, it was possible to imagine a culture of resistance as well as a reconstructive culture. By virtue of its affirming posture, this new view of culture became, in Malcolm's theory, a critique of oppressive reality. This critique was presented in Malcolm's rhetoric as a missile against the enemies of the African American people. Indeed his language epitomized the expression of the national culture. More so than Langston Hughes in poetry or Martin Luther King Jr. in civil rights, it was Malcolm who elevated the people's street language to a national style. Few passages in the history of oratory can compare with the straightforward logic and dynamic cadence of Malcolm saying:

> So when I come in here to speak to you, I'm not in here speaking as a Baptist or a Methodist or a Democrat or a Republican or a Christian or a Jew or—not even as an American. Because if I stand up here—if I could stand up here and speak to you as an American we wouldn't have anything to talk about. The problem would be solved. So we don't even profess to speak as an American. We are speaking as—I am speaking as a Black man.[33]

Indeed, one might argue that Malcolm's ground of contact with the people was so vast and his groundedness with the masses so profoundly human that he earned the title "spokesman" in a manner wholly unlike any other African American leader. He was not "spokesman" by virtue of his official status within the African American community, but "spokesman" because he actually spoke what was in our hearts the way we would have spoken it if we had been so eloquent. Language is never the invention of individual people but rather the creation of the community as a whole. Culturally, Malcolm tapped the most creative aspect of African American life, drawing upon the proverbs, the folklore, the nuances, the syntax, and the grammar of the people's creation to make his own discourse. Between his discourse and ours there was hardly any difference; he spoke and when he spoke, he took the words right out of our mouths.

Malcolm's discourse was African American cultural expression that changed with the economic and political conditions of a socially united people. This special form of speech, a rap tune of protest and action, enabled African Americans to reach for higher moral and political results. Speech became, for Malcolm, like dance—polycentric and polyrhythmic.

In reality, Malcolm X on culture was predictable. He could not have lived as an African in a racist society without wishing to come to terms with the contradictions of place. Racism is everywhere the same in its objectives, in the selection of its arenas of struggles, and in its means of attack. Its devastating impact on the intellectual, economic, and cultural life of Africans in America is everywhere evident. Malcolm knew, as others had known, that its effect on any people led to the same horrible outcome: the stripping of self-esteem and the creation of a population of consumers of a hostile culture. All anti-African attitudes that exist in racist culture become, if there is no corrective measure, the attitudes of the Africans. In such a situation the culture derived from Africans is considered secondary to the culture of the oppressors. Malcolm knew this process through his own personal experience and recognized the many facets of resistance. Indeed, it was necessary to build a culture of resistance, to strengthen Africans' self-concept, and to struggle for a liberated community.

Even with his great cultural commitment, Malcolm did not stand outside of space and time. He was bound to the past, present, and future. What is significant in his genius is the voice that created a unified and directed discourse that may have lain dormant in the masses. Thus, Malcolm's cultural idea is a universal vision based upon both what preceded him and what would follow him. This cultural picture opens to Africans a refreshing outlook on life. Humans are collective beings who are dependent upon predecessors, and therefore no one can really draw a line between what she has acquired by her own powers and what she has received from others. Every cultural idea, whether it is of a political, social, or spiritual nature, has forerunners without which it would be inconceivable. To truly appreciate Malcolm, therefore, we must embrace him in the context of his particular time and space. As heir to resistance, nationalism, pride, knowledge, and nobility, he was destined to be a cultured person as well as a teacher of culture. Perhaps his most authentic legacy to us is his fulfillment of the prerequisites of what it means to be "cultured" in our terms.

The criteria for culture derived from the actual life of the African American people are contained in Maulana Karenga's seven constituents: history, mythology, ethos, motif, social organization, political organization, and economic organization.[34] Those criteria constitute what Marimba Ani calls the *utaratibu wa kutizama:* African philosophy and worldview.[35] Malcolm walked in these criteria stronger than most public figures because he embodied—indeed, self-consciously embodied—these criteria in historical thought and language. For example, Malcolm's speech "Message to the Grass Roots Conference," held at the King Solomon Baptist Church in Detroit, Michigan, in 1963, employed history to "place the audience in the shoes of revolutionary and counter-revolutionary persona, transforming his audience into Bandung delegates, French revolutionaries, Russian peasants, field niggers, and betrayed black men."[36]

The heroic Malcolm championed African culture as the only corrective for an extremely misoriented people. Malcolm's cultural position might be seen as a self-conscious intervention against misorientation. An African American had to know that "he didn't come here on the Mayflower." Furthermore, the sane African "knows he was brought here on a slave ship. But this twentieth-century Uncle Tom, he'll stand up in your face and tell you about when his fathers landed on Plymouth Rock. His father never landed on Plymouth Rock; the rock was dropped on him, but he wasn't dropped on it."[37]

To be cultured in the traditional African manner carries with it the responsibility to use the language effectively.[38] In his heroic persona, Malcolm was the master of this cultural element. Numerous studies of Malcolm's ability to communicate suggest that his power was so elemental and essential in its efficacy that his voice remained unanswerable, fluid, pure, and fundamental. The best of our oratorical genius converged in his heroism, and we were always left with the feeling of having been in the presence of our purest self.

When Malcolm X spoke, his images were perfect; the cadence of his sentences was like poetry whose rhythmic structure harked back to the profound African sensibility of a people victorious against a million agonies. So full of his culture, it was as if he knew everything about us and wanted to teach us by sharing the depths of our experience. Malcolm could juxtapose "singing" and "swinging," "landless against the landlord," "grass roots versus grass leaves," "house negro versus field negro," and a "Black march on Washington versus a Negro march on Washington."[39]

The philosophical core of the African's relationship to reality is not conflict, not an antagonistic duality. Nevertheless, as Malcolm demonstrated, our condition in America was fraught with extreme danger because of the ideology of white racial supremacy. Therefore, he postured the one against the other, the good against the evil, the African versus the *diablo blanco*, as an instructive device rather than a philosophical statement. In the end, it was natural for him to show us the unreality of Hollywood and the basic reality of Harlem. The point was not lost on an audience of believers. This was an ethical lesson largely ignored at the time by the press.

Perhaps the principal clue to Malcolm's understanding of culture emerges when he demonstrates his rationale for action: the struggle against the condition of oppression. For us, culture has no other practical end. It must be the regaining of freedom in order to be truly effective as humans in history.

He had arrived at his analysis of the role of culture, by which he meant all of the seven constituents later conceptualized by Karenga as the Nguzo Saba, through testing the historical choices made by African Americans. The civil rights movement came under extremely close scrutiny, since it galvanized thousands and captured the imagination of the black establishment. What Malcolm discerned, however, was the ineffectiveness of a movement that did not address the cultural question. He spent his life asserting this theme and the varied implications of this theme. If some found his theses violent, it was because he laid them down without excuse, and because the system of white domination of African Americans was violent. What more could he do than present a direct challenge to Africans in America to take up arms and march into battle? How else does one approach a sustained physical and psychological assault? What else is real? Thus, Malcolm had gained his own sanity and was located in an Afrocentric mode before he broke with the teachings of Elijah Muhammad, teachings that had been a major bulwark against the indecencies of white Christianity. John Illo has written of Malcolm's rhetorical challenge to the American government in this way: "[T]he only useful attack is directness, which, opposed to outrage, is outraged and, to apologists of outrage, outrageous."[40]

Malcolm's cultural consciousness exalted resistance to outrage and became, by virtue of his commitment to the survival of his own culture, a key aspect of his nationalism:

> And the Motto of the Organization of Afro-American Unity is By Any Means Necessary. We don't believe in fighting a battle that's going to—in which the ground rules are to be laid down by those who suppress us. We don't believe that we can win in a battle where the ground rules are laid down by those who exploit us. We don't believe that we can carry on a struggle trying to win the affection of those who for so long have oppressed and exploited us.[41]

On another occasion Malcolm asked the African American community questions such as the following: Why should whites be running the stores in the African American community? Why should whites own all of the businesses in the African American community?

Malcolm's questions were unanswerable by the "so-called Negro" leadership of his day. He destroyed through a powerful rejection the logic of then NAACP Executive Secretary Roy Wilkins, that though the black man was a second-class American, he was still an American.

> I'm not going to sit at our table and watch you eat, with nothing on my plate, and call myself a diner. Sitting at the table doesn't make you a diner, unless you eat some of what's on that plate. Being here in America doesn't make you an American. Being born here in America doesn't make you an American.[42]

This passage, like so many of Malcolm's passages, shows him to be one of the most accomplished orators of his time because he was attuned to the deepest emotions of his own people. The Los Angeles uprising is a testament to Malcolm's analysis. He spoke the words that the Wilderness dwellers felt and wanted to speak. Indeed the Oxford Union Society considered him among the best of all living orators after he debated under their auspices about three months before his death. Always amused at the lack of reason of his opposition and assured of his own cultural and moral rectitude, Malcolm taught us the most majestic element in our defense was not meanness of spirit but the magnificent nobility of African American culture, derived from traditional African philosophical roots.

One reason we listened to him was because he possessed the virtue of recognition. Malcolm became us at our best, in our most authoritative manner, in our humanity, in our style, in our humor, in our secrets, and in the manner of our treatment of each other. In these things, collectively, and with specific qualities, we each could individually admire Malcolm's life as a testament to African American culture.

While we must admit that Malcolm resembled us in our highest cultural aspiration, he was also our cultural teacher. Creating a curriculum of culture from our own history, he elevated the art of instruction by serving as the model for what he taught. If he taught us that courage was more rewarding than cowardice, he demonstrated by his own life that he believed it. And as his pattern of growth demonstrated, if he taught us to respect other human beings, then he was never anti-Semitic or racist, or a disrespecter of persons. If he taught us to love one another, then he loved his people to the last full measure of his devotion. If the government was full of "tricksters," then African American leaders should not have coffee with the tricksters; he met the protectors and defenders of the establishment only to tell them of the grievances we rightly held. Thus, culture, for Malcolm, did not depend upon outside validation—rather, he promulgated the view that "by any means necessary" we had to advance from the oppressed state in which we found ourselves in America.

The broad dissemination of this message alone was sufficient to create for him a place in our contemporary cultural history because few had ever taught quite so effectively and so directly. He became, during and after his life, an icon equal to Marcus Garvey, Nat Turner, Harriet Tubman, Sojourner Truth, and Martin Luther King Jr. Malcolm was fundamentally a warrior who analyzed the woeful psychological and social conditions that disconnected Africans from themselves. Indeed, he was not a violence-preaching fanatic or a preacher of the lunatic fringe, as he was made out to be by the white media and some of the more conservative black newspapers. As a regenerator of racial pride and respect, Malcolm X articulated the feelings of millions of previously immobilized urban Wilderness dwellers and became, for some, an icon of the "in your face" rhetoric. America must pay us for the many Malcolm Xs who have forfeited all or most of their lives fighting for justice. What if Malcolm X could have served as a college professor somewhere, or been the leader of some formidable team of political negotiators seeking to bring peace to the world? Alas, this was not to be, and yet, for all of his grace and power, Malcolm has become the icon of the new generation in the Wilderness.

# CHAPTER SIX
# RACE AND THE
# RELIGION SITUATION

Perhaps one of the arenas in which Africans and whites in America share similar tendencies is religion. I have always believed that Africans in America have often been sidetracked from the issue of racial equality because of their adherence to religion, one of the worst addictions in the history of humanity. The connection between religion and racism is as old as the appearance of differentiation in the human species, and yet it retains a tremendous hold on the most oppressed masses of the human race. Religion and racism were established in the ancient past of human society when one group decided that it was better than another because of its god. In fact, monotheistic religions tend to have more virulent forms of racism and violence against others than any other form of religion. Religion is inherently a form of prejudice, that is, a xenophobic bias against the practices of other people. In this regard, it is much like racism, which is a particularly cruel form of the same xenophobia in which one group fears people of another race. Xenophobic people fear differences, or separations, in the physical, cultural, linguistic, or religious attributes of another person.

One form of separation is color prejudice based on skin hue. Another form of separation is cultural, which might be based on dress, cuisine, ritual, and fashion. Yet another form takes a difference of language as the reason for prejudice. One of the most bigoted forms of prejudice seems to be religious—a person is deemed worthy or unworthy because of the type of god he believes in, or the fact that he does not believe in any god. This is religious prejudice that prevents people from living together in society. But there is a more poisonous form of this bias against another person or group of people when it comes to religion practiced alongside racism, or when the religion itself appears to be based on certain ideological assumptions about other people.

Let's take the forced relationship between the Christian religion and black people as an example of how religion cemented the prejudices of many white people against Africans. The African's relationship to Christianity originates in the idea formulated by Europeans that blacks could be enslaved because they were not Christians. Therefore, to become closer to the white ideal, and perhaps to God, the black person had to become Christian. The idea was that our enslavement was good for us because it brought us close to the Christian god, notwithstanding the fact that the earliest examples of the Christian faith's encounter with Africa was catastrophic, where we were considered heathens and therefore outside the entire schema of good and god. In fact, the Christian idea was that Africans were not humans and did not possess souls, thus there was nothing to save. Although this telling belief was not practiced everywhere and was not always prevalent in every arena, it was strong enough as an accepted opinion that it created a deep-seated hatred for African people among Christians. Being "heathen" meant that we had no rights and privileges that had to be respected: the religion that gave the white man the right to enslave Africans had already dictated our position in the universe, and that position was one of inferiority by virtue of being soulless and without the Christian god.

One must remember, however, that such a position was unsustainable in the logical system that whites had devised for themselves. What happens to the child of a Christian man and a heathen woman? Is the child only part human? Does the child have half of a soul and so forth? These were questions that could not be answered by the men in cloth who preached silly doctrines adhered to by millions.

Soon there were transformations in the logic and differences among Christians about the possibility of an African soul. For example, when whites in the United States ceased using Irish people as indentured servants, they did so because the Irish had been declared to have souls. They were Catholic, although chastised for their love of the pope, yet they believed in a form of the Christian god. On the other hand, by the mid-seventeenth century it was clear that the black population in America held on to African ideas and rituals, so the political agenda was clear for the slaveholders: Africans had to be held in bondage in perpetuity because they were neither Christian nor did they have the capacity to become Christian.

There were no large groups of enslaved Africans practicing Christianity in the United States in the seventeenth and eighteenth centuries. By the end of the eighteenth century there were some organized Christian units, but the vast majority of Africans remained skeptical of the Christian faith until the late nineteenth century when white missionaries invaded the South to Christianize us in order to "civilize" us and make us ready for citizenship. The evolutionary road to Christian acceptance of Africans, which was never completed as a result of the attitude of some fundamental evangelicals, has been an uneven one.

Given the intricate interweaving of religion and racism in American society, it just might be that racism cannot be erased without erasing what goes for American religion. Encoded in the religion are ideas such as "the Chosen People," "the One True God," "believers and nonbelievers," and "Go into all the world and preach the gospel to all creation."[1] Add to this list the informal beliefs of white Christians that Africans are the children of Ham, who laughed at Noah during the time of his nakedness and therefore were cursed to be servants and hewers of wood forever. There you have the recipes for a powerful racist brew. On top of this, certain Christian groups, such as the Mormons, proclaimed for most of their history that blacks did not have spirits and could never be apostles, leaders in the church, because of some past deeds. The church changed this doctrine in the mid-twentieth century when it began an international push to bring Africans into the Mormon fold. This drive was first attempted in areas where blacks did not know about the previous history of the Mormon Church, certainly not among the African Americans who maintained their suspicion of a church only recently converted to the equality of all human beings. A revelation by a church leader is all that is necessary to change the basic doctrine of religious racism; this represents the new logic of a church in search of new members.

If we return to the idea of religion and racism, one thing is clear: xenophobia creates isolated groupings of people, whether they are Baptists, Mormons, Muslims, Jews, or Hindus. In the past, people stuck together to survive together. When we learn about new distinctions between one group and another, we are in the presence of the new logic of isolation. Religion, like racism, produces in-groups and out-groups with distinct boundaries, as we see in the case of Christians and Africans. Inclusivity and exclusivity create the type of boundaries in religion that predispose people to accept some and reject others. The idea that you are either with us or against us can lead directly to antagonism.

The role played by religious leaders in regard to racism is not much different from that played by the ancient priest or shaman who danced, performed, chanted, and formed a community of believers who were willing to do anything to maintain the group, including condemning members of other groups if necessary. In America during the late nineteenth century and the early twentieth century, a particularly violent form of the Christian religion was taken outside of the church buildings and into the meadows and onto the farms of rural America. There, group solidarity, anti-Africanism, and anti-Semitism were expounded, and racial iconographs were displayed to create awe in the believers and to cut fear in the heart of the out-group. This American religion was the Ku Klux Klan. Deriving its name from the Greek word "kuklos," meaning circle, the KKK established itself in the forefront of racist thinking in the American South for decades.

## MAKING CHRISTIANS
## AND DULLING INQUIRY

Immediately after the Civil War, white groups of Christians in the North sent massive numbers of moral carpetbaggers for political and religious purposes to the South to enroll Africans in both the political and the religious system of the ruling elites. Our people saw both of these systems as necessary for a citizenship acceptable to the white Americans. With little supporting infrastructure for our own African religious practices, we were nearly stripped from our identity by the evangelizing Christians whose purpose was to make us more present-able to the Lord.

Africans arrived in the United States as Africans, neither as Euro-peans nor as Christians. To be an African meant that the person followed the religious traditions of his or her own ethnic group. A Yoruba remained a Yoruba, and an Ibo remained an Ibo in this situa-tion, but both were Africans. With the imposition of the Christian religion, many Africans began to question their identity as Africans. They were told to get Christian names—meaning European names—and to practice the morality of the whites, many of whom had been slaveholders. For nearly two hundred and fifty years, Christianity had not been encouraged among the enslaved Africans; consequently, there was a strong ambivalence toward the Christian religion among African Americans. Christianity, therefore, had to be sweetened with concrete proposals such as building a church edifice, providing money for scholarships, assisting in the erection of schools, and encouraging missionary societies to teach those who had never seen the possibility of a Christian way of life. All told, this entire process discombobulated and corrupted the African man and woman to the extent that some African Americans became more fervent than those who gave them the religion.

I have always thought that the great problem of leadership in the black community was the omnipotence of *preacherdom*, that is, the overly esteemed position of any who stood at the pulpit. This is not to minimize the role played by the black church or the black preachers in the struggle for affirmative action and equality under the law, but rather to say that the preacher's authority is not derived from reason but from faith. Therein is the problem for African American people. In one sense, the election of Barack Hussein Obama—a law professor, and not a preacher—is a giant step forward in African American political expression. I say this while recognizing and appreciating the fact that some of the outstanding men of courage who have influenced me have been Floyd Rose, Jesse Jackson, Al Sharpton, Wyatt Tee Walker, Jeremiah Wright, Gardiner Taylor, Henry Mitchell, Samuel Proctor, Cornel West, and Martin Luther King Jr., all preachers of various talents and abilities. What they possessed and possess is the ability to use their moral authority with such prophetic rhetoric that the nation's hypocrisy is revealed. Their text of authority is the Bible, not the Articles of Confederation, Plato's *Republic*, or "The Tale of the Eloquent Peasant." These preachers have always managed to find a space in a bigoted nation that allowed them to be free enough of the white economic impact to assume leadership. This role is their great contribution and their unique niche in the struggle for justice. They have a different mission than most political leaders. It is rare, almost impossible, to show a white American preacher who rose to the pinnacle of political power.

The fact of the matter is that reason and faith operate in two different spheres of influence. As a free thinker, I seek knowledge from all sources in an effort to explain the human condition. When famous

African American theologian James Cone says that the difference between whites and blacks is "due exclusively to the failure of white religionists to relate the gospel of Jesus to the pain of being black in a white racist society,"[2] I find this an inadequate explanation of both racism and society. The failure is a human one rooted and grounded in the idea of white racial supremacy. We must examine racism from the perspective that it is a failure of society—a failure in the way we acculturate our children, and a failure in the political will of the nation to overcome racism. I think, also, black people must stop thinking and saying that the enslaved Africans listened to the Bible as it was interpreted by the slaveholders, and therefore found a reason for their own pain and also found a way to stay alive through the inexplicable suffering of slavery.[3] To say this is to minimize the resistance to brutality that is inherent in humanity. Even if one says that the Africans had faith to sustain them after the Civil War, it was not the Christian faith, but their faith in their own posterity to right the wrongs that they had experienced.

I have found no examples of Africans who worshipped with their white slave masters in the same churches as equals. Yet there are blacks who write or preach as if the white churches of the South were places of congenial relationships between blacks and whites. It is true that some white churches felt a need to advocate for missions among the enslaved Africans, but because these churches and their societies were symbiotic, they hardly ever thought of Africans as being equal to white people. In fact, the Civil War split some white churches into those who supported slavery and those who opposed it. Such a split occurred in the Restoration Movement when those who opposed slavery went in one direction and those who supported slavery chose another. Thus, the emergence of the Disciples of Christ, Churches of Christ, and Brethren Church may be the classic examples, although the Baptists and Methodists also broke apart over the issue of slavery.

African history in America had been stamped by the Denmark Vesey and Nat Turner conspiracies and rebellions in their revolutionary resistance to oppression. Vesey's plan was hatched in 1822 and

Nat Turner's in 1831, but by the time of their plans in the nineteenth century, thousands of Africans had risen up against their slaveholders as individuals exhausted by the oppressive slavery system. Although Vesey and Turner both couched their rhetoric of revolt in terms of religion, neither could be called Christian in any genuine sense of the word. Nevertheless, whites feared Africans and sought to curtail the Africans' ability to hold segregated worship assemblies or attempts to become literate. Increased efforts to convert Africans to Christianity accompanied this intense attack on the assembly of Africans and their rights for literacy. White anxiety invented various means for essentially preventing Africans from expressing any form of resistance to oppression. One of the most successful stratagems was to prevent worship, except under secure circumstances. A second plan was to teach Africans to turn the other cheek and to obey their masters. Both of these devices were used effectively to conservatize the African population. Evangelizing Africans became a contest among Christian churches during the late nineteenth century as the effort to "save the souls" of black folk. Campaigns with well-organized preachers sought to convert freed Africans from one area of large plantations to another. Some blacks were recruited to be preachers, and still others were motivated to volunteer as builders of churches. The praise houses were meant to sing the name of Jesus because as long as the blacks were concentrating on the Lord, they could not be worrying about what the whites were doing to them. There could be no possibility of revolution because religion served to prevent even insurrection. While one could never say that all the whites who worked to evangelize Africans were engaged in it for tactical purposes, it is true to say that many of them saw their work as preparing Africans for some far off acceptance as equal humans. Others did see saving the souls of Africans as a part of their earthly work for heaven, as fulfilling the purpose of God, or as something divine. Yet those who saw religion as a way to pacify Africans and to make my ancestors comfortable with second-class status, servility, and blind obedience to white authorities were actually doing the job of the white authorities.

Nothing in the religion of the American nation, from its beginning to the Civil War, could be considered free of racial implications. Those black churches that were established in the North—the African Baptist, the African Methodist Episcopal, and the African Methodist Episcopal Zion—were all responses or reactions to racism. Subsequently, the white denominations that admitted African Americans as members were determined to treat blacks differently from whites. These superficially accepted Africans were the victims of the racial attitudes of the religious people in their congregations.

On the other hand, Africans who were unfortunate enough to be enslaved in the South, as was the case with the vast majority of blacks in America, were considered outside of the possibility of salvation. Africans were spoken of as wretched heathens, loathsome pagans, or African idolaters. Some plantation owners saw Africans as full of superstitions that had not been eliminated by the enslavement. Indeed, the allegations and suspicions of African traditional beliefs, amounting to what the Europeans called fetish practices, were evidence to the whites of African paganism, which meant that there was no reason to teach them Christianity.

One could argue that the nature of African traditional beliefs was so different from Christianity that the whites did not have categories or concepts to explain African philosophy and therefore they could only see Africa as less than Europe and African beliefs as less than Christian beliefs.

To be sure there were different ways of looking at reality. Africans were the first to admit that they saw the earth as consisting of a plurality of strong forces that could be leveraged for good or evil. Nevertheless, all African people accepted the idea that there was one creation, not multiple events of creation, and that one supreme force must have been responsible for the bringing into being of all things.[4]

Furthermore, there could be no separations as one found in Western thinking between concepts such as monotheism and polytheism or secularism and the sacred. Everything was everything. One could not make distinctions between life that is and life that is to be, since there was no idea of community without the living and the dead as a part of the same community. This continuum was a way to explain the presence of the living and the dead in the same society. It was easy, therefore, for Africans to speak of the idea of a linkage between the living and the dead in ways that were different from the European idea of community.

Whites would eventually refer to all African beliefs as voodoo. Rituals of culture and ceremonies of blessings were referred to as pagan spirituality—names and concepts that Africans had never used in relationship to their cultural practices. However, this set the stage for a vigorous attempt by whites to eradicate these practices, and many of them were eliminated within the first forty years after the Civil War. By the turn of the twentieth century, Africans had been stripped of much of their cultural beliefs and practices. Thus, it is not correct to argue that the African cultural forms were stripped during the Middle Passage or during the 246 years of enslavement. Most beliefs, rituals, ceremonies, medicinal behaviors, herbal knowledge, and protective arts and acts were forced out of Africans during the generations after the Civil War.

Many scholars have contributed to this debate. Eddie Glaude, one of my former students, has argued in his book *Exodus!* for a position that I believe overstates the case for Christianity in the experience of the enslaved Africans.[5] On the other hand, the Afrocentrist Ama Mazama has contended that many scholars have stretched the hearsay notion that the Middle Passage stripped Africans of all culture.[6] Africanist Melville Herskovits argued that the success of some denominations, such as the Baptists, in attracting Africans to their church had to do with the mystery of immersion because it suggested connections to the idea of West African river deities.[7] But E. Franklin Frazier, a noted sociologist, took a different position, a contrary position, when he contended that the enslavement destroyed the social basis for religion and that the Baptists won many Africans converts because of the emotionalism of their appeal.[8] He advanced this thesis and similar positions in many sociological works, and he established an entire discourse tradition around the stripped culture perspective. Stanley Elkins, following the same line of argument and using the Holocaust as an example, believes that the Africans lost all sense of self and culture and were so demeaned and defeated by slavery that there was nothing left on which to hang any cultural clothing. Contrastingly, the position by the Afrocentric historian John Blassingame was that the evidence suggested Africans kept much of their culture as an act of resistance. His argument is much like that of the numerous African scholars who have claimed that ceremonies, rituals, and African cultural behaviors were direct assaults on the attempt to strip African culture from the masses. Indeed, in a contemporary sense, the aim of the African American community to celebrate and honor African cultural forms, Kwanzaa, for example, and African art, dancing, customs, fashions, and rituals, is to present a positive position of agency in the face of all endeavors to undermine the African nature of the community. Consequently, I side with Blassingame, Mazama, and Herskovits in this discourse, because I believe that Africans used every device, strategy, and philosophical belief and concept to combat all forms of cultural aggression. Religion, the Christian religion in particular, was seen as a stealth attack on the vigorous African culture that had sustained generations during the long enslavement.

The real problem of religion for African Americans lies in the basis of religion itself. Because there is a racial characteristic to Christianity as interpreted by whites and presented to blacks that follows the promotion of white supremacy, that is, God as white, it is a part of the religious message received by the African population. Racial features tend to be a part of all god concepts; people invent deities that are modeled after themselves. Thus, the god delivered to black folk by white evangelists was a white god, a single creator god in the image of the same white folk who had enslaved the Africans in the first place. The fact that Africans accepted this image and this god defies rational judgment! One could only understand it as the grossest form of cultural imperialism that can be imagined because while Africans were depressed, oppressed, and without economic or political capacity, whites entered with their god to offer consolation. Those who bought into the white offer, that is, accepted being instructed, converted, and baptized, swore allegiance to this white god and even placed drawings and paintings of the god's image over their own altars and baptismal pools as an indication that they had truly learned the lesson that was taught by their new white masters. Success was sweet for the white masses because it meant that the blacks would have no recourse to their own resources for mounting a challenge to the hegemony of white people. Furthermore, the white clergy had succeeded in teaching the Africans that the whites were God's chosen people because he gave them the beautiful continent of America, from one ocean to the other. All one had to do was to look at the evidence that the white man's god had defeated the Native Americans' gods and the Africans' gods, and it had shown a unique ability to maintain white control over the entire continent. Whites were God's chosen people. Whites had secured the selective advantage as the in-group, while, at the same time, allowing the African population to share in the honor of celebrating the white god and in promoting the white god's image.

Many whites who took strong positions against human slavery were atheists, infidels, or antireligious thinkers such as Benjamin Franklin, Robert Owen, Frances Wright, John Stuart Mill, and Abraham Lincoln, among others. They were often supported by demythologized religions such as the Quakers, Universalists or Unitarians. Highly religious people who believed in the superiority of white people and the cohesiveness of the white nation against outsiders tended to practice slavery and to support it to a high degree. This is not to say that all antislavery fighters were antireligious or that all religious persons supported slavery, but rather to emphasize that a sizable number of people who supported religion also supported the enslavement of blacks. One only has to look at the civil rights era to see that Martin Luther King Jr.'s "Letter from a Birmingham Jail" was written to ministers of the church.[9] They had been the ones who had counseled him to abandon his drive for equality or to slow down his movement.

Here is the dilemma of the black church and religion: how does the church explain that the most thoroughgoing practice of religion has gone hand-in-hand with the practice of racism for the past five hundred years? Whether it has been slavery or the Jewish holocaust, two of the most significant threats to whole populations in the past five hundred years, religion has sat at the front door. Christianity, of all religions, has been the most aggressive against other nations during this time. In previous epochs one might identify Islam as an aggressive, invading religion, such as it was after the Crusades and with the rise of the Ottoman Empire. However, for us, it is clear that Christianity has occupied the front seat, whether the promoter has been Protestant, Catholic, or Anglican. They all call upon the same god to protect the American, German, French, or British people. In a way, the Nazis were just a more organized version of the Ku Klux Klan; they both used their Christian identity to stir up hatred against certain people. The KKK consisted of religion and racism in one of its most hateful combinations: anti-Africanism and Christianity. Other smaller Christian movements that are also racist and American include Aryan Nations, the Order, the Church of Jesus Christ—Christian, and The Covenant, the Sword and the Arm of the Lord. They reinforce the idea of a religious tribe of whites arrayed against all others. Now the problem for black Christians is what to do with these so-called aberrations, since they express themselves in Christian terms and with so-called doctrines that make them "more Christian" than those blacks who also claim Christianity. After all, these racist religious groups seek to suggest that the African population could never be Christian because Jesus Christ, in their terms, was white.

To erase racism we will have to learn to judge people as parts of the human race, not as parts of a specific gene pool that might bio- logically determine the color of one's eyes, hair, and skin. Since the world is smaller in the sense that we live in closer proximity to each other, we must turn on our internal mute button when we hear the unwanted and unnecessary voices of religiosity and racism entering our world. We are all human, and we must change to be able to accept and appreciate all humans as such.

Religion fails to alleviate the interracial tension in our society because it operates on the same structural basis as the racist aspects of the society in general. All religious institutions in the United States reflect the dominant social patterns in the nation and reinforce the principal myths of white superiority. Clearly I am overstating the case because there are some churches and synagogues that have been actively antiracist. However, without more interventions, practical and active, the conversation about race among religious adherents will continue to be shaped by the centuries-old structure of white as good and black as evil. Heightened and reinforced by the construction of a supreme deity who could never have been black, religion in America has always been, and still remains, a bastion of racism.

Churches are among the most racist institutions in our society. By both choice and interest, they are either white or black. As I have already demonstrated, in the past blacks could not attend churches run by whites. Churches would take missionaries to the recently freed Africans during the nineteenth century to "civilize" those who had lived under one of the most brutally uncivil societies in the world. This was a contradiction between religion and society.

I grew up in Georgia, where my people attended church and showed their religion in great outbursts of orations and shouting, but I could not see any change in our condition, nor did I believe it made us better people because we were constantly struggling against one or another of the white man's oppressive laws and regulations. This was the era of segregation, and blacks were essentially sharecroppers, day-workers, or unemployed, since white Christians controlled all the jobs.

Historically the church has had a negative impact on African people. Many times we point to the church as one of the sources for black recruits during the civil rights movement's demonstrations. That much is true, in the sense that black people did not control large corporations or other institutions where one could find massive groups of people. The churches and the historically black colleges were the only available instruments of power. These were the sources of thousands of demonstrators. Thus, I think that any discourse about race relations must be moved outside of the churches and schools, and onto the grounds of rational discourse about a national—or global—response to oppression. What will people do if they find that their backs are to the walls?

What we have to say about the churches is that if their goal is to save souls, then let them save souls, but do not let them claim any other social advance. The churches, with their decline into designer religion with consumerist tendencies and pablum sermons, have become the greatest drag on free expression of will and creativity in the black community. African Americans who gather in churches have not been able to lift the communities surrounding their churches out of the muck and mire in which they are stuck. A strange relationship has developed in the African American church in which it has lost the spirit of resistance that we saw briefly during the 1950s and 1960s. Martin Luther King Jr., Wyatt T. Walker, Jesse Jackson, and Andrew Young are all well known; however, the resistance we saw in the church was really sparked by the driving force of the nationalist movement led by Elijah Muhammad, Malcolm X, and the many student and community leaders, such as Maulana Karenga, Bobby Seale, and Fannie Lou Hamer. The fact that Rosa Parks would not give up her seat in Montgomery, Alabama, is not disconnected from the awesome nationalist sentiments of Paul Robeson testifying before the House Un-American Activities Committee. The church may have been where the people were, but the people were fed up with conditions in the society and resisted in the spirit of national liberation. We must be clear in understanding that the civil rights movement would have occurred if all the blacks had been in cultural centers; the people had a will to freedom grounded in their real experiences every day. They were fed up.

Christianity did little to change the nature of the condition of African Americans during the nineteenth and twentieth centuries. One might argue that Christianity was useful for whites in the areas of art and culture, as shown in the creative energy of Bach and Mozart, the paintings of Michelangelo, Leonardo da Vinci, and Raphael, the presence of Milton's *Paradise Lost*, Dante's *Divine Comedy*, and Bunyan's

*Pilgrim's Progress*. If we were to interrogate African American culture in the same way, we would soon discover that the writers, painters, poets, and dramatists with whom we most identify are the ones who challenged this religious construction of reality.

Much of what was accomplished in African American civilization had been tied to the African cultures out of which we had come. Forgotten, shoved to the side by the dominating ideology of white supremacy—which endangered our mental state—African cultures asserted themselves in the 1960s in a powerful manner. Without a strong understanding of African culture, blacks and whites had limited views about the role Africa played in music, art, and language. Victimized by ignorance and stunned by unrelenting prejudice against Africa, the African American population often confronted Christianity in its rawest, most authentic form. Without a belief in God and Christ, Africans were often considered soulless, and when souls were granted, Africans were frequently condemned to the white man's hell. Without an acceptance of Christian values and mores, the idea was to dismiss black cultural values as primitive, heathen, and profane. Christianity had, and still has, ambivalence toward Africans that colors the way black and white people communicate in American society.

Freethinking Africans like organizer A. Philip Randolph and historian John Jackson resented the Christian assignment of Africans to the back of the bus. Believing that African Americans were equal to any other human being, these freethinkers became leading campaigners for equality. When Martin Luther King Jr. emerged as the leading orator against racism in the South, he chose the Indian philosopher Mahatma Gandhi as one of his philosophical mentors. Although Jesus was considered a pacifist, King recognized the compromised position of many of the Christian leaders, and he ultimately believed that the campaign for nonviolence, a strategy that could work where blacks were heavily invested in an area or industry, had to be founded on something other than Christian terms. King's selection of Gandhi as a philosophical mentor was an admission that the Christian ideology subscribed to by both whites and blacks could not bring the deliverance and salvation from discrimination and segregation that oppressed blacks in the South. King was, in effect, on the road to discover any means for black liberation.

Like the political and social leaders before him, King understood the role of the church, and while he had grown up in it and he had had a more intimate relationship to it than A. Philip Randolph or Bayard Rustin, he also saw its limitations. This is why, as I have intimated, King had asked the white preachers in the "Letter from a Birmingham Jail": What are you preaching? Whose deliverance are you seeking? Why don't you have the same moral outrage as black Christians?[10]

In the end, it was neither the church nor the church preachers that would end discrimination and segregation in the South. It was the people in the streets, the children of Birmingham staring down dogs and water hoses, and their readiness to struggle for freedom that would make the difference. Religion existed, but was, as always in these cases, an eyewitness to the victory over overt racism. Religion was almost as silent as it had been during the 246 years of enslavement. Christian religion was the dominant ideology of the white South and it became, after the Civil War, the dominant ideology of blacks in the South. Both groups were bound up in an unholy alliance that made genuine community almost impossible, given the segregation of the churches and the great gulf between the two groups of people in terms of their aspirations and inspirations.

I have come to believe that religious imperialism in the United States is a variant of the imperial racism that fueled the economic engines of Europe from the fifteenth to the nineteenth centuries and made Europe the major economic region of the world. Imperialism was heavily invested in the doctrine of "the white man's burden." The idea was that whites were superior, and the aim of white civilization was to uplift those who were childlike and backward. This meant that the Christian whites had a God-given right to rule, dominate, and otherwise control the lives of those who were considered heathen and inferior. It is this intellectual idea that sparked racism in the United States during and after the enslavement. White Christian Americans considered all black people inferior; therefore, whites believed they were superior and consequently responsible for blacks. This was a mythical responsibility that whites hated to give up. As David Walker understood and wrote in his pamphlet *An Appeal to the Colored Citizens of the World* in 1829, the white Christian Americans were the "most cruel people on the earth" and their subjects, the blacks, "were the most abject of humans" on the earth.[11] What was the value of Christianity for black people during this time? How did Christianity guide whites in regard to Africans? Which white Christians rose up en masse against the system of slavery to defend Africans against the brutality of their brothers? Wasn't the Ku Klux Klan a Christian group marching with the cross before them?

In my final analysis, we erase racism by restructuring the myths of society. An outpouring of reality checking can only do this if we refer to the existential condition of humanity at the present time. All myths must be based in some reality. Fighting to create a society free of racial, gender, sexual, or class prejudices is the great struggle of this century. We erase all forms of human subjugation, all forms of discrimination, and all forms of abuse of others and the environment by taking responsibility for our own actions. This is the moral imperative that will help save humans on earth.

CHAPTER SEVEN

# CHAPTER SEVEN
# THE FURIOUS PASSAGE

H e was a young boy, only twelve, when he went to a prominent "whites only" barbershop in Valdosta, Georgia, and asked permission to shine the shoes of the customers for twenty-five cents. His first customer, a white man in his thirties, agreed to the price and sat in the designated chair for the shoeshine. The young boy, preparing his supplies, stooped over to begin the shine and the customer spat on his head. Other whites, including the owner of the shop, began to laugh. Knowing precisely the disdain and hatred the men in the barbershop had for him, he gathered his shoebox with his waxes, cloths, and brushes and, without saying anything, walked out of the shop.

I, a descendant of enslaved Africans whose ancestry goes back six generations in America, was that young boy in Valdosta, Georgia. As a child I saw the difference between the white world and the black world from the standpoint of the South. Everything was in technicolor, clear and impressive in my young mind. Neither my mother nor my father had much to say about the situation; I came into it as other African American children, grown, mature, and prescient. Today it is different, but the evidence of double standards, white racial preferences, and opposition to affirmative action is all around us. Indeed, we are caught in an inextricable web of racial deceit.

Innocence has been lost millions of times as the Wilderness dwellers interact with those who see themselves as people of the Promised Land. I kept the memories of the African men and women, my uncles and aunts and cousins, working to shape some white man's wealth while their own wealth slipped farther and farther away. This was the beginning of struggle. I know that this must have been the experience of many other African Americans of my generation. Slapped down for no reason other than the anxieties and fears harbored by whites, the early rural Wilderness dwellers could ask the perennial question of the urban Wilderness dweller: What have we done to create such hatred in the whites? There would be no answer, because the white world hid its own head in the sand of time. Whites had removed the stones and could not put them back; they had opened the sores and could not heal the wounds.

One northern-born schoolteacher told me, "I never let my guard down with whites." I detected in his voice fear of disappointment, attack, and racism. Letting one's guard down is a risk some African Americans take, but others are not willing to take. During the great migrations from the rural South to the industrial North in the 1940s, many African Americans lived in urban areas and often had jobs at the same automobile factories as whites. But after work, whites drove off in one direction and African Americans in another. In the school system, the teachers were often white and many of the students were black, but they did not live in the same neighborhood. Betrayal by those who did not know you or could not fathom what was in or on your mind was common. So the questions of how to be open without being crushed, or how to be honest with whites without being betrayed, occupy a lot of space in the minds of African Americans who interact with whites on a daily basis.

In the American Wilderness, isolated from the same liberties as whites, we are often furious because openness, directness, and candor frequently produce more brutality, punishment, and impoverishment. And since there is an aversion to concealment in African American culture, we are left open to the world with our complaints and protests. Ours is not a culture of complaints, but a culture of long suffering, as if providence wanted us to learn a special lesson.

Those who conceal themselves or their attitudes are seen as sneaky, sinister, perhaps like the proverbial "snake in the grass." We even say, "Don't tell me your secrets if you don't want me to tell." Rather than praise the person who hides emotions and refuses to be open about his attitudes and ideas, we see him as suspect, broken, and different. Yet there is a dilemma, often based on the betrayals of the past, that creates dissonance in the African American: Can I really trust this white person to honor my opinions, beliefs, judgments, and actions, or must I take a defensive position, one of an emotional safety cushion?

I have always found African Americans, by virtue of experiences with terror, to be emotional people; our faces easily reveal our joy or pain. One has only to ask us and we will give a full description of our lives and circumstances, throwing in philosophical commentaries along the way. This reaction is justified historically as an appeal, an invitation for someone to listen. But the ability of other Africans to listen to us has increased with the passing of time, and now, as heard in the music of our youth, we want to share our victories with those who understand what it is to overcome anti-African attitudes. Our emotionalism is not irrationalism; we are also experientially rational because of our lived experiences. Put simply, we know evil and terror when we see it because we have so often been the victims.

Each goal, social or artistic, is achieved against unnecessary odds. A choreographer who is reviewed by a white writer complains because the lack of knowledge of African culture or African American styles produces a contorted, distorted, vile review. An African American playwright complains that a white reviewer misses the point of his play because the reviewer does not find anything European in it. We live in the Wilderness, and the only response to our circumstance that the white person understands is her own racial point of entry. Anything that shows the African moving closer to whiteness in attitude and behavior is attractive, but few whites appreciate, at the artistic or social level, the strictly African culture.

In the past, Africans often sought the commentary of one white person on the negative behavior of other whites. This was an important strategic move because during the period of segregation, Africans believed that if decent whites only knew what their fellows were doing, they would be horrified and condemn white brutality. If they understood and acted on the ignorance of their fellows, this would demonstrate a human concern. This procedure was irregularly rewarded with positive results. We asked and expected too much.

Yet our response to courtesy, respect, and sympathy is the awesome joy of reciprocity, reflecting emotionally, as James Baldwin knew and expressed in his essays, the need to be understood and taken seriously. Perhaps we laugh so easily and so strongly because we are a bruised people and our psychic pain is deep. We laugh, and our laughter is like a temporary gauze on our wounds. Those who mistake our laughter and easy joy for stupidity or gullibility, which has been done, are frequently stung by the severity of our reaction to insult.

We have often murdered insult with the sharp glance of our eyes, the sucking of our teeth, and the bold akimbo. But our reactions are often quick and knee-jerk, evidencing the hurt we have experienced. Those who do not understand the complexity of the historical self-hatred engendered by racism often question cultural nationalism and see it as a reactionary position of people who do not realize that they are already free. These questioners do not appreciate the extent of the social dehumanization that was meant to crush and destroy our hope. The historical situation we found ourselves in was past grievance, beyond petition, all the way to an abject defamation and desecration of our African ancestors. Our hope was turned to despair; our faith, to disbelief. Did some individual blacks escape to beat their chests and speak of their personal accomplishments? Of course, some did, and they represent the fish who found the cracks in the net—but have no appreciation of the dangerous waters in which they swim.

Zora Neale Hurston, speaking about the Wilderness dwellers, once said that it would take generations before we learned to love our children. Indeed, it may take generations before we learn even to love ourselves. Each generation must pass to the next the traditions it has learned. Our fury is intensified when most whites appear ignorant of the causes of our rage. Yet many of these whites are often responsible for the condition in which we find ourselves. To insist that we undo in one generation what has been done to us for more than seven generations—legally and by custom in this country—is to ask beyond a miracle. "Black is Beautiful" and other slogans of the 1960s were meant to help eradicate the self-hatred that had been engendered by white racism. Indeed, our victimization, degradation, and dehumanization had been necessary in order to enslave us and, subsequently, to keep Africans from ever conceiving of equal opportunity.

The checkered history of struggle against racism in the Wilderness has made some community actions predictable.[1] Thus, the response to a jury verdict, a police beating, a racial incident, or a perceived personal slight can set off urban unrest. After all, there is a volatile mix of good and bad, negatives and positives, and Africans and Europeans in this land. Andrew Hacker's suggestion that the entire American social drama turns on the issue of blacks and whites is not insignificant, because it underscores the nature of resistance and rebellion in the African American community.[2] It also highlights the difference in the responses to the police authorities.

Andrew Hacker writes that "when white people hear the cry, 'the police are coming!' for them it almost always means, 'help is on the way.' "[3] Hacker astutely observes that African American citizens cannot make the same assumption: "If you have been the victim of a crime, you cannot presume that the police will actually show up; or, if they do, that they will take much note of your losses or suffering."[4] One could add that the people of the Wilderness often see the police as part of the problem. Parents constantly warn their young boys about the danger of the police. Indeed, Wilderness dwellers must learn how to defend themselves against the police, who often see most African American males as potential criminals.

No wonder the Black Radical Congress came out with a withering report, "Contemporary Police Brutality and Misconduct: A Continuation of the Legacy of Racial Violence," declaring that "racial violence was fundamental to the creation of the United States. Moreover, force and violence are not options but necessary to the maintenance of racial oppression. Racist violence is the scaffolding upon which capitalist exploitation and white supremacy are erected."[5]

Whenever white police confront African American students on college campuses, they tend to bring with them a number of negative stereotypes. Examples among the problems reported on campuses in recent years include singling out African American males when a crime is committed and stopping African American men and women who are walking on elite college campuses. A review of newspaper reports reveal the following cases.

- The police department at the University of Nebraska singled out five African American males for questioning and photographing in a case of the disappearance of a white female student. Later, two white men were arrested and charged with murdering the woman.
- African American students at the University of Rhode Island complained that the police often stopped and questioned them for no other reason than that they were black.
- At Princeton University, male African American students said that they did not leave their apartments without a Princeton cap or a book bag for fear they would be stopped by the campus police.
- An administrator at the State University of New York College at Oneonta provided the names of all 125 African American male students to the local police, who were investigating an assault on an elderly woman in town.

Police treatment of whites contrasts with that of blacks, reflecting the racist character of the police institution. When the shootings happened at Santana High School in Santee, California, the white community—including the police—were quick to say that the community was good and the youth were good and that this was unbelievable in an "all-American city." After so many incidents during the past decade in which white youths have shot up schools or other venues, one would think that there would be outrage in the white community and among the police forces of the country. Instead, there is this denial that it could happen among white people: one more piece of evidence of the racist attitudes of the police. Imagine what would have happened if the Columbine or Santana or numerous other shootings by white youths had taken place in Atlanta, Philadelphia, Los Angeles, Harlem, Chicago, or Detroit? There would be all kinds of commissions created to deal with black-on-black violence or to discover the profile of the typical killer. I do not believe there was a single call by white police for some local or national body to investigate the reasons white high school youth are engaging in such horrible mass murders. No one rushed to claim that these kids were "monsters" who needed to be controlled, because the police were reluctant to claim that in suburban communities of blond-haired children there could be dangers once thought to lurk only in the poverty-stricken areas of the worn-down inner cities of the Wilderness. But isn't it true that the denial of what is possible in the white community is symptomatic of the racist classification of who is capable of criminal activity?

While geography may define certain high concentrations of people of the Wilderness—for example, the inner cities—the encounter between those of the Wilderness and those of the Promise is everywhere and inescapable. And the college campus—rural, Midwestern, or elite—seems to set up the same dynamic between blacks and whites as one finds elsewhere in the country.

One of the most horrifying ironies in America is that the Wilderness dwellers and the people of the Promise are so closely wrapped in the same historical contexts, yet are as distant as people of different countries. College campuses and segregated metropolitan spaces are, in major ways, so far away from each other, yet they often participate in the same dramas of Wilderness and Promise. Finding avenues to navigate the distance between where African Americans are and where we know others to be takes leadership. New and more intense voices come up from the Wilderness with every generation. They are the spirits of the vanguard, the ones with the new names and the different gaits. In some senses, the late Khalid Abdul Muhammad of the New Black Panthers was one of these voices. His death in February 2001 was a national event among African Americans committed to challenging police brutality. In numerous ways Muhammad, despite his controversial rhetoric and deep pathos, was a voice for many urban youth.

Leadership in the Wilderness must be proved through local activism to be considered authentic. Otherwise, a person may advance himself as a leader without any following. "What has he done for the community?" is a legitimate question in the Wilderness. I once heard a middle-aged guy with a beard on a street corner in Philadelphia list the current crop of entertainers and athletes, giving thumbs up on some and thumbs down on others, explaining that they either had or did not have community credentials like pouring money into visible projects in the African American community: "Oprah and Bill Cosby are all right, man, they have not forgot where they came from. O. J. and Whoopi Goldberg are just playing to the whites. They haven't done a thing for their communities." These are typical comments, and whether they are correct or not, they demonstrate an interest in finding leaders or role models who show compassion, concern, and commitment to improving the life chances of African American people.

While those who have led the black communities have often come from the arena of political activism, it is true in the Wilderness that the struggle is frequently wrested from the politicians and given to those who best express solidarity with the Wilderness. We can explain the comeback of Marion Barry as mayor of Washington, D.C., in 1994 by his commitment to serve the community. This overrode all other considerations. Barry may have had many problems, but he was a legitimate fighter for the ordinary African American.

In some instances, the struggle is wrested from the academic scholars and given to the lay scholars in much the same way. A host of influential local leaders, tempered by community disputes and often outside the major media circles, are created by the special knowledge and wisdom they bring. I believe that this is the Wilderness's magic, the sleight of hand, and the wand of social transformation. While the white media anoint black leaders, the Wilderness community chooses its own heroes from those who have been baptized in the fire of struggle.

This transformation happens because we have seen the limits of what anointed public intellectuals can do. They are often victims themselves if they are thought to be Wilderness dwellers or sympathizers. After he came out in support of Louis Farrakhan's right to speak at the African American Summit, Cornel West, one of the most visible black intellectuals, found himself increasingly under personal attack. Even politicians with commitments to equal opportunity and freedom are often unable to get their overwhelmingly white colleagues to act in accordance with the ethical and the moral principles which we believe will bring harmony, if not unity. Was Cornel West tarred and feathered by the white press simply because he spoke in support of Farrakhan's right to speak? Will Michael Jordan now be trashed in the media for finally finding his own political voice against racism and media oppression?

Jesse Jackson, for all practical purposes, has been the leading African American political voice for the past decade, though he has occupied no effective elected office. Prior to the revelation that he had fathered a child by his secretary, his strength was in the moral tone of his politics, where he demonstrated the combination of charisma and altruism that best describes our greatest leaders. During the 1990s Jackson's constant attempts to place the political message on a moral, ethical, and spiritual level gave him an advantage over most legitimate politicians in the Wilderness. His brand of populism spoke to the plain folk of the urban Wilderness of America, as well as to those whites who saluted his courage and conviction. African Americans were struck by his struggle for history, his commitment to principle, and his willingness, as it were, to suffer the slings and arrows of his country in order to save it. But alas, Jackson, like all of us, is human—all too human. The good that he did and continues to do must not be forgotten.

Take the work he did in bringing forth a black agenda during the 1984 political campaign. Jackson's presence in Philadelphia on numerous occasions during his 1984 campaign for the Democratic nomination allowed him to mediate and cajole, to discuss and debate the ethical positions on social and economic issues in the city. Jackson was a catalyst for conscience and transformation, even before the conflagration that engulfed the house of the MOVE organization and sixty other homes in Philadelphia. He campaigned vigorously in Philadelphia during 1984 and consulted with numerous local politicians in his quest to gain the Democratic nomination for president. In addition, he had become the interpreter of the plight of African Americans in the lowest socioeconomic levels. Jackson was, by all estimates, more in tune with the fury of black Philadelphians than even W. Wilson Goode, the first African American mayor of the city, was. Perhaps too eager to please and too centered on his history-making election to find the guidance he needed during his administration, Goode made the mistakes of a novice politician. More than that, however, was his inability to listen to the spirit of the Wilderness.

The Wilderness creates tensions that give birth to individuals with some of the most revolutionary responses to oppression. These are not the professionals but the working classes, who may be working or not working. They have found the relationship between economics and the quality of life and know the dignity of work and the honor of courage. They will not put up with disrespect. You might say that these are the battle-tested soldiers of the Wilderness. They combine many of the attributes of the warriors, rappers, and little Malcolms, many of whom have never heard of Malcolm, but who nevertheless live out his life.

Such a group of people was MOVE, people who opted out of the American system as far back as the 1970s and 1980s. Although they do not represent all people in the urban areas, the MOVE people who were not killed are still among the living-dead in the Wilderness who are detached, alienated, and disillusioned.

The origin of their concern is their perception of grievances, no justice, and no peace. Their position is as American as jazz. The Boston Tea Party is the prime example and symbol of a fed-up people. Can we imagine that these Americans actually threw overboard tea that had been shipped for their own consumption? Were they destroying their own drinks? Were they getting rid of the source of the livelihood of their own merchants? Were they really interested in principle or in harassing the British? Were those early Americans really serious about their rights?

The answers to these kinds of questions have meaning to the people in the Wilderness. Because the example of the early Americans is the best primer for the Wilderness dwellers, the urban organization called MOVE adopted its principles. Members of the organization developed a revolutionary consciousness that was often beyond the scope of the professional intellectuals to understand or to appreciate. But the abstract, elite intellectual, who has often separated himself from the critical elements of struggle that produce cultural commitment, can never develop a revolutionary consciousness without renouncing detachment. To claim objectivity in the face of brutality, terror, or racism is to be an enemy of peace.

The everyday engagement with life in a racist political system is itself a lecture-discussion course in consciousness and unconsciousness, racism and fellowship, crime and unpunishment, style and substance, and inclusiveness and exclusiveness. Those who pass the course are prepared to understand the relationship between the consent to law and harmony and the fairness of law. Living in the Wilderness, I know that the seams of society are held together by law—but by law that is respected because it is fair. In most cases, unfair laws are broken and ignored by the people. On the other hand, I also know that the social compact with neighbors must be agreed upon, practiced, and teased out of the most minute situations.

Wilderness dwellers believe that those who are authorized to keep the law—the police, the national guard, and the courts—are often outright enemies of African Americans. Ramona Africa, the only adult to escape the bombing-burning of the MOVE house in Philadelphia, told me of her suspicions of the police and the entire system of law: "Molefi, they are enemies of the MOVE. They don't want to see black people who are not supporting their white lifestyles. They are threatened by our very existence. This is why we must always be in struggle." Ramona has been through a lot in her lifetime just to express her own viewpoints and to live as the MOVE did, free from the constraints of the modern white society. She knows and believes that the police are, in every society, the guardians of the ruling classes. The logic of the Wilderness is severe. Thus, in a Marxist society, the police are the guardians of the Marxists; and, of course, in a racist society, they are the guardians of the racists. By knowing what kind of society we have, we can determine what kinds of remedies are necessary for collective national harmony.

Learning the rules of social respect are essential to survival in the Wilderness, but also useful in our dealings with each other on a national basis.

*He was young, not more than twenty-one. He walked into the bar, past three other young men who were talking and gesturing with great emotion. He accidentally stepped on the shoes of the short, stout man doing most of the talking. He must have felt awkward, because instead of saying he was sorry, he kept walking, probably not wanting to interrupt the conversation. He was shot dead. When asked why he shot the man, the short, stout man said, "Motherfucka did't say, 'Excuse me.'"*

Life can be treacherous in the Wilderness, but no more dangerous than the random violence one can find in shopping centers in the white suburbs. The rule, however, is simple: Show respect. Aretha Franklin spells it R-E-S-P-E-C-T.

Disrespect is the most serious offense that can be committed against a Wilderness dweller. And Wilderness dwellers, who have been trampled on, seem to always remember the disrespect they have received at the hands of others. In fact, this is the fundamental anger we have carried since the beginning of the twentieth century and the reason Ralph Ellison's *Invisible Man* was such an important book in setting forth the metaphor of ultimate disrespect. Disrespect in terms of the tension between the Wilderness and the Promise means that those who represent the Promise have been able to essentially trash the Wilderness dwellers—materially, legally, economically, and politically—and not be held responsible.

The enslavement and subsequent discrimination based on race and color have so damaged our psyches that we are forever cautious about disrespectful moments in American society. "Think you are better than we are?" asked the truck driver when the white insurance man pulled his Buick ahead of him at a rural Pennsylvania A&W drive-in. Respect is very important, but it is often hard for us to tell when we are being "dissed," as in "dismissed" and "disrespected," or when someone just does not have good manners. As it turns out, most black folk think that white folk don't have good manners. This is obviously a stereotype; some whites probably believe the same about African Americans. There is, however, the lingering suspicion among Wilderness dwellers that whites treat only African Americans, not each other, with a lack of respect.

The idea, that an African had no rights that a white man had to respect, first legalized in the 1857 *Dred Scott* decision, became a testament to our political powerlessness in the face of a judiciary or police force that sought to undermine our rights and our humanity. In other words, German Americans, English Americans, and in most instances other European American groups can and do demand respect. They possess political and economic power that in America has also meant racial or cultural power. Of course, this is not to say that the Wilderness dwellers are impotent. Our tradition is one of struggle and of battle; we have often set the tone for the fight against injustice in this nation by using a moral appeal based on justice, righteousness, and harmony—ancient African values translated as "dignity" in the contemporary world. In some ways our struggles against social and racial disrespect are at the base of our sometimes bitter encounters with whites. At a collective level as well as a personal level, in our minds, the residual impact of years of enslavement and racial segregation and discrimination dominate all possibilities. How to throw off the effects of this history is the constant debate in the Wilderness. Yet with the virulent anti-African and anti-Semitic rhetoric of a Patrick J. Buchanan or the more sophisticated and subtle white supremacist attitudes of many college deans and professors, African Americans realize that the struggle is long because the elements that support it are enshrined in the political and educational culture of the society.

America's history of white racial privilege has to be overcome in our imagination. The social and economic walls that must be scaled are vile, racist, violent, bitter, mean-spirited, anti-African, prejudiced, disrespectful, evil, paternalistic, and spiteful. In surmounting these walls, the Wilderness dweller operates on the basis of an intimate historical encounter with America itself. The people of the Promised Land must confront themselves at the core of their racism. These are times when the nation must seek the reasons for racism in the first place. Insanity breeds insanity and our situation in this country, black and white, is one of deep dysfunctionality.

I am not the first to point out these problems in American society and I will not be the last.

The idea of obstruction—obstacles and problems in the soul of this society—has captured the attention of some of our most brilliant thinkers, including Paul Robeson, Frederick Douglass, Tony Brown, Claud Anderson, Shirley Chisholm, James Baldwin, Harold Cruse,

Jeremiah Wright, and Ida B. Wells. In their own manner, they artic-ulated a vision of encounter between Africans and whites that sug-gested the possibility of a more human relationship. America, to them, represented negative sentiments that imprisoned Wilderness people in a vortex of racist actions, economic hazards, and active cultural conspiracies. Of course, we know that there are competing definitions of the American past, but in its fundamental sense, from slavery to segregation to discrimination, there has been an over-whelmingly economic, political, and social hegemony that has worked against Africans—whether articulated at the public level or carried out in the private arenas that collectively constitute the public behavior of a society.

Every sector of society has participated in the creation of our Wilderness. The assaults against African Americans may not be a con-scious activity on the part of any one individual, but so many whites—in their jobs, positions, and offices—are negating or have negated the life chances of Africans in obvious and not-so-obvious ways, that it is often hard to separate the "good" guys from the "bad" guys. The bad guys are definitely conscious of their intentions. The natural partici-pation in the denial of African Americans' access coincides with the intimate way in which the African American experiences racism.

The white person who says, "I have never discriminated against a black person," but who sits atop an office tower on Wall Street, Michigan Avenue, Peachtree, Market Street, or Rodeo Drive is a victim of the invisibility of decades of discrimination and layers of exclusion that have placed her in that position because of the advan-tage of race. Had we ever had an army of whites who, in their profes-sional capacities, worked for the equal opportunity of all Americans, we would have turned the tide on pessimism years ago.

What America means to the Wilderness dweller is the dynamic interplay of forces working to thwart African liberation that would mean freedom from inequality, social and economic justice, and inclu-siveness in the national agenda. Thus, only by overcoming that America—*white* America ensconced in false pride and notions of white supremacy—will we be able to regain the America of the Dream. No group of citizens understands this any better than the Wilderness dwellers who seek to survive and to prosper despite incessant assaults on their psyches.

The resistance to racism and the rebellion against oppression activate a fury that is neither wild nor savage; it is a slow-burning fury, like that of molten lava cruising down hillsides, clearing away the debris of generations of benign neglect. The Wilderness people are certain that this fury is purifying because it is grounded in experiences, in the things that have happened rather than in illusions.

The Wilderness is not our creation. It is invented by the system of white privilege and it is maintained by practices that we encounter with great intensity on a daily basis. Yes, there are courts, and we can and do sue, but sometimes the court system itself frustrates the securing of justice. Sometimes we win the human victories and sometimes we lose. There are some who would like to make us believe that what we experience is unreal, fantasy, and extraneous to our life chances. And indeed there are African Americans who have succumbed to that version of our experiences. However, the everyday experiences in the Wilderness tell us how much we yet have to resist. Even after nearly four hundred years on this continent, arriving long before the signing of the Declaration of Independence, we are still fighting bigots who think our styles, behaviors, language, and indeed our very lives are non-American. They believe that our cultural origin and citizenship are contradictory, when, in fact, *both* represent our reality. We have never denied either of our heritages, African or North American; nor should we. But we recognize that our fellow citizens have not always treated us as if they believed we were a part of the same country. Indeed, the history of the nation is that there have been many groups of whites who have tried to discredit our history. So we must continue to define our spaces, chart our courses, and make our pacts, hoping always to survive in the Wilderness.

Not only can our attempt to define space within a racist society be defined as resistance and rebellion, but the nature of that resistance and rebellion determines how and where we will take our stand. Importantly, different professions require different kinds of responses. Maya Angelou's performance at President Bill Clinton's inauguration in 1993 represented the highest form of African American inclusiveness. Her poem tied the nation's people together like no other poet had ever done. This was her resistance, her rebellion, and, ultimately, her transcendence.

Unfortunately, in some cases, precisely *because* we are up against the wall of the Promise, our hands are tied, our feet are shackled, and our minds are weary. It is not an easy struggle and there are no easy triumphs for the Wilderness dweller, even for those who sit in the highest towers of the American corporate structure. Quite frankly, the battle lines are drawn tightly around the privilege of whiteness, and even with one or two African Americans in a board room, on a commission, or in an executive meeting, racists can still have their irrational way.

There are still large numbers of African Americans who approach the Promise with hope and optimism—that is, willingly, but with one foot at a time. Invariably, if they are sensitive, they speak of the difficulty of maintaining that posture in the world when they see the terror of life in the Wilderness. Take the example of Leanita McClain, a brilliant journalist who worked for the *Chicago Tribune* and who was the first black person to serve on the editorial board of the paper. McClain wrote passionately about what she experienced sitting on the board, watching and listening to the debates and the discussions that often insulted the reality of her people but found that she was powerless to do anything about it. The frustration finally got to her, and at thirty-two she committed suicide. Few people have ever wanted to see human beings of all races, ethnic groups, and cultural backgrounds live together in harmony as strongly as the idealistic Leanita McClain. Apparently, a combination of factors led her to a depression where finally she could contemplate taking her own life. She became distraught because of personal agonies and the belief that racism was a permanent fact of American life. This belief was a major element in her psychological resignation. Bombarded by the call for tolerance yet seeing everywhere the practice of intolerance, the African American professional often is adversely affected by almost every encounter with whites who harbor prejudice against blacks.

A more subtle line of attack may be that which seeks to undermine the ancestral pride or cultural motifs of the African American professional. This happens when the values for a particular profession or the personal prejudices of a supervisor are played out in an individual case to the disadvantage of the African American.

For example, what am I to think if I am an attorney like John T. Harvey III in Washington, D.C., and I am told by a white judge, Robert Scott, that I cannot wear an African *kente* cloth scarf in the court? Whose country is this really, in the judge's mind? What standard of dress is he upholding? As reported, the judge said to Mr. Harvey, "Sir, I will not permit you to wear the *kente* cloth, which you say is part of your religious beliefs, before a jury." The same judge would probably permit a crucifix to be worn around the neck, but he has a problem with something out of African culture. Why? Has a judge ever asked a lawyer to remove a crucifix? What disturbs Scott is not the fact that *kente* cloth is worn, but that it reflects Harvey's African culture. Although it is easy to claim that the religious element is the key to the judge's resistance, many African Americans wear *kente* cloth on some occasion. The sartorial style of the lawyer, so long as it is appropriate and in good taste, should not trouble a judge. But the Wilderness dweller is often deprived of free will; particularly if it is viewed as a contravening measure against the established white order of things. One is up against the dictates of the Anglo-Germanic establishment as a definer of the way one should dress, walk, talk, eat, and behave.

I am a defender of pluralism, that is, the idea that this nation holds out to every individual or group of individuals an opportunity for self-expression, so long as that freedom does not damage, injure, or harass others. No more furious passage to the ends of possibility exists in any country. But the establishment of those rights remains a task unfulfilled in this nation, because too many citizens harbor too many notions of white supremacy. Tackling white supremacy would be a major advancement in every avenue of social responsibility. But you must protect my right to wear my *kente* cloth or my *agbada* as I protect your right to wear the Windsor tie!

How does the nation ensure the same rights for the Wilderness dweller as for the people of the Promise? How does it protect the constitutional rights of the African American as well as those of whites? This requires far more than altering rules and procedures; it requires a commitment to equal justice under the law and to equal freedoms. Justice demands that law takes into consideration the past harm heaped upon the African American population and the consequent devaluing, discrediting, and putting at a disadvantage of that community. This means that the police need special cultural and historical training. Racial profiling remains a problem to this day, such as the attack on three African American males shot by New Jersey State Police on their way to a recreational event in 1998. Their van was surrounded and they were shot and injured. Perhaps the police were scared of the black males; perhaps they just wanted to shoot some "niggas"; perhaps they thought they saw a gun. Whatever the perhaps, they were wrong to have shot into the van without provocation.

Fred Mazelis's "New Jersey Internal Records Document Widespread Racial Profiling of Black and Hispanic Motorists" demonstrated in detail the appalling record of the New Jersey State Police.[7] When ninety-one thousand pages of internal documents were released by the state of New Jersey, the report outlined a rigid pattern of searching cars driven by blacks or Hispanics. Although blacks and Hispanics made up only 13 percent of the population in the state, they accounted for more than 80 percent of the highway stops by troopers. Apparently approved and supported by the chief law enforcement officials, the practice of racial profiling of black motorists had gone on since 1989. When questioned, many troopers testified that coaches and consultants taught them how to profile blacks and Hispanics. Others spoke of parking their patrol cars perpendicular to the highway with their high beams shining, so they could see the occupants of passing cars. The racial profiling scandal is another part of the pervasive nature of racism in society. This particular project happens to have been encouraged by the law enforcement community itself. Indeed the troopers were *trained* to identify black motorists.

As Mazelis argued, "Continuous campaigns at the state and federal level for new prisons, an end to parole, and increased death sentences and executions have all contributed to an atmosphere in which racist harassment is considered permissible and racist cops are encouraged to vent their prejudices and hatred."[8]

Let me put it in another authentic form. Even if Rodney King had been found doing something illegal, or unlawful, or absolutely stupid, there was no reason for him to be brutally beaten by fifty-four blows to his body in eighty-one seconds. To understand how African Americans felt about the incident, one must understand how the memory circle in which we participate operates. Any brutalization of an African is enough to bring back thoughts of enslavement and whippings, of lynchings and late-night burnings of homes. Much like the Jews who remember the Holocaust, we experience victimization in our heads. This is why Ted Koppel asked a group of prominent African Americans on *Nightline* to talk about "lynching stories"—that is, to speak to the real physical and psychological ways white America has brutalized and terrorized us throughout history. We can never forget these stories, even as some of us have tried. And if the nation continues to be lulled into amnesia by shortsighted white politicians and careerist black intellectuals, the erupting consciousness of the Wilderness dwellers will be stunning.

Rodney King was every African at one time or another, either in reality or in memory, despite the rhetoric of the black conservatives against this argument. In many ways the Jewish cry of "never again" reverberates as a universal refrain in the mind of all persecuted people. To the degree that we feel the innumerable instances of violence and hate that crowd our minds, no matter how pervasive or how subtle, we are vigilant in the interest of social justice for all. Quite clearly, a Dinesh D'Souza would not have been able to eat at the lunch counter at Kress in Valdosta, Georgia, when I was growing up. It was the courage of African American men and women through antidiscrimination demonstrations, legal challenges, and strength to withstand physical assaults that helped liberate someone as colored as D'Souza. In a Vanderbilt debate I reminded D'Souza that Hindu Indians were liberated by Africans in this country just like we had liberated ourselves. Prior to the 1960s D'Souza would have had to drink out of the "colored only" fountain in Birmingham and would not have been able to live with his white American wife in any of the southern states. D'Souza argued in the Vanderbilt debate that he did not support affirmative action, even for the Dalits, the so-called Untouchables, of India, because they would take away places from the higher castes. This is the language of racism, hierarchy, and intolerance of other human beings that resonates with the American political right wing.

Some African Americans have also had amnesia about the struggle for equality. During the Reagan and Bush administrations it was fashionable to speak of blacks who believed in the Reagan Doctrine. These were supposed to be "good black people" or, as white southerners often said in the past, "good Negroes," who understood that their individual achievements made all things possible for themselves and for other blacks. Detaching "Negroes" from a group identity or a sense of collective feeling became the major enterprise of right-wing whites. The Republicans and others made the mistake of assuming that the ideas of these new black right-wingers were innovative or creative when, in fact, they were black reactionaries who imitated the arguments of white reactionaries and racists using the same basic arguments made since the middle of the nineteenth century. They were and are conservatives who, ironically, like many of Marxists, are without roots and without fruits in the Wilderness.

What is new is the fact that there are finally blacks, thoroughly convinced of the power of the white right, who have become racists against themselves, antiblack blacks who do not see from within but who see blacks as objects from without. This is the initial form of disorientation. The final stage is when a person of African descent rejects any identity with Africa—which is viewed as negative—and declares that she is not black but white, or half white; anything but African. This final stage is called *ultimate misorientation* because the person has abandoned her own identity and taken the identity of the other.

Misoriented Africans also suffer from a sense of historical discontinuity, an incomplete consciousness of African social and economic history, and a bitter, obscene phobia of being African. But therein is the critical problem of being African in America. How does one interpret the domination, the subjugation, the discrimination of Africans? If you are an ultimate misoriented person, you run away from the historical reality and blame the other victims for maintaining their allegiance to something that obviously does not benefit them with whites. Such Africans represent the most successful examples of the Eurocentric domination of the victim, when the victim takes the arguments about his or her inferiority from the oppressor and restates those arguments as if they are new.

I have found the bizarre nature of racism in America more stunning in its ability to disorient and misorient African Americans. Keith Richburg, a black journalist, has written a book called *Out of America*,[9] which is a sad testimony of an individual who is caught in the spiral of psychic pain produced by what Frantz Fanon and Robert C. Smith call *internal inferiorization*. Richburg sees Africans as his enemies and this is the beginning of his problem. He is of African descent and, given the fact that he works for a major media institution with political clout, is probably quite astute. But he is in trouble with himself.

Richburg, who was a correspondent and bureau chief for the *Washington Post* in Africa for three years and is presently Hong Kong bureau chief, has indicted the entire African continent for the bad times he had there. In fact, his book raises numerous questions about the objectivity of the dispatches he sent to Washington from his post. The book is a diatribe against Africa and, much like the books of African American conservatives during the Reagan years, it attempts to show that he is big enough to be critical of black people. The only problem with that is the ax he has to grind has been overused. You cannot get too much mileage out of such an exercise among people who really know Africa. They also know the historical roots of many of the problems Richburg cites. If there ever was a reason for journalists who report from Africa or who write of African Americans to take courses in Afrocentricity and African American studies, Richburg has given the best reason. He has written a superficial, headline-grabbing attack on the African continent, and many of us who have lived, studied, and travelled in Africa find his book offensive and obscene.

He is at once intent on explaining that he is happy to have had an ancestor on the slave ship because he does not identify with what he saw in Africa, but at the same time calls into question the history made by African Americans who have fought against racism and discrimination in this country. He likes neither continental Africans nor African Americans who are proud being of African origin. Therefore, he sought out African Americans at the Gabon Summit organized by Rev. Leon Sullivan—Jesse Jackson, Louis Farakhan, and others—to criticize in an effort to ridicule the leadership of the African American delegation. So if he does not identify with the continental Africans and hates the historical opposition of Africans in America against white supremacy, what are we to make of Richburg? This is not to support everything that Jackson or Farrakhan say and do; they have both had their problems with getting the record straight, but I believe they are genuinely interested in the eradication of racism in our society.

I imagine the internal inferiorization that insinuates itself over and over again in the African American mind and that must be expelled by intellectual and psychological exercises is one of the abiding legacies of our enslavement. But Richburg has availed himself of neither the antidotes to racial self-hatred nor to history, which might have saved him the terror he felt about his Africanity.

Richburg's book came on the heels of *The End of Racism*, *The Bell Curve*, and *Not Out of Africa*, and was simply one more attempt to confuse the American public and to subdue African opinion on matters that affect Africans.[10] Richburg's angst depends on two specific errors in his nativistic thinking: (1) that Africans do not kill each other, and (2) that Africans are not susceptible to political corruption. That is, his arguments and disappointments tend to turn on these assumptions, although he is clearly convinced that Africans have killed and have been corrupted to an extraordinary degree. But his pain, if one can call it that, when he sees the killing and the corruption is surreal. He denies to Africans what he gives to white Americans and Europeans: humanity. Why should he expect that Africans, given a set of social and political circumstances, should be different from other humans? Did he beguile himself into believing a racist lie that Africans were somehow better than Europeans or white Americans? The logic of his thinking is racist.

But how can Richburg feel superior to the Africans he confronts in the rawness of their ordinariness, when he does not confront the same ordinariness in either white or black Americans? Does Richburg understand anything at all about the historical events that unfolded right here on this land? Was he not taught somewhere of the absolute slaughter of the indigenous people who fought to defend what was theirs? Does he know anything about the enslavement and murder of African people over a 250-year period, and has he not learned about the Red Summer of 1919? Had he not read the *Washington Post* itself? Not only is violence against Africans in this country terrible and terrifying, it is constant and consistent in a country that tries to deny that it is based on white supremacist ideology. In 1997 a headline in the *Chicago Tribune* read, "3 Whites Charged in Attack on Black." The story begins, "As a 13-year-old lay unconscious in a Cook County Hospital bed Sunday night, authorities charged three teenagers with trying to beat him to death. Their motive, police said: to rid the neighborhood of blacks." The police charged Frank Caruso, seventeen; Michael Kwidzinski, nineteen; and Victor Jasas, seventeen; all apparently sons of immigrants whose families were probably no more than three generations in the United States, with taking a baseball bat and trying to smash the head of a thirteen-year-old African American. Then, according to the *Tribune*, a witness said, "they bragged to their friends that they had taken care of the niggers in the neighborhood."[11]

How could Keith Richburg or any other African American not understand the subterranean currents of anti-African hostility in the

American society? Does Richburg understand his own history? If he understood something of the history of this country he would not be so happy to declare that he is grateful that his ancestor was a slave. What does he know of the enslavement?

Even more, Richburg has only to read his own newspaper and others to get a steady diet of African Americans in the United States killing each other at a phenomenal, and often with callousness equal to what he saw among continental Africans. Yet he does not want to abdicate his position as an American. Is it only his blackness, and perhaps the ultimate misorientation that comes when the oppressed view the world too long through the eyes of the oppressor, that scares him?

Every objective presentation of the political, social, and economic situation of African Americans points to the previous condition of enslavement as a principal reason for our contemporary predicament. But the misoriented person tries to negate this history, when it is illogical to negate the source of the problem if you sincerely seek to find a solution. It is poor science as well as poor conceptualization to misstate the historical foundations of the situation. When a scientist wants to find a cure for a disease, she must begin with the nature of the disease, its origin, its causes, and its behavior. This is the logic of science. You can more adequately prescribe therapy once you have identified the causes; otherwise you are practicing what Plato called "quackery." I have been most struck by the myopic vision, a sort of distorted discontinuity, of some contemporary writers, because they remember some things more than others and this selective memory often leads to a disregard for historical fact. Perhaps because most of them, unlike Cornel West, have a limited vision of history, they are unable to see the relationship between history and the human condition. Of course, lack of training is not an excuse for those who would speak on the issues confronting the Wilderness dwellers. To paraphrase something I once heard Malcolm X say: Of all our studies, history is best qualified to reward our research.

The fact is, we cannot dispense with 250 years of involuntary servitude and sweep it under the rug. We cannot dispense with nearly one hundred years of official segregation. These years count for something, even at the psychological level of what goes through the mind of a five- or six-year-old African American child sitting in a kindergarten classroom when the subject of slavery comes up for discussion. Does this child put himself into the frame of mind of the white child? Does this child become white in the middle of this history?

We are not just in America; this nation is our history and whether you take the Congo Square of New Orleans or the Missouri Compromise or Mark Twain or the Alamo, you cannot get away from the African presence. This is not history as a moral bludgeon, it is history as a fact that must figure into every serious equation about racial harmony in America. If we are not prepared to do so, we will inherit the windstorms of innumerable Los Angeleses. If we listen to the conservative black feel-good artists, those who make money from rich white groups who want to hear a black person say they are all right, then we will misunderstand the meaning of Los Angeles and the numerous other examples of fury.

What does the history of white enslavement of Africans have to do with the destruction of languages, the loss of spiritual beliefs, the breakup of families, and psychological disorientation? No cute intellectual exercise can obliterate the damage done to the African American community, because the moral issues are inseparable from the historical issues. Therefore, nothing is so important to the Wilderness dweller as resistance to intellectual, cultural, and political oppression, even if this means opposition to African Americans who are dislocated. Clearly, the resistance to oppression, as viewed by Wilderness dwellers, is not simply a matter of confronting whites; it has also become the struggle against modern-day surrogates for the racist system.

There is no mass movement in the white community to educate

itself out of ignorance regarding the question of race. The white community appears to most Wilderness dwellers to be leaderless in social ideas except for occasional intellectual hessians like Dinesh D'Souza, Shelby Steele, Linda Chavez, and Anne Wortham. Steele and Wortham are African Americans from interracial families. Steele is mixed African and white and Wortham calls herself "colored," but both are inclined to speak about issues dealing with African Americans and trade on their "blackness" with white audiences while at the same time condemning blacks for attacking racism. D'Souza, on the other hand, calls himself a "person of color," which tells you nothing about his relationships to the Dalits of India or anything else. These hessians have learned how to provide the white community with a mirror of its own rhetoric. Their identity is important because it helps to explain some of the confusion they have spread among whites and why they have little legitimacy in the African American community. They are, in many ways, more "white" than African or people of color; this is particularly true because they appear to have a limited understanding of their own history and experiences or have opted out of those experiences, appropriating white history as theirs and becoming illiterate in the history and culture of African Americans.

The fact that the Patrick Buchanans and Rush Limbaughs are often glorified as intellectuals and enjoy popularity on television and radio demonstrates to the Wilderness dwellers that a large segment of the white population thrives on prejudicial rhetoric. Furthermore, the racialized thinking that characterizes too many in our country allows individuals to publicly and regularly criticize those like Leonard Jeffries and Khalid Muhammad—but not the several hundred paramilitary and hate groups of whites. From the vantage point of journalists and others who care to comment on the state of race relations in this country, the Wilderness dweller in the urban area is far more dangerous than the white militiaman in the Idaho forest. But is this really so? Certainly, one's position often determines what one will answer in given situations.

Location, as Afrocentrists say, is everything.[12] Soon after D'Souza's polemic *Illiberal Education* came out, I debated him at Vanderbilt University under the auspices of the Center for Black Culture. He made the arguments he had made in his book, namely, that African Americans seemed disinterested in education and that federal monies could be better spent educating Asian and white students who scored high on the standardized examinations and were essentially willing to work without raising cultural questions.[13] In effect, for him, the Asian, whether American or alien, is the model minority. D'Souza's aim, it seems to me, is twofold, as revealed in his arguments: (1) to provide white conservatives with an alternative "minority" strategy, and (2) to solidify the negative and false stereotypes of African Americans as disinterested in competing in the educational arena. The political correctness issue is used as a smokescreen, with D'Souza and others arguing that some ideas seemed to be off-limits in the universities. But the real issue is an attack on so-called black entitlements. Furthermore, D'Souza argues that the emphasis placed on culture in the academic arena is misplaced because the main idea is to teach students skills—not culture.

I find D'Souza thinking unusually shallow. In the first place, he has almost no understanding of the history of the United States. Not to say that historical inaccuracies or geographical misstatements are defining characteristics of a person's mental capabilities, but when there is a degree of sloppiness in these matters it suggests that the person has not thought through many of his clichés. And most of what D'Souza presents are new angles on old clichés.

Furthermore, African Americans have *never* been disinterested in education. Not even during the harshest period of enslavement were Africans disinterested in learning. Of course, it was illegal for an African to be taught or for an African to learn how to read for almost 250 years. But just as soon as the Civil War was over and Africans were freed, schools and institutes of learning sprang up throughout the South. No people ever had a greater thirst for information and knowledge than the Africans after the end of enslavement. Our ancestors took up collections of nickels and pennies and built, sometimes with the support of white philanthropists from the North, more than two hundred colleges and schools! More than one hundred of those schools still stand as monuments to our interest in education. Actually, illiteracy went from 98 percent in 1865 to 45 percent in 1900. Thirty-five hard years of struggle and victory over illiteracy from a people for whom it had been a crime to read and write!

D'Souza's problem and, as he interprets it for some whites, their problem, is that African Americans demand quality education—that is, education that does not project the Eurocentric experience as the only human experience. D'Souza suffers from the displaced Asian syndrome. Born in a part of India dominated by colonial influences, rejecting his Indian identity, and adopting a Portuguese name, D'Souza seemed to have rejected everything that is not European. Furthermore, he has failed to distinguish between Asian groups. The results of the self-selection of Asians, such as Japanese and Koreans, who arrive in this country shows up on test scores and in colleges. But one group of Asians is not like the next. Cambodians and Vietnamese, many of whom are in the United States as refugees from war, tend to have different test scores than Japanese and Koreans.

When D'Souza came to America in the 1980s as a student, he was struck by the fact that many African Americans were claiming pride in African culture at a time when he was abandoning his own Asian culture. This became an existential problem for him. He soon adopted an anti-African posture and became one of the favorites of the right wing.

D'Souza is not alone in his quest to lay the blame for racism at the feet of blacks. There are a number of conservative black authors who have taken up the same position. Chief among them have been Shelby Steele, Thomas Sowell, and Anne Wortham. Shelby Steele's book *The Content of Our Character* contains some interesting ideas, but it is tragically flawed.[14] Steele's problem is that he cannot bear to see Wilderness dwellers who are still wallowing in the so-called victimage of the postenslavement period. In his mind, there must be something wrong with the way we approach our reality, and the something wrong is that we have not become "white." I think he means white in terms of ideas and views, not in social or biological terms—although a great many visible black conservatives seem to suggest in their own personal choices that biology is the only way out.

One of Steele's main arguments is that the quest for power comes from the assertion of innocence. What he allows with this argument is the claim that African Americans pushing for legitimate respect are really trying to demonstrate innocence so as to deflate white entitlements. Of course, Steele sees this idea in other areas as well, and he writes, "Our innocence always inflates us and deflates those we seek power over."[15] Yet African Americans cannot be accused of seeking power over whites. Our response to hatred and bigotry is nothing more than the assertion of our fundamental right to defend ourselves and to live in peace. It is neither more nor less innocence that is claimed in this situation, but the right to live free of racial domination. Furthermore, the people of the Wilderness have nothing more than their moral power, since they do not control the economic sphere; this may not be merely innocent power but the imperative of human decency. One cannot claim, as Steele seems to want to, that African Americans hold equal responsibility with whites for the economic condition of the Wilderness. This is really nonsense. Unfortunately, there are whites who accept such misguided theories about race relations because they desperately seek a way out of the burden of accountability. However, as long as 89 percent of the people whose wealth is over $200 million are white males, while the same white males make up only 39 percent of the population, the responsibility and the accountability for the Wilderness must remain with white males.

Thomas Sowell is the leading black conservative writer. He has been engaged fully in a campaign against identity politics, black nationalist thinking, African cultural values, and liberal ideas for more than forty years. In his book *The Economis and Politics of Race*, his thesis is that human cultures are not equal and some of them are better than others.[16] This view is obviously rooted in an arrogant location based on Sowell's own estimation of American society. In fact, it is the epitome of autobiographical analysis to assume that your historical and cultural view is the standard for the rest of the world. Sowell assumes a white identification but condemns a black identification as a restraint on assimilation into the American mainstream. One could argue, as many authors do, that there is nothing in African American history and culture that should preclude national unity. In other words, it is not the subjugation or the obliteration of the national identity of the African that brings about national unity, it is the acceptance of all Americans, regardless of cultural heritage, that constitutes a positive step forward.

Shelby Steele and Thomas Sowell may be the most prominent voices on the conservative black right, but Anne Wortham may be one of the most confused. She found her niche in the conservative movement during the administration of Ronald Reagan. Her defense of white cultural and social values has added to the theories of white domination.

Wortham has been featured at the Heritage Foundation as a speaker against the Afrocentric movement in education, the civil rights movement, and African American nationalism. As the most well-known "colored" (her preference) woman on the conservative platform, Wortham, a follower of Ayn Rand, has attacked every conceivable "progressive" idea. Her argument usually centers on the belief that individual rights are more important than group rights, and therefore she does not care so much about the African American community but about "colored" people as individuals. This argument coincides with some of the leftist arguments for the individual as well.

Civil rights organizations and African American nationalists are condemned as group projects, as a collective consciousness, by both the right and the left. Wortham's criticism might be different in tone from that of Manning Marable or Henry Louis Gates Jr., but she argues, essentially like them, that there is an essentialism to cultural nationalism that bothers her because it talks about "African American people" as if all African Americans are the same. But to speak of African Americans is not to speak precisely of each and every one of us, but rather of the totality of the people in the sense of history and experiences. Although not every African American is a descendant of enslaved persons, we cannot get away from the fact that our *history* and *experience* here is that of the formerly enslaved.

However, the cultural nationalist position has been stated well throughout African American history and needs no defense from me: African Americans have a right to seek the preservation of history and culture within the context of our American citizenship. The fact that this disturbs Anne Wortham and other modern-day hessians likely has more to do with their own sense of inadequacy—that is, loss of cultural identity—than it does with what is correct for greater national harmony.

The viciousness of the poverty in our community is related to the nature of our existence in this country. What are we to think when we are accused for our poverty when we know that in the 1830s and 1840s, while we were still enslaved, the Armed Occupation Act gave whites the right to claim 160 acres of land in Georgia and Florida, if they would agree to farm five acres and kill the Native Americans who owned the land? Are we to think that whites are better than we are? More intelligent? More hard-working? More humane? What are we to think when we read that after Gen. Andrew Jackson's massacre of the Muskogee people, whites were given their lands and the Muskogee people were forced to march to Oklahoma along the Trail of Tears?

It is no wonder that the condition of the Native Americans today is directly related to their historical encounter with whites. A moral crisis based not on hypothetical issues of innocence, but on the concrete realities of white settler encroachment of land, is another open wound in the body politic. How the debts of land and labor will be paid will constitute the great discourse of the twenty-first century.

Our fury is the collective moral outrage of a people whose very existence calls for repentance. Indeed, our fury may also represent that of thousands of Native Americans whose blood is mixed with our blood, whose history is often twisted with ours, and whose pain on this land is as great, or greater, than ours. Thus, the Seminoles, those runaway Africans and Muskogee people who comprise the bulk of the Native Americans in Florida, are modern-day descendants of those who were left from the occupation of Florida. And those of us who went—and many did—with the Native Americans on the Trail of Tears in 1835 to Oklahoma, eventually established our own towns, like Boley and Langston, there.

Every oak and willow weeps with the Native Americans and Africans whose blood was spilled on this land. Perhaps there is a reason for our spiritual strivings, our mysticism, our relationship to nature, and our quickening desire for justice and peace. That reason is found in the abiding love that we have for the soil of our fathers and mothers, the metaphysical meeting of their personalities, temperaments, and bodies with this land. In this way, perhaps, we African Americans are double relatives of the Native Americans.

The Wilderness dweller seeks every opportunity to subvert the oppression, to change the ground rules, to move the boundaries, and to free himself from the expectations of defeat and failure. One of the unfortunate facts of life in America is that the talents of some of the most brilliant individuals remain unutilized or underutilized because of aggressive anti-African behavior on all fronts. From time to time we hear the questions: Do you believe that they could find only ten African Americans for the space shuttle program? Why don't we see an African American political scientist from a historically black college on television on a regular basis commenting on international affairs?

The answer in the African American community, among those who consider themselves historically conscious, always centers on the maintenance of white supremacy as a system. If few African Americans graduate from Duke, it has less to do with the ability of blacks and more to do with the structure of white supremacy. If an outstanding African American teacher is passed over for a distinguished teacher award, it has more to do with white racism than it does with the teacher's worth. If Wilderness dwellers live in the most squalid conditions in the cities, it has more to do with the manner in which whites have structured banking and housing privileges than with the desires and wishes of the African American people.

I am certainly not alone in making such claims. Andrew Hacker, Derrick Bell, Joe Feagin, and many others have elucidated the roots of structural racism with great clarity. The worst attitude for us to have is that racism does not affect people's life chances. Acceptance of that attitude means that the unutilized and underutilized Wilderness dwellers remain separate and outside of the possibilities of the Promise, or, if they are brought inside the various institutions, they must be careful lest the institutions are turned against them.

This is as true in politics as it is in other sectors of the society. Driven by the same racism one finds in the general society, the assault on African American politicians who resist hegemony and who support the interest of their community can be unrelenting. Wilderness dwellers have come to believe, with enough anecdotal support, that politicians who feel our pain and who are willing to defend our interests are threatened in their offices and in their persons.

Perhaps no one African American disturbed the peace of the people of the Promise as did Congressman Adam Clayton Powell Jr. of New York. He believed that the American pie was large enough for everyone and that if he had anything to say about it, the Wilderness people would share in the largesse of the nation.

Harlem was his home and he used his church, the Abyssinian Baptist Church, one of the largest congregations in America, to rise to the top of the political world. He embodied all the attributes of Africans that seemed to upset whites. He was fun-loving, in pursuit of the music of life, free, boisterous, and loud. He did not fawn over whites, as so many blacks of his day did, and he made it his business to exercise the power that he had attained as chairman of the House Education and Labor Committee.

Before Malcolm X, Powell was the great challenge to the white establishment on its own terms and with its own logic. African Americans throughout the nation felt good when Powell spoke because we believed that he understood our sentiments and held our interests close to his heart.

The downfall of Powell may have been the belief that he could get away with his power and style in white America. A libel suit by a black woman brought Powell down. He had referred to her as a "bag woman for the police," meaning essentially that she collected money from gamblers and took it to the police. The woman sued him. He was disgraced and convicted. Although he was thrown out of Congress, his constituents reelected him, but the end was short in coming. The venerable journalist and professor Chuck Stone, who worked for Powell, said that among the adjectives used to describe the congressman were "arrogant, audacious, flamboyant, irresponsible, self-centered, elegant, witty, charming, exciting, paranoid, perpetually happy, uncommonly brilliant and disturbingly handsome."[18] In fact, Stone says, "he ignited deep resentment in the ordinary little white men who were his peers and were forced to tread in his shadow."[19] So the persecution of Powell, as his followers saw it, despite his own self-destructive tendencies, was the work of whites. They did not appreciate his popular strength with his community, his arrogant distaste for racists, and his sharp logic and oratorical flair.

Born in New Haven, Connecticut, on November 29, 1908, he was the son of Adam Clayton Powell Sr., a preacher of immense talent, who moved his family to Harlem in 1909 and built the Abyssinian Baptist Church into one of the most influential institutions in the city. The young Powell attended Colgate University and Columbia, finally succeeding his father at the church in 1937, at the age of twenty-nine. Fully aware of the relative vacuum that had been created in New York by the decline of Marcus Garvey, Powell became an activist minister with the aim of ending racism in Harlem. He led picket-bearing marchers against white merchants who would not hire African Americans.

Successful at the picketing of large stores, Powell turned his attention to the semiskilled areas of employment such as the utility, police, and transit sectors. In 1940 Powell forced Mike Quill, the leader of the Transport Workers Union and an Irish Catholic who had made a practice of hiring only Irish, to open the union to African Americans, hiring 210 African Americans as bus drivers and grade I mechanics.

Powell's political road was now paved with victories. Harlem sent him to the city council in 1941 and to the United States Congress in 1944. He had no significant problems with his electorate until he made his "bag woman" comments in 1960. He had previously made detailed remarks about the gambling syndicate in Harlem on the House floor. His televised remarks were based on newspaper articles he used from the *New York Times*, the *New York Post*, and the *New York Journal-American*.

On February 25, 1960, Powell said Mrs. Esther James was "extorting money from gamblers" for the purpose of dropping it off to police officers. Her suit cost Powell $46,500 in fines, reduced from a judgment of $210,000, in addition to legal expenses. Powell became the perfect target for every major newspaper, journal, magazine, and network in the nation. The "big, bad black" could now be tamed. He was hounded out of Congress, he was criticized for travels, he was condemned for absenteeism in Congress, and he was ridiculed for his personal lifestyle.

I think it is necessary to recount this information not to praise Adam Clayton Powell Jr.'s lifestyle, but to give a backdrop to the anger he must have felt, just as we felt fury when he was persecuted. We knew then that few African Americans could stand firmly against white racism without being punished. And so we waited to see if our prophecies would be fulfilled. And then, before we knew it, Marion Barry of Washington, D.C., came to power, lost it in a drug raid, and returned in triumph because of his organic connection to the fundamental wishes of his community. The drama began again and we watched in the Wilderness, knowing all too well that the views of those of the Promise would be different from our own.

# CHAPTER EIGHT
# THE DRAMA OF RACISM

B arack Hussein Obama's ascension to the presidency of the United States of America in 2008 transcended the Republican appointments of Colin Powell and Condoleezza Rice as secretaries of state in the American government. Major American corporations and universities are now headed by African Americans, yet there are still taxi cab drivers who will not take black passengers, and there remain men and women who believe that blacks are inferior to whites. What is often at stake in any discussion of race in the United States is the African American's sense of her own cultural self. To what degree, for example, is the African American willing to divest herself of culture, tradition, resistance, and the rhetoric of freedom for the oppressed in order to join a white agenda that might be antithetical to her history? What dangers lurk in the common, everyday places where some believe in white supremacy? What kinds of racial profiling will Barack Obama confront during his presidency?

❊❊❊

Consider two cases with which I am familiar. The first I heard from a former colleague; the second I learned about from an interview with a young professor at a major university.

According to my friend and former colleague, a medical scholar and professor at Morehouse Medical College, a young African American male graduated from medical school at the top of his class, secured a major university professorship in medicine, and had a reasonable practice until his white colleagues thought he was making too much money and systematically cut off his referrals.

In the medical profession, I was told, it is essential for a specialist to receive referrals from other doctors. This is a problem if you are black and do not fit into the small cliques that often govern the medical profession. A medical degree and a license to practice will go only so far in an anti-African environment. While the African American surgeon might do well vis-à-vis other African Americans, it is rare that he will reach the very top of the profession in terms of material rewards because such ascendancy depends upon the referrals of white doctors.

Excellence, graduate degrees, and specialties aside, the African American surgeon, despite his intellectual capabilities and skills, is not afforded the same recognition or material rewards as white doctors.

Not long ago I was discussing this issue with a neighbor, a relatively well-known physician in Philadelphia. I asked him, "Do you think the African American doctor is discriminated against?" He replied, "I don't think it, I *know* it." He went on to explain that in perks, such as samples from pharmaceutical and medical supply companies, and appointments to medical boards and community or civic organizations, African Americans were often the victims of discrimination. If medicine is subtler in its prejudice against African Americans, education regularly produces clear-cut cases of either harassment or outright unequal treatment of African Americans.

Consider the case of a female African American professor in the

German language department at a Midwestern university. She had published six books and many articles, yet was refused an evaluation for early tenure by her white colleagues in a department where no one else was so widely published. They suspected that she, being black and a woman, could not have written "all those books" because it flew in the face of their beliefs about African Americans and women. Of course, they had hired her because she was intelligent in the first place. Her genius was not unexpected. What was not anticipated was the fact that she felt her genius should have been rewarded as it would have been rewarded were she white. This annoyed her colleagues.

The chair of the department had flown to her previous city of residence to recruit her. The young woman held degrees from the University of Michigan and from German universities. Her doctorate had come from Princeton University and she had taught in European and American universities. Most universities have policies that allow professors who make extraordinary achievements to be considered for early tenure. So there was nothing out of the ordinary when she asked to be considered for tenure after four years, since she had already spent two years researching and teaching at the University of Pennsylvania when she was hired.

Early tenure considerations, while not common, have been made in other cases at that university and are made routinely at most schools. But the professor's department fought against her, the dean's office refused to intervene, the provost's office turned her appeal back to the dean's office, and the president's office listened but refused to intervene. In effect, in a department with more than twenty faculty members, the young black professor was left with only one active supporter—a fairly well-published female professor who herself had struggled for recognition in the same department. Counsel advised the African American professor that since the department had refused to seek outside evaluative letters, it was probably acting in a racist way because it suspected that the outside evaluators would have affirmed the superior work of the professor, thus forcing the department to promote her. Ultimately the young professor had to fall back on the

African American affairs office and the protest mode with which African Americans have become eternally familiar as a staple in the Wilderness. She did not prevail and decided to leave the university.

In such a situation, where the African American woman was clearly superior, by the publication records, to her peers, why was there such a fight against her?

The fury is that had she been white, the department probably would have pronounced her a supernova, paraded her before many university and external bodies, and given her numerous awards for her merit. In the end, the department chair argued that she was a brilliant scholar but that her teaching was not up to par. Certainly white female professors have often heard this same answer to their attempts at promotion. However, this professor was both black and female, and although one white female professor supported her, others did not support her. Thus, the reply remained undefined, contradictory, and a lame excuse, because she had clearly outstripped her colleagues at the scholarly game. Her teaching stints at the University of Pennsylvania and at Princeton had been unquestionably successful.

Since the department had never had a tenured African American faculty member, one would think they would have done everything possible to keep her on the faculty, but the threat of having a superior black faculty member was, it seems, too much for the department to consider.

This professor's bitter struggle must not be viewed as a unique odyssey, because at this very moment scores of black faculty members are undergoing similar experiences in American universities. I recall seeing the film of Harper Lee's *To Kill a Mockingbird* and remarking to a friend that whites rarely take on the role of an Atticus Finch today. Yet the most positive alliances between blacks and whites have always been based on a united front against racial discrimination, and sometimes against white supremacy.

To be a Wilderness dweller means to live under a siege of disrespect, whether you are a person of high visibility or of no visibility. The attempt on the part of the prisoner is to escape the Wilderness by rearranging the field of struggle—that is, to find one's own ground.

Challenged by racist assaults and feeling pressed to the wall, the Wilderness dweller will often turn to religion—but not always the Christian religion, since that is often seen as the crux of the problem with whites. "They kidnapped us, brought us to America, and enslaved us," a young sister explained to a group of youth in Milwaukee during a Kwanzaa celebration.

A storm of suspicion greets each action of the white power structure reaching its hand into the lives of African American people. Disrupting the economic and social lives of black people appears to be the principal purpose of whites when they consider African Americans, otherwise we remain invisible to them. And consequently, each of us, if we think about it, could pour forth story after story of the very nature of these vicious interventions.

The problem is endemic. In almost every profession, the record is the same. In dealing with the persistent nature of anti-Africanism we must not evade a discussion of the relentless way it insinuates itself into every field of art or science. Often, unless an African American engineer works for a white firm, she will find it difficult to secure private or government contracts because the people most often in charge of awarding the contracts are whites, and if they are also racist, the African American will not receive the contract. While the nation is fortunate that all agencies do not operate on the basis of race, enough of them do that African Americans develop profiles of racism and a company's history of contractual relationships that seem to tell the story of bias in every sector. The memory of these cases is long and troublesome.

A few years ago, a firefighter in a rural Tennessee town filed a federal discrimination suit against his city and the fire department, claiming that he was fired from his job because he was African American. Roland Hamilton of Martin, Tennessee, contended that his firing was based on racial discrimination. When I first read the story of Roland

Hamilton, it occurred to me that this was in a small town, isolated in the South and away from the urban communities where racism seems so prevalent.

Upon reflection, however, it becomes clear that racism is not just an urban American problem; it is an American problem. Hollywood and the media have served in some important ways to show us how prevalent racism is in the nation. Even so, continued racial discrimination in Hollywood itself was the main topic at the fifteenth annual convention of the National Association of Black Journalists. Hundreds of African American journalists heard panelists outline the continuing plight of screenwriters, directors, and producers in Hollywood. John Horn wrote in the *Call and Post* that the association of black journalists had concentrated on the Hollywood sector as a central theme because of the impact the movie and television industry has had on popular conceptions of reality. When Halle Berry and Denzel Washington, two veteran actors, won the coveted 2002 Oscars for best actress and best actor, Hollywood seemed to be attempting to right a wrong. Nevertheless, the overall impression of the industry is that it still lacks a commitment to the African American community. One rarely sees movies, for example, that reflect African history, culture, or situations in a well-rounded light. Screenplays reflecting African history are obviously not accepted at the large movie studios.

What can the Wilderness dweller do to prevent the abuse of his person or the disruption of his professional ambitions? This question centers the issue of resistance in the powerlessness Wilderness dwellers have often felt. Only through the boycott can the African American convey a national response to injustices, such as the fact that during the 1999 television season of nearly seventy new shows, not one featured a black cast.

Not long ago, a popular Philadelphia journalist was removed, over the objections and protests of the African American community, from a television show because the station saw her as too outspoken, too opinionated. The television station's message to the black community was that we did not count, either economically or politically, in their assessment of their audience and ratings. The perceived attack on the Wilderness community creates anger that we do not control our own destiny and cannot dictate the terms of our own communication interests. Some people considered the demotion of the journalist a corporate decision, not a racist one. But for the Wilderness dweller it is difficult to tell if the decision is merely corporate, based on economics, or racist, based on prejudice, when the only perceivable issue with which the corporation could disagree was the journalist's opinions.

I have never considered media corporations perfect—or any different from the rest of American society in terms of race and racism— so the incident in Philadelphia was, for me, another testament to the fury that rages in Wilderness dwellers' hearts. This travesty of respect for our community, perhaps made in the name of money, underscored the fragility of the already strained relationship the African American community had with that television station.

Several days before the demotion of the journalist, I was invited, along with four other African Americans from government and business, to a luncheon with the new station manager. We found the manager to be relatively unimpressed with our message about the journalist and about the value of her program. He seemed to believe that the only thing that mattered was his decision to demonstrate to his corporate bosses that he was in control of the station. His bottom-line position seemed to be, How much money can the station make by putting a popular football player in the same time slot as the community program? What the community felt did not seem to matter. To some degree, this search for the most thrills in order to reap the greatest amount of money is true of much of television as witnessed by the *Survivor* series or *The Bachelor* being besieged by scores of lovely ladies.

The people of the Promise, those with the money and ownership, had spoken, and the station would not change its opinion because it did not care what the African American community wanted. The television journalist may have been popular in the African American community, but she was not popular with the media managers because they believed she alienated a portion of the white community by concentrating on issues in the Wilderness.

Our anger, vented in the usual letters and telegrams, did nothing to change the verdict. We only hoped that it would cause the station manager to pause the next time he thought of doing something that went against the best interest of the community. But even that was not guaranteed, because the people of the Wilderness are often without real economic power. But this is power that can only come from a renewed sense of agency on the part of the African American community. Such an agency, however, cannot be, as Cornel West seems to think, granted by external forces; it must be grasped by African Americans themselves. Using Malcolm X's corpus as his principal paradigm of black nationalist theory, West accuses Malcolm of nearsightedness in the claim that nationalism is a legitimate response to white supremacist policies.[1] However, on closer reading one finds that it is not Malcolm X's logic that is problematic, but West's. Neither political nor economic agency can be created without a reclamation and a restoration of the centeredness that was stripped from African people over the past four hundred years. We reclaim by initiating and maintaining our own activities against racism.

Those Africans who remain sane and who exercise either economic or political will do so because of self-love and self-determination. They see themselves neither as victims nor as spectators of white achievement. Furthermore, for Malcolm X to have articulated his views without the historical background of white supremacist rhetoric and action would have been for him to abandon reason and operate as if racism was a temporary phenomenon in American society. So when West contends that Malcolm used whites as "the principal point of reference," he misunderstands both Malcolm's location in his own culture and Malcolm's orientation toward white people in America. So clearly did Malcolm X challenge blacks to claim heritage and history that we cannot even speak of him as being anything but centered on the cultural question; he was preeminently culturally located and that, not white people, was his principal reference point.

On the other hand, Malcolm's orientation toward white people was based on what he saw as the origin and maintenance of a system of oppression and exploitation in the Wilderness that was controlled by whites. To disregard this hegemonic situation, either economically or politically, would have been rationally impossible. Malcolm said, "They have a system that's known as gerrymandering, whatever that means. It means when Negroes become too heavily concentrated in a certain area, and begin to gain too much political power, the white man comes along and changes the district lines." Anticipating a cynic's question about why he was speaking about whites so much, Malcolm said, "Because it's the white man who does it. I haven't ever seen a Negro changing any lines."[2]

Take this case: A Pennsylvania businessman-farmer was able to secure a contract to supply vegetables to a major fast-food chain, but when he sought to purchase produce from white farmers in order to help meet his orders, the white farmers decided not to sell to him and forced him to cancel his contract. He had spent several months lining up the white farmers to supply him, since his farm, while significant, could not satisfy the new demand. They had all led him to believe he could depend upon them for the vegetables, but just as he needed to deliver to the fast-food chain, his suppliers failed to deliver. His reaction was that they did not want to see an African American with the principal contract. Some of the whites even wanted to approach the fast food-chain for the business.

A few years ago, when I taught at the State University of New York at Buffalo, the sociologist Sidney Willhelm came by my house. We lived about two blocks from each other and he had been in the neighborhood much longer than I had, so since we both taught at the university we often found good occasions to sit and share ideas. I recounted to him some of my experiences as a young man growing up in Georgia and Tennessee, and he told me how far in his thinking he had come from his Texas background and since he first wrote *Who Needs the Negro?* considered in the 1960s as one of the standard works of liberal sociologists. As we talked, I noticed that tears came into his eyes. Always a sensitive individual, Willhelm spoke quietly but with great emotion about the work he was doing that demonstrated that racism was the principal factor setting African Americans behind the rest of the society. He believed that William Julius Wilson was misguided in publishing *The Declining Significance of Race*, in which he claimed that class was a more significant factor in the life chances of African Americans than race.[3]

Willhelm became a forceful opponent of this view and believed that Wilson had misread the data on the condition of Africans in this society. He discussed this with me at length and, with tears in his eyes, said, "I find it difficult to see how African Americans can take the psychic, social, and economic assaults from this society." He recounted incidents, stories, and anecdotes of his years in the university, where his colleagues seemed consistently to miss the point about the cause of the anger in the African American community. Willhelm's early works were prophetic because he understood the nature of racism.[4] Along with Joe Feagin of the University of Florida, who writes in the same vein, Willhelm abandoned many of the traditional liberal and Marxist tenets for new syntheses in race studies.[5] Unfortunately, one has to search long and hard for good sociological work in the area of racism. *Racial Formation in the United States*, a work popular in the sociological field written by Michael Omi and Howard Winant, seeks to outline a theory that conceptualizes racial identity without biology.[6] The problem with sociological theories of this type is the same problem found with race studies generally: They do not want to deal with deconstructing white racial supremacy. It is rather easy to examine microlevel issues of the African's response to prejudice, discrimination, and racism; it is equally easy to discuss the macrolevel issues of politics, economics, and culture to describe racial identity. What is more difficult, it seems—and this is the problem with Omi and Winant's work—is to create a theory that deals with white people.

The capturing of the American imagination by a wave of conservative authors over the past few years has set back the progress of studies in racism as well as race relations by a decade. Unleashed as a new interpretation of social policy, the conservative line in political science and sociology is not new, but rather a straightforward attack on affirmative action. Contending that affirmative action cannot be defended on grounds of justice, the conservatives push the agenda that affirmative action is unjust. With the arrival of Linda Chavez, John Bunzel, and scores of others, sometimes as regents or trustees at state universities, the reactionary right has contorted the very program that was advanced during the Nixon administration as a conservative response to the historical injustice done to the Africans in the United States. What was once thought to be justice is now defined as injustice. What was once an attempt to correct the problems of inequality for Africans is now being pressed as inequality to whites. The argument is appealing to those with short historical memories, but it remains a wrongheaded argument and the nation will always reap the whirlwind for abandoning the legitimate goals of a more equitable society for Africans and other historically discriminated persons.

John Bunzel's examination of affirmative action policy at the University of California at Berkeley concluded that affirmative action on college and university campuses must be viewed in relation to other competing and legitimate values.[7] What this amounted to was an assault on the principle that African Americans had been especially victimized by enslavement and discrimination, and therefore the nation, to overcome the negative impact of racism, should act affirmatively to redress the situation. Bunzel was not the first, or the last, to take this line of thinking; others have taken it even further, arguing that no special privileges ought to be given for historical racism. The Bunzels of this nation have tried to promote affirmative action as a drag on competing aspects of educational institutions. Unfortunately they have been joined by some African American writers who seem not to understand the dilemma that brought forth the affirmative action paradigm.

One such book, *Reflections of an Affirmative Action Baby* was published by Yale University professor Stephen Carter.[8] Carter's complaint seems to be that he was stigmatized by the affirmative action label, and therefore it was not a good idea. Meanwhile, Carter has recently received a major advance for a novel on the black middle and upper classes, showing that his stigma is more in his own mind than in the minds of those who would hire him. Race stigmatizes him more than affirmative action. For some whites, however, to see him as black, regardless of what program paid for his education, is to see him as inferior.

It is a mistake to assume that any program can eradicate the stigma of blackness in a racist society. Carter could have been an honor student in an honor club and yet felt the stigma of racism. As Malcolm X put it so succinctly at Harvard, "What do they call a black with a Ph.D.? Nigger." Malcolm understood that neither education nor money could change the status of the African in the minds of whites who had been imbued with a sense of our inferiority based on race and the condition of enslavement. So the African who is in the honor society is considered "rare," "different," "unusual," "special"— but is still stigmatized by race in ways that whites would not stigmatize themselves.

The problem with the "progressives," as used by Cornel West, is that they have bought into the conservatives' position on affirmative action.[9] They argue that class-based affirmative action would be better than race-based affirmative action because class is now more important than race. This argument is fallacious. If a Serbian peasant came to the United States tomorrow and changed his surname from Milosevic to Miles, he would immediately be accorded greater "racial," hence social, status with all the "rights, access, and privileges" of whiteness than Cornel West, a Princeton professor. This would be so despite the fact that West is urbane, articulate, and well traveled.

The present educational deficit is not an individual deficit but a collective and national deficit. This is not the same as saying that Kim Su or Ted Vaclav came to this country and could not read, but look at him now. Immigrants who choose to come to America are in no way enslaved, and they have different orientations and reasons for feeling support in the United States, where many citizens are sympathetic to their plight. Our coming was different and our struggle was epic because we were brought on slave ships and often worked nearly to death, and where we did not die we wrote elegant and passionate phrases in our hearts and minds about justice and love. We African Americans are the children of the ones who could not be killed by heatstroke from the sun, frostbitten hands and feet from the bitter cold, the overseer's lashes, the lyncher's ropes, the stone thrower's venom, the bloodhounds' pursuits, or the petty violence of verbal and emotional abuse.

Despite the curious attempt to claim for all Americans the same heritage and the same history, the record of the country speaks for itself. From education to prison, the evidence of racial bias in interpretation of data as well as in the data themselves show that African Americans have been treated unfairly. The United States General Accounting Office confirmed in a study of racial bias in the death penalty that in 82 percent of the cases the race of the victim made a difference in whether the defendant was sentenced to death. Furthermore, the study showed that those who murder whites are more likely to receive the death sentence than those who murder blacks.[10] Thus, the likelihood of a black man getting the death sentence for killing another black is far less than if he killed a white. Since we know these things, the question is really, Why is it impossible for us to deal with the issues? In a real sense this is a problem of focus. We have been unable to direct the attention of the nation toward the need for redressing the wrongs committed against its African American citizens.

Many whites would typically argue that racism does not exist in their workplaces. Yet in almost all cases where African Americans work with whites, the African Americans believe that whites frequently operate on the basis of race. This is the case whether the person is a veteran or not, a teacher or not, and a professional or not. Black men —even those who graduate from high school, earn college degrees, pursue careers, escape serious health problems, and raise families— say they face racial discrimination that often prevents them from reaching their highest potential. When an African American rises to the top of a large corporation it is usually seen as an example of progress. And while it does reflect changes within the business culture, it cannot be taken as a sign that we have erased racism. African American women speak of the difficulty white men have in being supervised by black women. In this case it is a double whammy because the white male reacts to both the issue of race and the issue of gender. Of course, black men have shown the same sexist attitudes toward female bosses as white men have. However, racism is virulent in this situation because white men often believe that they should be in positions of leadership by virtue of their race, particularly in the case of black women, the descendant of enslaved Africans. This is why Andrew Hacker is right to argue that the bottom line in race relations is the institution of slavery.[11] How whites feel about the condition of servitude forced on blacks, and how *we* feel about that condition or how we feel about the attachment of whites to the perpetration of that condition, are the central issues affecting race relations in this nation.

One cannot speak about discrimination in isolation from history. We have not had extensive antiracism training in this country. Instead, we have situational "sensitivity" training: When the Holiday Spa Health Club chain agreed to settle allegations that it discriminated against African American customers, the agreement stipulated that employees had to be trained not to discriminate. Furthermore, the company's advertisements had to include blacks and explain the club's nondiscrimination policy.[12]

Without some ethical transformation, there is very limited instructional value to simple "don't discriminate" training. Discrimination is morally indefensible. Nondiscrimination must become more than a technical adjustment; it must be seen as morally correct. In the health club business, where appearance is considered important, many club operators had the habit of turning away black customers so as not to "frighten away" white customers. Neither the operators nor the white customers would likely express their reactions as racist, yet they were discriminatory actions. In some circles it is believed that to have more than 10 percent of customers identified as black is to have a black club in the minds of many whites—even though they still comprise 90 percent!

In 1993 the Denny's restaurant chain faced the first of several lawsuits for racial discrimination. The first site sued was the San Jose, California, store, where several black teenagers were refused service unless they agreed to pay in advance. Subsequently, in 1994 at the Syracuse, New York, Denny's, six Asian Americans were made to wait for more than thirty minutes before they were served, while white patrons were served immediately. When they complained, they were physically ejected from the establishment by two security guards. Once outside, they were beaten by a white mob. Three black students were threatened with mace when they attempted to assist the Asian Americans, and a white student accompanying the black students was also threatened. Two of these students were knocked unconscious. A third incident occurred at a Denny's in Annapolis, Maryland, where six black Secret Service agents were forced to wait for an hour before they were served, while their white companions were served promptly. Numerous other incidents happened at Denny's restaurants across the nation, and thousands of black customers claimed discrimination at Denny's. The management company, Flagstar Companies, signed a pact with the National Association for the Advancement of Colored People (NAACP) to get the problems out of the headlines.

The company pledged to hire more African Americans and to participate in a program to ensure that customers were treated fairly. This solution did not address past discrimination, and when it was all over Denny's had paid out $54 million to nearly three hundred thousand customers and their lawyers.[13]

When Cynthia Wiggins of Buffalo was struck and killed while crossing a busy thoroughfare to get to her job at a suburban shopping mall in 1995—because the mall refused to allow a city bus to enter mall property—the African American community cried foul. The Walden Galleria and its developer, Pyramid Company, contended that they decided not to allow city busses onto the property because they would cause excessive wear on mall roadways. In a $150-million lawsuit against the companies, attorneys for Wiggins's family noted that busses carrying Canadian tourists—busses larger and heavier than Buffalo city busses—were regularly allowed onto mall property. The suit, buoyed by testimony that the companies believed that "the people who rode the Walden Avenue bus were not the kind of people they were trying to attract to the Walden Galleria," charged the Galleria and Pyramid with banning the number 6 bus from mall property because its riders were predominantly black.[14]

Racism appears to be alive and well in many sectors of the society. Confronted with the possibility that blacks might seek membership in the country club he headed, the founder of the all-white Shoal Creek Country Club in Birmingham, Alabama, said that whites would not feel comfortable playing golf at a club that admitted blacks.[15] Why wouldn't whites feel comfortable? What is the phobia in the minds of whites that drives them to such extremes about human relations? Is this a particular problem of certain ethnic groups of whites? Is it a problem of certain regions of the country? In particular religions? I believe that many Wilderness dwellers remain baffled by the hatred or fear that whites feel. At any rate, the president of the Shoal Creek

Country Club apologized for his remark about whites feeling uncomfortable with black members.

Commenting on racism in private clubs, an editorial in *USA Today* went right to the point with the statement that "if private clubs want to bar minorities or women, they must live with public scorn and without public tax benefits."[16] Furthermore, according to the editorial, "it's time for private clubs and pro golf to join the 20th century, because their discrimination is unacceptable."[17] Tiger Woods has made some difference, but there are still too many clubs across the country that practice discrimination. Just a little over ten years ago the Los Angeles Country Club was investigated because of discrimination. In fact, Don Jackson, a citizen, sought an investigation because, in his words, the club did not admit African Americans. Why wouldn't African Americans be concerned about the implications of a club refusing to admit blacks, even though it is located in one of the most racially diverse cities in America?

A similar situation was discovered in New Orleans, and an editorial comment by the *Times-Picayune* declared that clubs that discouraged or prohibited blacks from joining did not have ground to stand upon if they based their exclusion on racial, ethnic, or sexual discrimination.[18] Obviously there is a moral consciousness on the part of the media that was not seen years ago. We are on the verge of erasing some of the offenses of racism.

Discrimination in education has become synonymous with the most pervasive form of racism. Although discrimination abounds in education throughout the nation, the South is at the center of the struggle around school discrimination and desegregation. Around the beginning of the twentieth century, southern blacks lost the right to vote, which had been granted after the Civil War by the Fifteenth Amendment. However, once whites returned to power in the South, the local governments intensified discrimination, often killing blacks who attempted to vote, passing the Jim Crow laws and making segregation the rule of the South. The most obvious symbol of this discrimination was in the locally segregated schools. Since the Jim Crow period in the South was so intense, it had a profound impact upon the shape of educational relationships in the South and throughout the nation. A California Department of Fair Employment and Housing report that two black administrators at the Centinela Valley Union High School District had been unfairly charged with wrongdoing when they were accused of misconduct, and that the school district had practiced racial discrimination, demonstrates that racism is still operative in education. Now, obviously, some decisions by school districts and school boards cannot be called racially motivated, but those actions ought to be clearly seen as fair to all concerned. If, for example, a school board closes schools in a city but chooses to close schools only in the predominantly black community, it seems racially motivated, even though the school board may argue an economic reason.

The old adage that African Americans are "the last hired and the first fired" is increasingly changing to reflect the downturn in the economy and the shifting structure of our society. Now the Wilderness dwellers are often "the never hired and the left to the side." But those who are still able to find positions in industry or education must face the music of discrimination. General Motors recently settled a class-action suit for discrimination against African Americans. The suit alleged discrimination against black employees in pay and promotion. Under the settlement GM will pay about $3 million to thirty-eight hundred past and present employees, and will set up an unusual computer model to monitor future personnel practices, comparing career advancement of blacks and whites while taking educational backgrounds and job experience into account.[19] One can already predict what the model will find with regard to race: Blacks have been consistently discriminated against. When one of the largest corporations in America, one with an international reach, is found guilty of discrimination, one must ask: If gold rusts, what will happen to silver?

Smaller, less visible firms often try to avoid antidiscrimination laws. For example, the Andrew Corporation allegedly attempted to avoid racial discrimination laws because it was located in a predominantly white Chicago suburb. However, the US Equal Employment

Opportunity Commission won a discrimination ruling against the firm, charging that it discriminated against blacks in hiring for clerical jobs. The pattern is remarkably similar: In both large and small companies, there is a clear attempt to avoid hiring African Americans.[20] This is not a situation limited to American companies or corporations. Foreign companies that have set up in America often follow the same discriminatory practices as some American companies. For example, Volkswagen of America Inc. agreed to pay $670,000 and the United Auto Workers will pay $48,000 to settle claims that they discriminated against black employees.

African American economist Julianne Malveaux has written that despite antidiscrimination laws, thousands of black workers experience racism daily.[21] Discrimination remains a problem nationwide. Take four examples of discrimination from different cities and states. Six employees of the Holiday Spa in Washington, D.C., alleged systematic discrimination against them while they worked at the firm. Three employees of Northwest Airlines filed a class-action suit against their employer for discrimination. Seven employees of State Farm Insurance Company filed suit against their employer in Texas. Nine Domino's employees, all black, sued the pizza chain and twenty-one of its Atlanta franchises owned by Michael L. Orcutt, charging racial discrimination in the denial of raises, promotions, and other opportunities. Discrimination in some franchises in terms of job opportunities is clearly part of the traditional, slow process of equality. With jobs scarce in a downsizing economy, African Americans have often had to choose their pride over their employment. One can take mistreatment for only so long before retaliating; this is the history of abuse. But there is also a price to be paid for pride in a society that has made a habit of disrespecting African Americans.

There is always the threat of retaliation if the Wilderness dweller speaks up for rights. Those who are seen as "uppity," a term common in the South and often compared to the South African word "cheeky" to refer to persons who are willing to seek fair play, often are punished. Zina Garrison, a black deputy, filed a racial discrimination suit against the Jefferson Parish, Louisiana, Sheriff's Office, and was fired immediately by Sheriff Harry Lee.[22] Ostensibly Lee believed Garrison had violated the protocols of his office; but more than that, a black man had brought charges of racial discrimination against the sheriff's office. Or take the case of Bobbie Fisher, a black woman and former legal secretary at CBS in Hollywood, who faced misdemeanor charges of petty theft from her company. Fisher maintained that the charges were in retaliation for a racial discrimination complaint she had filed.[23] The effect of some retaliation measures is to silence the complainer. Other African Americans, who may be discriminated against in promotions and assignments, may decide not to pursue their complaints if they see that others who complain lose their jobs or incur considerable legal debt.

Even with the threat of harassment and the loss of a job, thousands of racial discrimination actions are filed each year by African Americans in every conceivable type of profession. For example, three black employees of the US Army Corps of Engineers in Pittsburgh charged that government agency with racial harassment and employment discrimination.[24] African American agents at the racially and politically troubled Bureau of Alcohol, Tobacco, and Firearms filed a lawsuit in the fall of 1990 saying the agency discriminated in its hiring, promotion, and evaluation of blacks.

Unions, both public and corporate, are not exempt from charges of racism. Three clerical workers for the American Federation of State, County, and Municipal Employees filed a class-action lawsuit charging the union with discriminating against blacks. The increasing boldness of Wilderness dwellers in challenging the institutions of the nation suggest that there is a perception that our voices matter; this is an indication that racism will be confronted.

Police forces have not been immune from charges of racism and discrimination, in both their public faces toward African and Hispanic communities and their private, internal relations with African American police officers. New York City, with the largest urban police force in the nation, has had heated, tension-filled discussions about the nature of a police review board. Former Mayor David N. Dinkins supported a civilian review board with the power to investigate cases of police harassment of civilians or any other misconduct. He was roundly criticized during the fall of 1992 for suggesting that civilians could evaluate what the police did. Indeed, Phil Caruso, the leader of New York's police union, argued that a civilian review board could not adequately judge a police's conduct. Caruso's response created apprehension among African Americans.[25]

Former Mayor Ed Rendell of Philadelphia, a leading Democrat long supported by black voters, vetoed the Philadelphia City Council's initial establishment of a police review board in 1993.[26] Intense reactions to his decision in the African American and Latino communities underscored the wide gap in perception between those of the Promise and those of the Wilderness. Within the African American community there is the very real belief that most police departments in the nation are agents of white supremacy. Furthermore, blacks know that two different standards usually operate when police are confronted with situations of unruly white and black teenagers. Whites, the police have been known to say, are "feeling their oats," but blacks engaged in similar behavior are "wilding."

Internally, tensions between white and black officers threaten to create intolerable situations in the maintenance of law and order. What African American patrollers are seeking in their capacities as peace officers is equal protection of the procedures of the force, fair treatment of African Americans, and nonracialism in promotions and assignments. These are important concerns, since African Americans remember the "point man" punishment that was occasionally given to African American soldiers in the Vietnam War. As the first truly integrated war, veterans say the Vietnam War allowed the full dimension of the American social scene to come to the front on the battlefield. Being the point man meant encountering danger or the enemy first, and many soldiers claimed after the Vietnam War that some African Americans were killed because they were given the duty of being point men. So when it comes to the case of the police, a sort of military force within urban communities, blacks often wonder about the type of assignments they receive.

The issue is complicated by the consistent racism in promotions. Eleven black deputies filed claims against five cities that subcontract with the Ventura County, California, Sheriff's Department for their municipal services, charging they were denied promotions on the basis of race.[27] The fact that the eleven deputies believed that they had been discriminated against shows the widespread nature of the fury against perceived racism.

Of course, being denied a promotion or being fired improperly can lead to changes, damages, and consciousness raising. This is particularly true for those who have sought to avoid any identification as African.

A black employee who was fired as part of an effort to cut costs won a lawsuit against Texaco. The employee claimed that she didn't receive a proper performance evaluation because the company was afraid of giving her any grounds for a racial discrimination lawsuit. On May 14, 1991, the *Wall Street Journal* reported that the employee had no previous problems with the company. Nevertheless, in refusing to give her a proper performance evaluation the company was attempting to circumvent the possibility that it would be accused of racial discrimination.[28] But by its circumvention of the regular procedures for evaluation, the company demonstrated discriminatory actions.

This is not an unfamiliar situation. On May 5, 1991, Robert C. Newberry wrote in the *Houston Post* that he was saddened and frustrated that the great majority of African Americans will never reach certain positions because of employment discrimination.[29] He cited research that found black job seekers were denied equal treatment about 20 percent of the time. Most African Americans would argue that this is more like 50 percent of the time. Whites might argue that they never mistreat blacks. I once told a dean at a university that it was a racist institution. She became rather annoyed and said it was not a racist institution. I said to her, "The society is racist, the synagogues are racist, the churches are racist. We live in a racist country. That does not mean that you personally are consciously practicing racism, but the institution is racist."

The Urban Institute report "Opportunities Denied, Opportunities Diminished: Discrimination in Hiring" marks the first major study directly measuring unequal treatment of black and white job seekers.[30] The study underscored what we already knew about hiring discrimination. In fact, the conditions in society push African Americans toward a nationalistic solution; that is, to turn increasingly toward the development of separate institutions and businesses. Thus, a dual objective in the economic arena becomes the integration into the white-controlled corporations and business areas while developing black businesses that open up job opportunities. Until there are enough jobs created by Wilderness dwellers to employ themselves, the jobs in the public and private sectors ought to be open to all fairly.

At one time we believed that the utility companies, like the federal government, were areas where there would be less racism. However, the recent complaint by Oliver Washington demonstrated that utility companies are just like other American firms. He filed a complaint with the Equal Employment Opportunity Commission (EEOC) regarding his job with the Chicago Department of Water, claiming that his supervisor used pressure tactics on blacks.[31] This is one of scores of complaints filed by African American workers against utility companies that have pressured them to leave by giving them poor work assignments or harassing and threatening them. Nothing in the history of this nation suggests that this kind of pressure and these kinds of tactics will end soon. However, our fury cannot be misunderstood; it is a reasonable fury.

In a letter to the editor, James W. Compton of the Chicago Urban League cites findings of significant, pervasive employment disparities between inner-city blacks in Chicago and suburban whites, and says that an easing of residential segregation in the suburbs is needed.

Nearly one out of five federally sponsored programs under the Job Training Partnership Act discriminates against women and blacks, according to a General Accounting Office (GAO) study.[32]

Wilderness dwellers have seldom received a fair share of good jobs even when their educational qualifications are equal to or exceed those of whites. In fact, taking the construction industry as an example, even when educational barriers are removed, employment discrimination against African Americans is common. In an article in *Politics and Society*, Roger Waldinger and Thomas Bailey showed that the perception that the construction industry is doing better than other industries in hiring and promoting African Americans is dead wrong.[33] Every industry has problems because society's fabric has supported an anti-African posture. Take the dispute involving former African American employees of Pepsi's Exeter, Michigan, plant who claimed that Pepsi hired only four people from their plant, all of them white, when the company relocated to Detroit.[34]

This represents the kind of unnecessary situation with which African Americans are often faced, situations that could be alleviated if whites did not practice racism. However, the Pepsi plant gave African Americans every reason to complain. All of its black employees were laid off and eventually fired. Michael Wimberly reported that the white employees were allegedly no more qualified than the black employees, yet Pepsi hired them over all blacks.[35] When whites have the opportunity to choose other whites over blacks, it seems that the logic of race dictates that they will choose whites over blacks. This is the crime of racism, for which there has never been a sufficient remedy in American society.

Fury for the African American is often wrapped in the cloak of the employment environment. We are most at risk in the job market. Like the African American employees of the Exeter Pepsi plant, the masses of black people react in fury. And all our fury is turned back on us by whites who ask, "Why are you angry?" We are once again reminded that we may be the only people in the United States who deeply believe in the ideology of an equitably integrated society. In some senses it may be said that during the period of segregation we were better off with our own businesses and employing our own people. Yet the attraction of an integrated society actually destroyed many of the businesses and much of the entrepreneurship that had been the bulwark of African American economic progress. Now we see ourselves as the most ardent promoters of an open society at a time when the doors to an integrated society are barely ajar in many sectors.

Discrimination in employment is bad enough, but many employment agencies have been known to discriminate themselves. In 1991 the Cosmopolitan Care Corporation, one of New York City's largest employment concerns, agreed to pay more than $1.75 million to settle lawsuits that it discriminated against black and Hispanic job applicants.[36] What infuriates the African American community is that this type of lawsuit should never have to be filed in the first place. But the evidence is clear from many sources that much of the poverty in the African American community is related to discrimination. Tom Larson wrote an article for the *Review of Black Political Economy* in 1992 in which he showed that African American male migration is constrained by discriminatory practices in employment.[37] Often when companies move from one standard metropolitan area to another they leave behind many African American workers. Past and present discriminatory practices help explain the labor market problems confronted by young African American males.

Discrimination against African Americans appears to be pervasive and is not limited to one or two sectors of the society. In fact, universities, the leading repositories of American civilization, have fared no better on average than other institutions in the hiring of African Americans. Some major universities have no significant numbers of African Americans in their tenured ranks. This is particularly evident at the Ivy League universities, where no institution approaches an African American faculty percentage equal to the African American population of 12 percent. At most universities, many departments have no African Americans at all.

At prestigious private universities, with less federal intervention, fewer African Americans hold tenured positions. Derrick Bell, a distinguished African American law professor, resigned his tenured post at Harvard Law School because the school would not commit itself to hire an African American woman as a tenured professor. This was one of the most poignant protests in academic history. Bell said that Harvard disproportionately excluded black women and African Americans from its faculty.[38] White academics like to believe they do not hold the same racist views as their less educated brothers and sisters, and therefore must not be judged in the same way. Yet colleges in America are the preeminent bastions of bias. They contain, in their structural and symbolic memory, all the worst elements of white supremacy, and because of their arrogance they are often unable to encourage major transformations. Every possibility of transformation in the character and composition of the curriculum or the faculty is more dishonored than honored. If you ask why there aren't more African American graduate students in engineering schools, you still get racist answers: for example, "African Americans cannot handle mathematics" or "Blacks have no inclination for mathematics."

Meanwhile, those same schools are able to find hundreds of Asian students for enrollment. Take the example of the Health Careers Opportunities Program (HCOP) at Temple University, which was designed to have a student population of 80 percent African American, 10 percent Hispanic, 5 percent Asian, and 5 percent white in order to overcome the many years of discrimination against African Americans. By the summer of 1993 the HCOP class consisted of nearly 50 percent Asian students, almost half of whom were foreign born. According to the program's mentor, this increase in Asian students was directly related to the way the white and Asian supervisors ran the program. The black and Hispanic population did not decrease because the pool of worthy candidates decreased in those communities; they were simply not selected.

It may be true that African Americans find social, political, and philosophical ideas more necessary in terms of intellectual growth at this juncture in history, but it is unfair and untrue to claim that

African Americans are uninterested in mathematics or any other science. Uri Treisman of the University of Texas has demonstrated that African American and Hispanic students excel in mathematics if one takes group culture into consideration when teaching. Treisman and I had a discussion at Kalamazoo College about the importance of culture on learning. We had both been invited by Prof. Jeanne Baraka-Love to hold a discourse on culture and black learning styles. At the end of the day, the students and faculty of the college understood the relevance of culture to education. Nothing is more important in learning than recognizing the cultural foundations of the learner. If Treisman could use what amounted to Afrocentric principles to teach mathematics, why can't other teachers do the same?

Mathematics was created in Africa by Africans. It is a part of the intellectual heritage of Africa. The oldest mathematics books in the world are African books, the *Rhind Papyrus* and the *Moscow Papyrus*. Both of these books of mathematical principles and propositions are the works of African minds. They predate anything else in the world in mathematics. The African continent claims as much legitimacy in mathematics as any other continent. If African Americans do not enter the mathematics field in the numbers that we expect, then the answer must be in the conditions of the Wilderness itself; indeed, on the continent of Africa thousands of students study the higher principles of mathematics.

To transform education it is necessary to take definite ethical positions. Administrators must begin with the idea that racism is intolerable in a decent, progressive, and humanistic society. This sentiment must be conveyed to all administrators and must become a natural part of all decision making. Racism in education cannot be overcome by the expression of goodwill; it must be confronted constantly in every conscious way. When he became the president of the State University of New York at Albany, H. Patrick Swygert, who was later president of Howard University, declared a war on bigotry. The university *had* to actively seek to improve the educational and social chances of all of its students. While there was no great fanfare to this campaign, Swygert gradually gathered around him a group of academic leaders who understood the value of transformation. There are other such successes, but it is a difficult job in a divided society. How do you educate all the citizens who need to be educated in a pluralistic society? You cannot do it by depending upon the patterns of the past, which are designed to maintain the status quo. You must draw new lines around admissions and interests, create new symmetries in academic leadership, and underscore at every useful moment the educational mission of the university. Thus, whereas some administrators do not provide leadership in this area, the department chairs and academic deans often follow suit. On the other hand, it *is* possible to gather energetic and progressive leaders who understand the mission of a university. Such individuals can lead an institution to transformation. While this may work well in a university setting where the leadership is fairly clear-cut, it is more difficult in amorphous situations like the housing industry, where there is not one all-powerful guiding force.

Housing discrimination is still a major fact of African American life, even in the most affluent sections of the nation. The legacy of the slave's shack and the white planter's mansion remains with us. The Villas, a Virginia Beach, Virginia, family, filed a $1.7-million discrimination suit in which they alleged they were kept from buying a home because they were black. The Villa family also filed suit against Womble Realty Company. Obviously, this is not an isolated case. In 1990 a Maryland fair-housing agency filed a lawsuit against four companies, alleging that advertisements for the rental or sale of properties discouraged blacks because of the near-absence of black models. Here the idea was to show by symbolism that Africans were unwelcome and thus did not choose to live in those residences.

George Anderson examined the racism and discrimination that has produced de facto segregation in the United States in spite of the rhetoric and laws of the past fifty years.[39] He found that despite the advances made since the 1960s, African Americans are still confined to disadvantaged residential areas characterized by inferior schools, higher crime rates, poorer public services, and isolation from expanding job opportunities.

Racial discrimination in the housing field is pervasive, and the activity on the part of African Americans to counteract it is persistent. In 1991 a US Circuit Court of Appeals upheld the right of a black woman to sue an all-white Baltimore neighborhood, even though she never bid on a house because a real estate agent said the privately controlled neighborhood did not admit blacks.[40]

Private conventions and agreements to break the law of the land still exist in many communities. Unfortunately, there is no listing of such privately held agreements and African Americans learn about them only when we prepare to purchase a home. The fact that privately controlled neighborhoods can refuse to admit any citizen of this country is unacceptable. Although this practice is illegal, enough whites live in such racist enclaves that de facto segregation has become a matter of style.

Consider the fact that a HUD study found that housing discrimination occurs in the majority of cases in which African Americans attempt to rent apartments or buy houses. Hispanics encounter discrimination half the time when seeking apartments and most of the time when looking for houses. Discrimination in housing effectively keeps the nation segregated and isolates blacks, Latinos, and whites in ethnic and racial enclaves. In *Enemies: The Clash of Races*, Haki Madhubuti, poet and professor at Chicago State University, argued that the conditions in America as a result of white racism made it difficult, if not impossible, to think of how we shall overcome. Of course, Andrew Hacker makes much the same point in *Two Nations*.[41] These writers express their despair that racism continues to be an abiding problem in society long after slavery was abolished and segregation declared illegal. My argument remains that the generation of racism is a result of white racial supremacy as an implicit or explicit doctrine in the American society. Thus, we see racism in the housing industry as in education, in employment as well as in health care.

Housing issues represent an array of attitudes and behaviors. Since whites, according to an Urban Institute study, are no more tolerant of integrated housing now than a decade ago, there has not been and cannot be any decrease in discrimination against African Americans seeking to rent or to buy a home.[42]

Many white people who otherwise consider themselves enlightened practice subtle forms of racism such as avoidance, membership in clubs that implicitly exclude other races, blaming societal problems such as drugs and poverty on blacks, supporting exclusive residential communities that do not permit African Americans, and refusing mortgage loans to blacks who seek to purchase houses. One of the major complaints during the 2000 election debacle in Florida was that the police stopped African Americans and steered them out of their own districts to nonexistent polling places. The police could not believe that blacks would be voting in the same neighborhoods as some whites.

Martin Luther King Jr. once articulated the African American's position with great clarity on this issue. He wrote: "The question of the character of the potential Negro neighbor is not a matter of inquiry. If it were, a Cicero, Illinois, would welcome a Ralph Bunche into the community rather than an Al Capone."[43]

I can think of no sector in the American society that harks back to the days of outright racial hostility and vocal white supremacy more than the housing industry. Whether in whites' response to the possibility of a middle-income black family—or any black family, for that matter—is moving into a predominantly white neighborhood, or in the lending community for mortgages, housing is a bastion of racist attitudes. Banking regulators have yet to find a solution to end mortgage discrimination against blacks. Yet neither the presidential leadership nor Congress has made a strong case against the banks. Fear of the electorate is one reason leaders seek to avoid the issue of nondiscrimination in mortgage lending. In the minds of Wilderness dwellers, there has been little support at the highest government levels for policies that would eradicate some of the last vestiges of racial discrimination.

A host of opinion leaders can be found who are ready to condemn the victim and criticize African Americans who complain about unethical Realtors and racist homeowners. Such political leaders and intellectuals do not see African Americans as members of the nation in the same way that whites are members of the nation.

Conservatives usually frame the argument in terms of values. They complain that African Americans would neither be treated unfairly nor criticized if only we possessed the proper values, just like white people. What they mean is that blacks must be made "acceptable" to whites in order to be fully integrated into the American nation. Of course, I reject this framework for citizenship and participation in the national life of this country. There is no "standard" American.

Some whites see blacks as "enemies" and therefore cannot accept our legitimate demands for constitutional rights. Occasionally the government will investigate complaints even if there is limited national leadership in this area to exhort the nation to political unity. In 1991 the Justice Department agreed to a sting operation to uncover racist practices in the Detroit housing market because African Americans were being rejected for mortgages twice as often as whites.[44] This is not a unique situation; landlord and mortgage company bias is rampant across the nation.

An investigation into landlord practices revealed that bias against African Americans was very strong in Washington, D.C., even in the 1990s. There are still enough racists in the nation's capital to cause African Americans to harbor deep anger. We know that the perpetrators of these crimes know what they are doing, and those who benefit from their racism also know what they are doing.[45]

Housing may be one of the sectors where the steady toll of discriminatory acts has the greatest visible impact, because we can see the segregated neighborhoods. However, the judicial experience is the most sobering. Because of its place in the American mythology as fair and unbiased, we are stunned to see a Supreme Court that consistently rules against the interests of the nation's least powerful citizens. Even with the appointment of women and blacks, the Court has demonstrated anachronistic interpretations of the law in social situations. Clarence Thomas, only the second black in history to hold a seat on the Supreme Court, has shown that he can be as reactionary as the most conservative white justices. Clearly seeking to abandon the philosophy of the venerable civil rights lawyer and former Supreme Court Justice Thurgood Marshall, Thomas wasted no time showing his true colors by becoming one of the most conservative and reactionary judges in the Court. Since the Reagan-Bush court appointees gained ascendancy on the bench, African Americans have not felt the sense of hope experienced during the days of the Warren Court. I believe the judiciary has failed the American public and has often contributed to the distress African Americans feel. Indeed, US Civil Rights Commissioner Francis Guess has called for African Americans to renew the common struggle against racism to counter the attitude of a Supreme Court that has supported discriminatory acts.

Outrages of all kinds continue to happen despite the rhetoric of progress. Two angry mothers of African American male students at the University of Illinois–Chicago said that police indiscriminately took a white youth on a door-to-door search of dorm rooms looking for black males after three white youths were allegedly beaten. There is only one explanation for behavior that singles out African Americans: racism. A habit of seeking more subtle reasons for discrimination has led many writers to avoid the discussion of racism. Of course, I am not the first to recognize the complexity of the social and political issues involved in human relations; yet this move away from a discussion of racism has resulted in a proliferation of all forms of discriminatory behaviors. According to a Washington, D.C., lawyers' group that filed a federal suit to stop what it called pervasive discrimination among some of the city's cab companies, blacks in the area are seven times as likely as whites to be passed while trying to hail a taxi.[46]

In Boston, Massachusetts; Milwaukee, Wisonsin; Rock Hill, South Carolina; and Camden, New Jersey, there have been cases of whites committing serious crimes and blaming them on blacks. In the Boston case, Charles Stuart murdered his pregnant wife, Carol, in a brutal attack. Scores of black men were picked up by the police and interrogated, some ruthlessly, in an effort to secure a confession. Stuart claimed that a black man got in the backseat of his Toyota, shot Carol in the head, and shot him in the abdomen. When the smoke cleared around the investigation, Stuart was the key suspect and all evidence pointed to his guilt. In the meantime, Stuart, sensing that he had been caught, leaped to his death in the Charles River. The Rock Hill case involved Susan Smith, who killed her two young sons by drowning them in a lake and then blamed the murders on phantom African Americans. She was later shown to be lying and was convicted of the crime. The case in Milwaukee was similar. Jesse Anderson stabbed his wife, Barbara, twenty-one times, stabbed himself three times, and claimed that black males had attacked them. He was arrested by police and charged with murdering his wife. In Camden, New Jersey, a district attorney, distraught over the prospect of losing his job, manufactured an incident in which he was supposedly shot at by several black males. He was later found guilty of fabricating the entire scenario. There have been other cases of this type, including white men who have raped women and then claimed that black men did it. Or, as was the case a few years ago in Delaware, a high school girl who was raped by her white boyfriend claimed it was done by a black man. What these cases show is a racial sickness that reaches all levels of the society. The Boston, Milwaukee, and Camden incidents were perpetrated not by poor whites, but by middle- and upper-class whites who believed that they could get away with murder by convincing a public inclined to believe the worst about black males that they and their loved ones were victims of the stereotypical violent black male. As this litany shows, racism makes all of us its victims. The legacy of the lynching of African Americans during the early years of this century is exacerbated by the violence of codes, personal and corporate, against the African American condition.

⊠⊠⊠

Racial discrimination creates inordinate blocks to political and economic leadership for African Americans. This is true despite the superhuman efforts that have been made and are being made by increasing numbers of blacks. But the highway of leadership, in most areas, has few access lanes for African Americans. We see this most sharply in the area of sports management. Since the presence of African Americans in major-league sports is well known and well respected, it would seem that leadership positions would be available to more African Americans in management. Nevertheless, in 2002 attorney Johnny Cochran sued the National Football League for having only two black head coaches in the organization. Patrick Reardon has written that "no matter how rich and famous a black athlete becomes, his chances of getting a coaching or managing job are almost nonexistent. The inequalities in sports begin as early as high school, and some African-American athletes think they are valued only as long as their physical capabilities last."[47]

Remarks made on April 6, 1987, by Al Campanis, then general manager of the Los Angeles Dodgers, on Ted Koppel's *Nightline* were considered classic racist language. Campanis told Koppel that he did not think prejudice had anything to do with the limited numbers of blacks in management in baseball. He said, "I don't believe it's prejudice. I truly believe they may not have some of the necessities to be, let's say, a field manager or perhaps a general manager." When a powerful sports figure, someone with decision-making power to hire or to fire, makes such remarks, it is an indication of the depth of the prejudice against blacks in positions of management. A few years later Fay Vincent, then the commissioner of Major League Baseball, was quoted as saying, "Here we are, 17 years after Frank Robinson became the first black manager in the major leagues, and today, in 1992, we have only three minority managers in the major leagues, only three black assistant general managers in the major leagues and not one black manager in the minor leagues. That is unacceptable." Two of the three "minority managers" referred to by Vincent were leaders of Canadian teams: Cito Gaston of the Toronto Blue Jays and Felipe Alou of the Montreal Expos.

No more than five black head coaches have served in the National Football League; in 2002 there were only two. While we can applaud the hiring of African American coaches, we cannot afford to ignore reality. Although 65 percent of the players in the league are African Americans, the head offices do not reflect that concentration of players. A true transformation in values must be placed at the head offices; that is, general managers and partners must see the morality and the practicality of having a front office that is consonant to the goodwill on the team and makes sense ethically.

The National Basketball Association (NBA) was the first professional league to have a black managing partner, Peter Bynoe of Denver. Bynoe sold his shares to the company in 1992. There have been six black general managers in the NBA, but of a total of seventy-nine vice presidents, only five have been black. In addition, there are only five black head coaches. African Americans remain the last hired. For example, the last thirteen coaches to be hired by the league's teams have been white with the exception of one. This is so despite the fact that the athletes are 80 percent black. Jason Kidd, Tim Duncan, David Robinson, Michael Jordan, Allen Iverson, Kobe Bryant, Shaquille O'Neal, and other superstars seem to have no impact on the hiring in the front office. Of course, no one is asking these athletes to be unduly involved in their front offices, but I cannot think of a similar situation where superstar athletes would not seek opportunities in the front offices for others in their community. If you had a team that was 80 percent Korean with no Koreans in the front office, you'd have a problem, a perception problem and a management problem—perhaps even a racial problem. It is no different with African Americans.

The issue of race is complicated, as Cornel West tells us in *Race Matters*, but it is extremely simple at the level of personal racism, where individuals in the society bring their biases to work or to play.

Race, skin color, class, and national origin are all wrapped into the same fabric, but skin color is the marker that initially sets African Americans apart. Yet the issue of skin color is tricky: An East Indian may be darker than an African American, but since he is not of immediate African origin he is not subjected to the same atrocities as the African American. The African American's hair texture brings to the mind of whites the idea of involuntary servitude. While Indians may have served as indentured servants or virtual slaves in the Caribbean, South America, or India under English rule, there is no identification of them with servitude in America; hence, the color of the skin is only one criterion for racial victimization. Some Indians may also have British accents, a throwback to India's colonization, that, ironically, in a white racist society, might give them an advantage.

While racism may suggest a system of discrimination based on racial or national origin, the violent attacks on African Americans often because of the color of their skin is akin to the lynching phenomenon. Yusef Hawkins was killed in the Brooklyn neighborhood of Bensonhurst on August 23, 1989, by a gang of bat-wielding, gun-toting white youth. It was a case of mistaken identity in the sense that the whites had intended to murder another black who was dating a white girl, but Yusef Hawkins happened to be coming along the street at about the time they thought the other man would be arriving. Yusef lost his life because he was black and walking through a white neighborhood. But is this America? Why shouldn't a black be able to walk through *any* neighborhood? Of course, the same question could be asked of any neighborhood and any ethnic or racial group—and it *should* be asked.

African Americans commit less than 10 percent of all racial bias crimes. This has been consistent for the past fifteen years. If one looks at a typical year in New York City, one sees that of more than four hundred racial bias crimes in 1987, only twenty-three could clearly be said to be crimes by blacks against whites. In the New York City area, the case of policeman Gary Spath, who was accused of shooting teenager Phillip Pannell in the back after a foot chase, contributed to the racial and social breakdown of what was once thought to be a harmonious community.

Similar incidents pitting the police against black males have been recorded around the country. A few years ago the death of Rick Rankin in Phoenix underscored the tenderness of racial harmony in that desert city. Rankin was apprehended by security guards in a store because he was suspected of bouncing checks. The security guards caught him in a choke hold around the neck. He was thrown into a car and taken to the hospital, where he died. Rankin never got his day in court. The security guards got off completely, with no indictments.

In 1991 former Los Angeles Laker star and businessman Jamaal Wilkes complained of being harassed by the police. Wilkes was stopped and handcuffed during a routine traffic stop, allegedly because a light over his license plate was out. Wilkes complained about being handcuffed during the incident. It did not matter that he was a visible personality, well known, and very rich. Being black in America was his crime. And the intensity of his apprehension, his sense of self being violated, fan the flames in the many Los Angeleses of the nation. Wilkes's case could easily be glossed over, his clothes brushed off, and apologies given, but in too many instances others have been criminalized and sent to prison. It is a simple process. Some of us are able to avoid it by appearing obsequious or by feigning ignorance of an infraction, but none of us escape the scarring of the soul that is meant for us.

Not long ago Ngugi wa Thiong'o—in many critics' estimation one of the greatest contemporary writers—was a guest of mine in Philadelphia. As I drove him to Temple University to give a lecture, we came upon a police car parked in the middle of a narrow street near the university. Its location made passing it on either side impossible. My first inclination was to blow my horn so that the officer would move his car to the side of the street so I could pass. However, three hundred years of history haunted me from the moment I saw that white policeman sitting in that car in the middle of the road. I am not sure Ngugi, a Kenyan, who had written of police brutality and official mistreatment in Kenya, felt the same weight of history, but I suspected he might, because of the cruelty of his own treatment in Kenya. I know he did not understand the American history of danger that was in the catalog of my mind. After several minutes, aware of the rush we were in to get Ngugi to his speech, I blew my car's horn gently. Of course, the sound came out the same way as if I had leaned on it.

The officer laid his newspaper aside, got out of his car and came to the driver's side of my car. He looked at Ngugi and myself, two short black men in a red car, pointed his finger in my face, and said, "Boy, if you ever blow your horn at a policeman again you will be arrested." Ngugi had just recently come out of the Kenyan jails, and I could sense his distress at this situation. My distress was probably as great or greater—and I had not been in prison. I had only lived in the United States. So I said to the officer, in an effort to calm him down, "I'm sorry, I won't do it again." I was scared to say more, fearing he might take any word I said as a reason to harass us more. He asked me for my driver's license. I obliged, and he looked at it and returned it to me, then got in his car and pulled it to the side of the street. Relieved, I drove into the parking lot at Temple University. I am not sure if either Ngugi or I said anything more until after his speech. I often wondered if he thought I should have contested the officer's right to occupy the street. At any rate, Ngugi gave me no indication one way or the other; it was as if he had seen this scene many times in his own life.

I have chosen the metaphor "potholes of racial hostility," because they are often unexpected. You are minding your own business, with whites far away from your mind, until you read the newspaper, watch a television program, hear a radio commentator, or run into someone on the job whose only purpose that day is to try to reenslave African Americans. Here, I do not literally mean to physically enslave, but to "put Africans in their place," as the white southerners used to wish. Our place is wherever we are and, at this moment, African Americans are domiciled in the United States. This country has become, through our blood, sweat, and tears, one of the lands of African nationality.

# CHAPTER NINE

# THE NATIONAL SURVIVAL

W hen I was twenty-two years old I drove in my old 1956 Chevrolet from Oklahoma to California, seeking to enter graduate school at Pepperdine University. On my way West I experienced many adventures, stopped in numerous small towns along the highway, veering off always in search of the African American communities in places like El Paso, Gallup, Albuquerque, Flagstaff, and Barstow. There was a solace I enjoyed about seeing the mountains, the streams, and the big skies as I drove leisurely across the country.

One day, in the late morning, I saw an eagle hovering high over a stream, and although I knew that eagles could fly thirty miles per hour, I was not prepared for its next action. In a moment the large, mottled brown-and-white bird swooped down toward the stream faster than I could see while driving. I pulled to the side of the highway and watched the ensuing drama as the eagle caught a fish in its talons but struggled to get its prey out of the water. The eagle began swimming, using its wide wings as paddles, toward the shore. After several minutes of struggle with the fish, apparently too large to vanquish, the eagle, the mightiest of birds, abandoned the large fish. It caught a smaller one and flew away with the fish in its giant talons.

For the sake of our national survival there are some necessary actions we have to take as a nation. Like the eagle, we must see clearly our realities and our possibilities.

The first action that must be taken is a national apology to the descendants of enslaved Africans for slavery itself. This is the moral thing to do. It can only be done by the national legislature, Congress, passing a resolution of apology. The president of the United States should take the lead in securing the passage of such a resolution and it should be made a priority on the national agenda. To apologize is noble; not to apologize, in the light of the horrors of enslavement, segregation, and continuing discrimination, is arrogant. A proper apology is an expression, written or spoken, of regret, sorrow, or remorse for the suffering, insult, degradation, and injury experienced by Africans at the hands of Europeans in this nation.

African Americans have been wronged by the nation itself. This is not an indictment of any one individual or of any one state or civic organization. No one should take the issue of an official apology per-sonally; it should be seen as a collective quest for national unity. There are those who are quick to say that they had nothing to do with the enslavement of Africans, and consequently they have nothing for which they should apologize. This is the attitude that undercuts the Promise for all Americans because it obscures the fact that whites have used color, race, and economic privilege as a way to achieve advantage. The colossal guilt, often blocked from our view, is collec-tive. It was the American nation that supported, by laws and customs, the enslavement of, segregation from, and discrimination against Africans. An apology from the government of the United States would signal to those retaining vestiges of racism that the national vision is for a united nation.

After this apology is made, I believe that five additional steps must be taken in order to solidify the national spirit toward unity. These are not impossibilities; they are practically within the grasp of most communities in the United States. They are: (1) Embrace all of the nation's history; (2) Choose the present as the arena of action; (3) Rewrite our understanding of the national story from the standpoint of the Wilderness in order to see the whole picture; (4) Support the human and cultural rights of every ethnic group; and (5) Open up discussion on reparations to find a way to repair the wrong.

In suggesting these five steps I am guided by the belief that patriotism is, first of all, a national commitment to each other. When the soldier on the battlefield says he is willing to lay down his life for his fellow citizens, he is exhibiting what we say is *patriotism*. In peacetime, what the African American wants to hear, indeed, is what the nation needs to hear—that as citizens we are all willing to give our lives to defend the rights of our fellow citizens. This cannot come and will not come while some feel that they must distinguish between citizens on the basis of race. Consequently, I offer the steps suggested above as a way to ensure our national survival as a unified nation. It is rare that solutions come from the same minds that create the problems. I do not believe I have ever read a solution to the problem of white racial supremacy offered by a white author. Indeed, most of my white colleagues are full of analyses that infer something wrong with the *victims* of white racial domination. Thus, I humbly offer these solutions.

# EMBRACE ALL OF THE NATION'S HISTORY

In 1999 I flew to Texas to narrate a segment of the TNT film *The Faces of Evil*. Phil Tuckett, the film's producer, and his crew picked me up at the Beaumont airport and we drove to Jasper. This is the place where James Byrd Jr., a black man, was dragged to his death behind a pickup truck operated by three white men. Here I was, early one morning at the very site of Byrd's death, deep in the backwoods of Texas with six whites!

My mind raced easily to James Byrd even before we got to the spot where he died, where he was decapitated by the culvert. As I was narrating the events, I noticed a car stopping on the country road. An elderly black man got out and walked over to the site where we were filming. Looking at me, then at the whites, who were rather casually dressed, the old farmer asked me, "What is going on?" I assured him that I was safe. A couple of other blacks came by to ask the same question. So deep was the lack of trust that I had to convince them that Phil Tuckett and the crew meant me no harm.

Only by embracing all of America's history can we be on the road to national social survival. Our history is brutal and bloody. But it is the story of this land, and no amount of trying to hide it from our children or ourselves will ever solve the problem of racism. The history must be confronted in a mature manner. The decimation of the native peoples and the enslavement of the African peoples are twin testaments of the birthing pains of our national consciousness. Understanding both of these blights on our past and present is critical to our survival.

I couldn't get James Byrd off of my mind for many weeks after the filming. He must have lost all sense of time and place when it became clear to him that he was going to be murdered. The victim of racism is often a victim of context: smothering reality. How fast can you run? What were the other cases like when Africans had to run for their lives? There is nothing before you but life and death—no frills, just survival. Soldiers must feel this experience when confronted with imminent danger. The phenomenon attacks the perpetrator as well as the victim.

Racism blinds the racist, too, to the world around him or her. A racist may see certain signs of an impending storm, but when told by an observer that a storm is brewing, may refuse to heed the warning. The racist is not rational and does not make sense in his own decision about what to hear and what not to hear.

Racism is a pathology, a mental and social disorder, and many African Americans have taken on the responsibility of compensating for the white abnormality. So some of us change our hairstyles, or wear three-piece suits with watch and chain, or call other African Americans fascists, or affect accents, or alter our manner of walking, or fuss over certain foods, or oppose affirmative-action programs—all to please whites, and perhaps even to secure a job, hoping that whites will validate us because of these changes. This is a sickness and it stifles the real possibility of human maturity or of good interracial relationships, because the problem is not how we look, speak, or wear our clothes. No—we are persecuted, discriminated against, or abused because we are considered inferior to whites by virtue of our heritage or history. *Racists do not like black people because we are black.*

What is blackness? It is only secondarily a color. It is fundamentally a relationship to the Promise, a condition, an experience, and a heritage.

The problem whites have with us is much more than our blackness or our poverty. This is why the official explanations surrounding urban unrest are often inadequate. The official line often reads that Wilderness people rise up because of poverty. Certainly poverty is *an* issue, but *injustice* is *the* issue. When Los Angeles exploded after the first Rodney King verdict, some claimed that it was because there were no jobs. This explanation evades the fundamental issue of a nation dealing with a history of racism. What do we do as a nation to teach people not to be bigots but to embrace justice?

## CHOOSE THE PRESENT AS THE ARENA OF ACTION

Cornel West claims that "Afrocentrism, a contemporary species of black nationalism, is a gallant yet misguided attempt to define an African identity in a white society perceived to be hostile."[1] He goes on to say that Afrocentrism does not "link race to the common good."[2] West, correct in some of his observations, is wrong in these comments about Afrocentricity.

In the first place, Afrocentricity is as different from black nationalism as deconstruction is from white nationalism: One is a theoretical position useful for analysis, and the other is a political ideology maintained with religious fervor. Second, Afrocentricity does not seek "to define an African identity" any more than deconstruction or existentialism or General Systems Theory seeks to define a European identity; it is simply a theoretical perspective. West argues in *Race Matters* that to the so-called race-embracing rebels among African American intellectuals, "rhetoric becomes a substitute for analysis, stimulatory rapping a replacement for serious reading, and uncreative publications an expression of existential catharsis. Much, though not all, of Afrocentric thought fits this bill."[3] This is an unfortunate statement by a writer who understands the seriousness of a challenge to scholarship. West has written without citing any references to the Afrocentric works that fit his bill as rhetoric, stimulatory rapping, and uncreative publications. Thus, he serves up gratuitous commentary that has little substance as analysis of any of the works by Afrocentrists such as Maulana Karenga, Wade Nobles, or Ama Mazama. Nobles, the single most important voice in African American psychology, has written several books and scores of articles on African psychology and has led the restructuring of curricula in several school districts. Karenga is the founder of the Kwanzaa celebration, Kawaida philosophy, and the author of *The Introduction to Black Studies*.[4] Mazama's growing corpus in the philosophy of Afrocentricity is impressive from theoretical and methodological points of view. For West to disdain them and other Afrocentrists for their commitment to working toward uplifting those of the Wilderness is misguided. Self-love and self-determination are not evil; they are the beginning of national reconstruction. To speak about race or racism in the context of the common good, it is important to remember that race is linked to the common good because of the acceptance of self. I am a link to the common good and so are my people, and I cannot distance myself from my community in the

Wilderness and still speak of the common good. What is good for the Wilderness is good for the Promise. The defining moments of self are healthy not just for the African American community, but for the peace and harmony of the society.

Afrocentricity is against disharmony; it is preeminently an intellectual and practical search for harmony. While I understand that race is more a political and social concept than it is a biological concept, it nevertheless has memory in the context of the American Wilderness and Promise. Those who are defined as Africans have different life chances than those who are defined as Europeans.

The position of popular intellectuals like Henry Louis Gates Jr., Glenn Loury, and Shelby Steele who seem to argue for the capitulation of African ideas, that is, cultural abnegation in literature, philosophy, and science, creates unnecessary confusion. While writers such as August Wilson, Charles Fuller, and Martin Kilson have responded vigorously to those who deny that they are black writers, the attitudes of Gates, Loury, and Steele toward the masses of Africans remain troubling. To say that they have, in Cornel West's language, "an elitist attitude" is perhaps useless because it is not so much that they see themselves as representing a certain intellectual position above the rest of the Wilderness that creates the problem; rather, it is their misunderstanding of the Wilderness dwellers that undercuts any useful thought they may advance. There is a saying among the Wilderness dwellers that one should beware those who speak evil of their mothers—meaning one cannot divest oneself of one's culture and then parade as if speaking for it.

I am reminded of the story of a nineteenth-century group of enslaved Africans on a plantation in the piedmont region of North Carolina. Rebuked by the overseer of the plantation as being unworthy of freedom because they were imitative, copycats of whites, several of the enslaved Africans grew angry, and one of them said to the overseer, "What's wrong with being like the master? The master gives us everything we want. He even treats us like his own children. After all, what can we do apart from the master? We have nothing and we know nothing." Whereupon a young African man stepped forward and said, "My freedom is mine. I determine what I want to say, where I will stay, and what I will eat. I may be here now but tomorrow don't look for me here, look for me in the wind, in the storm, look for me in the clouds."

# REWRITE OUR UNDERSTANDING OF THE NATIONAL STORY FROM THE STANDPOINT OF THE WILDERNESS

The Afrocentrists are like the young visionaries, committed to finding their own centers: to inquiring about their own identities, their own culture, and their own history as a way of contributing to the grand flow of humanity without being mere imitators who follow others without first essaying their own experiences. The European Afrocentrists, white people who believe that black people must be viewed as historical subjects and not as objects, seek to understand the way Africans understand reality, history, experiences, and culture without imposing European concepts and ideas.

Afrocentricity is a legitimate understanding of the process of human maturity; we learn from others but we do not have to imitate them. Perhaps the literary figures and conservative pundits who criticize African Americans who are proud of their culture and heritage are victims of a structure of knowledge that detaches them from the actual lives of the Wilderness dwellers. Of course, many whites—and, by extension, some black writers—associate Wilderness dwellers with crime, violence, incompetence, lack of discipline, and emotionalism. None of these things has to be true to the extent claimed by the detractors. The detractors are clever enough to know that once they have made the association of black people with negative traits it is easy to go from the stereotype to the dismissal of the African's Wilderness voice on any subject.

Consider the gruesome tales told in Milwaukee, Wisconsin. The case of Jeffrey Dahmer demonstrates the danger of fear and trepidation rather than of courage and humility. In Milwaukee, Jeffrey Dahmer held a young Asian man who could not speak English against his will and later murdered and cannibalized the young man, as he had done to several other Asians and Africans. Although African American neighbors had complained to the police about the white man who had held the young Asian in a virtual prison, the white police who investigated the situation went to the house and were told by Dahmer that it was a homosexual lovers' quarrel that had caused the young Asian man to attempt to run away from the house, where the neighbors had seen him in distress. The police believed the white Dahmer over his black neighbors.

This is the Wilderness, and the response of the officers to Dahmer represented the standard procedure when white officers are confronted with a black version and a white version of an incident. It is a classic case of the white police assuming that African Americans do not know what they are saying. Hence, the dismissal of the voice of the African American in a situation in which it would have shed light. The tragedy is that Dahmer was a criminal and that the young man was eventually murdered. The police disregarded the African Americans' complaints, showing just how the police force had internalized their discrimination against Africans: In a situation where blacks were accusing a white, the police were inclined to believe the white; which was simply a matter of race. Moreover, had they investigated the apartment they would have found evidence of previous murders. Law enforcement, unfortunately, has often been one of the most stubborn venues of racism. We have often come to believe that law enforcement agencies either seek to ensnare, to entrap, or to ignore African Americans—but rarely to serve. Our fears are heightened when we discover that independent investigators confirm our worst anxieties about the police.

In February 1990 an investigation revealed that the New Jersey State Police had a special campaign to arrest African American and Hispanic drivers.[5] It would be nearly ten years before the State of

New Jersey would indict any police officer for entrapment. Traps, often set on highways throughout the country, were set in New Jersey specifically to entrap black and Hispanic travelers. How much are we African Americans expected to take without anger, indeed, without hatred? What troopers lurk in the dark of highways just for us? Who are these people who devise such attacks on us? What have we really done to harm them? Do they really want to force us to cry, "I give up"? These campaigns and attacks may injure our souls but they will not prevent us from championing justice and decency. We have pushed, as a vanguard people, for justice and equal treatment in America for more than a century. In the case of highway traps, we are doubly victims because the people least able to pay end up having to pay for tickets and finance all the white speedsters.

If Wilderness dwellers seek relief from the federal agencies that supply social security benefits, they must be on guard against discrimination. The Social Security Benefits Agency discriminates against blacks: According to a report in the *Philadelphia Inquirer* on May 12, 1992, social security disability was twice as likely to reject black applicants as compared to white applicants.[6] In everything we are being dispossessed of our health, our wealth, and our lives. One might assume, if one does not reflect too deeply, that the federal agencies would not discriminate against American citizens because of their race.[7] But as the social security benefits story illustrates, racism is alive and is flourishing in the Social Security Benefits Agency. Yet we should not be surprised by any of this, since there are now many documents that attest to the unequal treatment of Africans by the legal institutions of this nation.

## SUPPORT THE HUMAN AND CULTURAL RIGHTS OF EVERY ETHNIC GROUP

In his powerful book *Black Robes, White Justice*, which was scarcely noticed by most of the public, Judge Bruce Wright detailed what has happened to African Americans in the justice system.[8] When people no longer have faith in the justice system, believing that it has become, as people say in the 'hood, "an injustice system," and when people feel that the police are the enemy of the community, those people are in a state of volatile readiness. How to defuse a volatile situation that is already lit by the conditions is the subject of greatest concern to the government. I want to know—most Africans want to know—when will the racketeers and hustlers who hide behind the law be brought to justice for the indignities measured out to Africans? This is not a cynical, hostile, or angry question; it is one derived from a sincere concern about the quality of life in the Wilderness. By bringing to justice those who discriminate on the basis of race, religion, and creed, we might be making a difference in the Wilderness. In fact, it is this concern regarding justice that is at the root of the intellectual and academic debate about the quality of psychological life in the United States. Why can't we raise the issue of African agency in the making of historical events and the creation of ideas and concepts? The same obstacle to the expansion of justice for the African American is the one that stands in the way of appreciating a multiplicity of cultural centers.

There are students in schools who cannot bring books by Afrocentric authors to class without being criticized. At a university in Philadelphia, a student who brought in *Stolen Legacy* by George G. M. James was publicly condemned by the teacher for bringing in such a controversial book.[9] When the student asked the professor if he had read the book, he replied he had not; he had heard enough about it to know that it attempted to claim that the Greeks received their knowledge from the Egyptians and everyone knew this was not true. When the student protested that the book deserved to be read, the professor replied that he would not allow his classroom to be disrupted by a student. Of course, the professor had the right to control the direction of his classroom, but to dismiss the student's attempt to bring a scholarly book by an African American to the classroom as a disruption was totally off base. Much like President Clinton's nomination and withdrawal of University of Pennsylvania professor Lani Guinier's name from consideration for the civil rights post in the Justice Department before she had a hearing by the Senate Judiciary Committee, the attempt to censor Afrocentric ideas and to keep them out of the educational programs of students is a part of the current intellectual climate. Some whites use the guise of quality and standard maintenance to deny equal opportunity to African Americans. Furthermore, there have been outright racist commentaries in classrooms. Black students have lodged numerous complaints on hundreds of campuses. Certainly victims have legitimate complaints.

But our catalog of grievances is infinite. We walk into an automobile showroom and we are quoted higher prices than whites; we work as cooks in restaurants where whites with less skill and less time in the job are paid more; we step into employment agencies and they direct us away from jobs, high school guidance counselors direct us away from college, and college counselors direct us away from African American Studies courses where we can learn about our history and culture. We are told that there are no apartments available, but when our white friends call the same agency they are told there are several apartments available. We change our names to reflect our African identity and whites still insist on calling us by English or Scottish names.

The Afrocentric idea demands that the Wilderness dweller seek no undue deference and give no undue deference, because only a return to and an acceptance of ourselves as agents will create a new reality. There is a certain accountability that comes with this kind of freedom, because it is ultimately a freedom to be responsible for oneself. I have called this positioning of ourselves squarely in our own history a relocation, a repositioning, but it is not a physical action because it manifests itself only in our psychological reordering. Since the existence of this Afrocentric idea demands a new way to examine who we are and where we are, we are much closer to an understanding of our own motivations. Our problem is found in the diffidence toward our culture as expressed by some of our opinion leaders. Our problem is that we have inherited much of the white opinion and attitude about ourselves and we have therefore often become black versions of whites.

In "Black Demagogues and Pseudo-Scholars," Henry Louis Gates Jr., following most of the arguments of an Anti-Defamation League (ADL) research report, *The Anti-Semitism of Black Demagogues and Extremists*, exaggerated what he called "black anti-Semitism."[10] In a personal letter to Gates I challenged him to find one example of a black organization that made its principal mission hatred of Jews—or hatred of anybody. He could not; yet he had left the impression in a widely publicized article (it was distributed as an advertisement by the ADL in several African American newspapers) that African American intellectuals were on a campaign to attack Jews. This may have been opportunistic rhetoric but it was surely meant to create a rift between Africans and Jews, who have both participated in the struggle against bigotry. I wrote to Gates that an article on bigotry would have been more realistic and credible, since neither I nor colleagues I spoke with knew of *any* African American scholar who had written any attacks on Jews. Unfortunately, Gates wrote the piece quickly, with reference from another source and without much historical reflection. In charging that a victim was looking for a victim, Gates popularized a tragic illusion that will do more damage to the relationship between Africans and Jews than any of the people he alluded to in his article. While there are more than 550 white hate groups in the United States with declared missions against Jews and Africans—that is, they are both anti-Semitic and anti-African—neither Gates nor African American conservatives have attacked these groups. African Americans have not been enemies of the Jewish people, and Gates knew that—or should have known that—before he wrote his article.

There are African American anti-Semites, as there are Jewish anti-Africanites but I do not believe there is a campaign among either group against the other. The fact is, African and Jewish Americans have both fought to expand the idea of America to be inclusive. Finding an odd person out and then claiming that the part represents the whole borders on demagoguery of the worst sort, that which feeds racial animosity. It becomes the ultimate postmodern tactic to pit a victim against a victim and then argue that the victims' squabble, however manufactured, is the source of national discomfort.

In fact, the prolific white Canadian writer Michael Bradley, whom Gates cited in his article as saying that whites are vicious because they, "unlike the rest of mankind, are descended from the brutish Neanderthals" responded to Gates that "the stock in trade of any good demagogue is the use of emotionally charged words to distort fact."[11] Bradley then contradicts Gates by saying that in his book *The Iceman Inheritance*,[12] he never described Western culture as "vicious" and that his thesis concerning the aggression of Neanderthals is not "news to anyone but Henry Louis Gates, Jr."

African Americans are not, by and large, anti-Semitic; they are antiracist. And to be antiracist in American society means that one condemns any form of racial chauvinism, including white chauvinism. Immediately after the 1992 Los Angeles uprising, a producer for a television program in New Jersey called to ask me if I would sit on a panel to discuss the origins and causes of racism. I told the producer that I believed she would ask an African American to do that only if she wanted to avoid questioning whites about the origins of racism. Her request was a form of white chauvinism and had to be rejected in light of the fact that whites were the perpetrators, not just historically but in the current situation, of racial policies. Did she really understand my refusal to participate? She had asked the victim to explain the actions of the perpetrators of racism. I cannot explain what makes a white family condemn its children for calling the name of God in vain while it ignores pejoratives directed against Africans or Jews. What makes a white family angry about abortion but not about the death of African American children on the Wilderness streets?

Since racist ideology operates at all levels of society, many people do not know that they are racist in the priorities that they set, in their involvement in exploitative schemes that rob Wilderness dwellers, or in the way they teach the educational curriculum. Perhaps what we need is a general antiracist education mobilization.

One of the most predictable responses to the educational crisis, since American education is seen as falling behind that of several other information-age societies, has been the devising of major plans, initiatives, and corporation cooperatives to assist the school systems. But almost none of these plans involve an antiracist education.

It reminds me of a story about hunters among the Sotho in southern Africa. The hunters went on a long journey to hunt antelope for their village. They knew exactly where to look for the animals, because other hunters had looked in those places for many years. After a couple of days en route, they saw a limping antelope off to the side of their path. One bright young hunter suggested that they cap-ture and kill the limping antelope, cook and eat it, and then continue on their journey with more vigor than before. This suggestion was accepted, so the hunters ran after the limping antelope. They ran for hours, over the savanna, through the shrub forests, around the boulders, but they could not catch the limping antelope. They soon discovered that even in its crippled stage, an antelope could still outrun a man.

The plans to reenergize the educational system of the United States so that African Americans can "catch up" to the rest of the information societies sound like excellent ideas. And certainly we should always be doing things to make the system better. But the plans that are thrown around are all limping antelopes, and to chase them is to run for years after the wrong solution. The solution is not school choice, or corporate control of local schools, or some diverse new project to include parents. To make the system better we have to provide better connections between the student and the learning process. Motifs, icons, and symbols mediate what we learn and how we learn.

Education in the United States can be greatly advanced vis-à-vis other nations by simply providing the resources, curricular and finan-cial, to African American, Hispanic, and Native American schools—as we already provide for other schools. Rich suburban schools neither score below the schools of other societies nor lack imaginative, scientific, and artistic projects and interests. We are locked into a situation in which our schools, collectively, are doing worse than the schools in other information nations. The leading government analysts and policy experts respond to that situation with a limping antelope; they want to have industry take over schools, or have corporations pour millions of dollars into certain schools, or have groups of superplanners plan new schools. These are Band-Aids applied to the wrong problem. The competitive edge in education would return to the United States overnight if we brought every inner-city school child up to the standards of the suburban schools in the nation. Many principals and teachers know how to do that and do not need businesspeople or government officials to tell them how to educate children.

Some principals, such as Jan Gillespie—formerly of the Hatch Middle School in Camden, New Jersey, but now a deputy superintendent in Camden—have begun to turn the situation around even though they have schools in some of the most troubled urban communities in the nation. Gillespie instituted multicultural, civic, and science institutes in her school and brought the scores of that inner-city school to levels equal to those in suburban schools. But if she had the money, the corporate support of the richer schools, Hatch Middle School would do even better because the school has adopted the Afrocentric model of education, in which the child is the center of the content of the classroom.

The fury in the Wilderness is exacerbated by the machinations of the white Anglo-Saxon powerbrokers, who claim that they are helping schools when they are really helping businesses. Education ought to be a bridge between separate cultural islands through the sharing of ideas and values. Education should not be the imposition of Eurocentric ideas as universal on everybody.

Andrew Hacker sees the social and economic division between the two nations as being difficult, perhaps impossible, to bridge.[13] He shares this view with Derrick Bell, who, in a similar vein, believes that African Americans have quite a bit to be outraged about.[14] While I certainly understand their arguments and believe they are correct about the pathology of racism in this country, I do not have the luxury, as an Afrocentrist interested in humanizing the world, to believe in the impossibility of a resolution. Yet I see both Hacker and Bell as envoys of reality who are much closer to the facts in their analyses of racism in America than the so-called transformatives (Marxists turned radical Democrats), as defined by Manning Marable. Both Bell and Hacker seem to have examined the Wilderness in all of its depth and complexity, rather than merely present superficial observations of what is wrong with African American nationalism, as the Marxists have done.

One thing is clear and certain: African Americans must become more centered, more accountable, and more responsible to and for our own communities. Some will label this attitude *nationalism*, others will see it as an emphasis on separatism; in reality, it is simply the only way to move forward for a people too long dependent upon others. We cannot guarantee change in the attitudes of whites, but we can change our own attitudes and behaviors. This is the centered vision, and it is different from the socialist or capitalist vision.

In the first place, there is nothing more correct for African Americans than the historical and ethical experiences of our own history. Part of the antagonism some people have toward Afrocentricity is its philosophical unity, a unity without seams that supports the centeredness of African people. One cannot disconnect pieces and parts from an automobile and then expect it to run the same as if those pieces were not taken away. The objective in the African American community cannot simply be *Homo economicus*, but humans capable of spiritual and moral advancement with regard to the treatment of their fellow human beings. We achieve this holistically, not with pieces.

There is nothing broken in the Wilderness that cannot be fixed by African Americans themselves, *all other things being equal*. Indeed, that is the problem: All other things are *not* equal and the array of forces against the success of the African American community creates pain.

The Afrocentric philosophy insists that African people be viewed as subjects of experiences and not as marginals in a European enterprise. Those who will assist the Wilderness in realizing the Promise must know that their assistance can be based only upon seeing the Wilderness dweller as centered; nothing less will work or be acceptable in the long run. African Americans cannot be given the intellectual leftovers from the European table. No more books meant for white children will be given as second-hand copies to black children.

A philosophy such as this answers the questions of displacement, dislocation, and decentering in a positive manner. If a person is off-center, the only way to bring congruence between that person's reality and society is to relocate the person psychologically. That is why neither Los Angeles nor the greater Wilderness can be fixed through jobs and housing alone. People who have jobs may not show up for work if they do not have grounding in cultural values; if they get a house they may destroy it without some sort of value reconstruction based on culture and identity.

The Afrocentrist believes that four hundred years in the Wilderness have profoundly affected the way African Americans respond to the Promise. The Afrocentrist is distressed by the absence of Africans who appreciate the variety and diversity of the African culture as expressed in the Americas. But we are convinced that we will eventually dismantle the fences that have kept us away from the Promise. We know that the beginning of the dismantling, however, will be our own creation: centeredness.

## OPEN UP DISCUSSION ON REPARATIONS TO FIND A WAY TO REPAIR THE WRONG

While a paralysis of national resolve may now exist at some levels, there is no lack of national culpability, involvement, guilt, and interest in reparations. Millions of African Americans are already meeting and discussing this issue with increasing fervor. As the August 12, 2002, Reparation March on Washington, D.C., demonstrated, sentiment is growing among African Americans that the time to discuss the disinheritance of our African ancestors has come. Every reason seems to exist for the United States to shape and frame a platform for a true discourse on reparations that could become an increasingly powerful moral and political issue in the twenty-first century. Will the nation's politicians have the ability, intelligence, and moral courage to take a leadership role?

The highest form of law exhibits itself when a system of law is able to answer for its own crimes. Nothing should prevent men and women of ethical and political insight from making an argument for an idea whose legitimacy is fundamental to our concept of justice. We must act on the basis of our own sense of moral rightness.

Affirmative action had to be based on race because race is the source of the inequities between blacks and whites in the American society. Now, I do not deny the inequities of class and I believe that they, like those of gender, must be resolved as well; however, since we have not inherited a class nobility in this country, but a racial nobility, economic and social problems will be lessened if we can confront racism. I don't believe that this will be achieved through the Marxist solution proposed by respectable radical Democrats like Cornel West or democratic socialists like Manning Marable. A redistribution of wealth as they propose, even if practicable, would not eliminate racism. In fact, the socialist country most aggressive against racism, Cuba, has not eliminated racism.

Affirmative action must be seen as an attempt on the part of the nation to repay Africans for 244 years of enslavement and almost 100 years of legal discrimination. Of course, it is a debt that affirmative action can never repay; this is the frustration of whites and, indeed, of blacks. Even in the best examples of affirmative action—that is, when those in charge of the programs sincerely believe they can make a difference—it seldom works the way that it should. In other words, there are few examples where African Americans have honestly and earnestly been sought for positions wherein an agency, an institution, or a corporation has emerged with a ratio of African Americans in higher-level positions equal to our percentage in the nation. Since affirmative action, a good idea when it was first framed, cannot redress centuries of racism against blacks in a way that establishes the principles of fair play and justice, what can be done?

I believe that it is necessary to establish a national commission, perhaps a National Commission on African Americans, to examine all aspects of the impact of enslavement and legal discrimination against Africans and to promote the idea of reparations to resolve the lingering vestiges of deprivation and disadvantage to the descendants of enslaved persons. Such a commission should last for twenty-five years, doubling the time of the Reconstruction, which lasted from 1865 to 1877.

Richard America told us in his brilliant monograph *Paying the Social Debt: What White America Owes Black America* that reparations for Europe's enslavement of Africans in the United States is an idea whose time has arrived.[15] Almost a decade before Randall Robinson's powerful book *The Debt: What America Owes to Blacks*,[16] America's book laid out the economic bases of the debt owed to African Americans. While the argument for reparations is a Pan-African one, in this section we are most interested in the discourse surrounding enslavement and its consequences in the American society. There are those who will immediately say that the people of the United States will never accede to reparations. I am of the opinion that the discussion and debate surrounding reparations has never occurred until recently in any serious way, and my position therefore is offered as an attempt to raise some of the philosophical ideas that might govern such a discourse. Robinson's *The Debt* has been one of the most popular and important books written on the general subject so far, because he has captured the necessity for reparations in very clear and accessible language. What he has demonstrated is that while a paralysis of national will may exist at the present time, there is no lack of national guilt and interest in this topic.

When Raphael Lemkin started in 1933 to gain recognition of the term *genocide* as a crime of barbarity, few thought that it would soon become the language of international law. When genocide was adopted as a convention in 1948 with an International Criminal Court to serve as the home for judging genocide, it was a victory for those who had fought to put genocide on the world agenda. My belief is that the current discussions about reparations undertaken by scholars, political activists, and the United Nations will advance our own plan to place reparations at the top of the agenda to redress wrongs for African Americans.

The argument for reparations for the forced enslavement of Africans in the American colonies and the United States of America is grounded in moral, legal, economic, and political terms. Taken together, these terms constitute the payment of reparations to the descendants of the Africans who worked under duress for nearly 250 years. The only remedy for such an immense deprivation of life and liberty is an enormous restitution.

When one examines the nature of the terms amassed for the argument for reparations, it becomes clear that the basis for reparations is interwoven within the cultural fabric of the nation. It is not un-American to seek the redress of wrongs through some form of compensatory restitution. For example, the moral terms of the argument are made from the concept of rightness or righteousness as conceived in the spiritual and religious literature of the American people. One assumes that morality, based in the relationship between humans and the divine as well as that between humans, constitutes a normal warrant for correcting a wrong, if it is perceived to be a wrong, in most cases. Using legal terms for the argument for reparations, one relies on the judicial heritage of the American nation. Clearly, the ideas of justice and fair play, while often thwarted, distorted, and subverted, are representative of the legal ideal in American jurisprudence. Therefore, the use of legal terms for the reparations argument is not only expected but required for any thorough appreciation of the need for America to deal with the internal question of reparations. The Great Enslavement itself showed how legal arguments could be turned upside down to defend an immoral and unjust system of oppression. Nevertheless, justice is a requirement for political solidarity within a nation, and any attempt to bring it about must be looked upon as a valid effort to create national unity.

Of course, we recognize that justice may be both retributive and restorative. In one instance, it seeks to punish those who have committed a wrong; in the other, it concerns itself with restoring to the body politic a sense of reconciliation and harmony. I believe that the idea of reparations, particularly as conceived here, is a restorative justice issue. The economic case is a simple argument for the payment to the descendants of the enslaved for the work that was done and the deprivation that was experienced by our ancestors. To speak of an economic interest in the argument is typically American and is an issue that should be well understood by most Americans. Finally, the political term is wrapped in the clothes of the American political reality. In order to ensure national unity, reparations should be made to the descendants of Africans. It is my belief that the underlying fault in the American body politic is the unresolved issue of enslavement. Many contemporary problems in society can be thought of as deriving from the unsettled issues of enslavement. A concentration on the political term for reparations might lead to a useful argument for national unity.

One of the ironies of the discourse surrounding reparations for the enslavement of Africans is that the arguments against reparations for Africans are never placed in the same light as those about reparations in other cases. This introduces a racist element into the discourse itself. For example, even if a racist thought it, one would rarely hear the questions, "Why should Germany pay reparations to the Jews?" or "Why should the United States pay reparations to the Japanese who were placed in concentration camps during World War II?" If someone even tried to make arguments against those forms of reparations, the entire corpus of arguments from morality, law, economics, and politics would be brought to bear on them. Furthermore, they would be embarrassed to have even thought those irreverent things in the first place. This is as it should be in a society where human beings respect the value of other humans. Only in societies where human beings are considered less than human do we have the opportunity for enslavement, concentration camps, and gas chambers. It might be observed that when humans are considered the same as other humans, the questioning of reparations becomes moot. We expect all the arguments for reparations to be used in such cases. This is why the recent rewarding of reparations to the Jews for the Nazi atrocities committed against them is considered normal and natural. Any situation where humans are given the same values as other humans would result in a similar response. In Nazi Germany, Jews were considered inferior and had Germany won the war, any reparations to Jews would have been unthinkable. It is because Nazi Germany lost the war and that other humans with different values determined German culpability that reparations became possible. One can make the same argument for the Japanese who lost their property and resources in the American West. A new reality in the political landscape made it possible for the Japanese to receive reparations for their losses. Eminent African and Caribbean scholars such as Ali Mazrui, Dudley Thompson, and others have argued for an international examination of the role the West played in the slave trade and the consequent underdevelopment of Africa. This is a laudable movement and I believe it will add to the intensity and seriousness of the internal discourse within the United States.

A strong sense of moral outrage has continued to activate the public in the interest of reparations. In early 2001 a lawsuit brought against the French National Railroad in the Eastern District of New York Court charged the Société Nationale des Chemins de Fer with transporting seventy-two thousand Jews to death camps in August 1944. The case was brought to court on behalf of the survivors and heirs. A French court held that French banks that hoarded assets of Jews had to create a fund of $50 million for those individuals with evidence of previous accounts.[17] Similarly, on May 30, 2001, the German Parliament cleared the way for a $4.5-billion settlement by German companies and the government to survivors and heirs of more than a million forced laborers. This is in addition to much larger awards to Israel and the Jewish people for the Holocaust itself. The Swiss government has agreed to pay $1.25 billion to those Jewish persons who can establish claims on bank accounts appropriated during World War II.

Whenever people have been deprived of their labor, freedom, or life without cause (except their race, ethnicity, or religion) as a matter of group or national policy, then they should be compensated for their loss. In the case of the Africans in the American colonies and the United States, the policy and practice of the ruling white majority in the country after the 1640s was to enslave only Africans. Prior to that time some whites had been indentured as servants and some native peoples were pressed into slavery. However, from the middle of the seventeenth century until 1865, only Africans were enslaved as a matter of race and ethnic origin.A growing consensus suggests that some form of reparations for past injustice on a large scale should not be swept under the table. We have accepted the broad idea of justice and fair play in such massive cases of group deprivation and loss; we cannot change the language or the terms of our contemporary response to acts of past injustice. Our recognition of reparations in numerous other cases, including the Rosewood, Florida, and Tulsa, Oklahoma, burning and bombing of African American communities in the early 1920s, means that we must continue to right the wrongs of the past so that our current relationships will improve.

Africans did not enslave themselves in the Americas. The European slave trade was not an African enterprise; it was preeminently and solely a European enterprise in all of its dimensions: conception, insurance, outfitting of ships, sailors, factories, shackles, weapons, and the selling and buying of people in the Americas. Not a single African can be named as an equal partner with Europeans in the slave trade. Indeed, no African person benefited to the degree that Europeans did from the commerce in African people. I think it is important to say that no African community used slavery as its principal mode of economic production. We have no example of a slave economy in West Africa. The closest any scholar has ever been able to get to describing a slave society is the Dahomey kingdom of the nineteenth century, which had become so debauched by slavery due to European influence that it was virtually a hostage of the trade. However, even in Dahomey we do not see the complete denial of the humanity of Africans as we see in the American colonies.

Slavery was not a romantic system; it was evil, ferocious, brutal, and corrupting in all of its aspects. It was developed in its greatest degree of degradation in the United States. The enslaved African was treated with utter disrespect. No laws protected the African from any cruelty the white master could conceive. The man, woman, or child was at the complete mercy of the most brutish of people. For looking a white man in the eye, the enslaved person could have her eyes blinded with hot irons. For speaking up in defense of a wife or a woman, a man could have his right hand severed. For defending his right to speak against oppression, an African could have half his tongue cut out. For running away and being caught, an enslaved African could have her Achilles tendon cut. For resisting the advances of her white master, a woman could be given fifty lashes of the cowhide whip. A woman who physically fought against her master's sexual advances was courting death, and many died at the hands of their masters. The enslaved African was more often than not physically scarred, crippled, or injured because of some brutal act of the slave owner. Among the punishments that were favored by the slave owners were whipping holes, where the enslaved was buried in the ground up to the neck; dragging blocks that were attached to the feet of men or women who had run away and been caught; mutilation of the toes and fingers; the pouring of hot wax onto the limbs; and passing a piece of hot wood on the buttocks of the enslaved. Death came to the enslaved in vile, crude ways when a psychopathic slave owner wanted to teach other enslaved Africans a lesson. The enslaved person could be roasted over a slow-burning fire, left to die after having both legs and both arms broken, oiled and greased and then set afire while hanging from a tree limb, or killed slowly as the slave owner cut the enslaved person's phallus or breasts. A person could be placed on the ground, stomach first, stretched so that each hand was tied to a pole and each foot was tied to a pole. Then the slave master would beat the person's naked body until the flesh was torn off of the buttocks and the blood ran down to the ground.

I have written this brief description to underscore the brutality that existed on slave plantations. Africans on the plantations were often sullen and difficult, as far as the whites were concerned, hypocritical because they would smile on command and frown when they left the white person's presence, and plotting.

It is not my intention to enter the debate over Phil Curtin's numbers, except to say that I find the numbers quite conservative given the estimates made by other scholars and given the fact that Curtin has demonstrated a penchant for minimizing African agency. Curtin's estimate of the number of Africans brought to the Americas is 15 million. The figure has reached as high as 100 million in the estimation of some scholars. I believe the numbers are important only to ascertain just how deeply the European slave trade affected the continental African economic, social, physical, and cultural character. However, for purposes of reparations the numbers are not necessary, since there can be no adequate compensation for the enslavement and its consequences. The broad outline of the facts is clear and accepted by most historians. We know, for instance, that the numbers of Africans who landed in Jamaica and Brazil were different from those of Haiti and the United States. Yet the establishment of concrete numbers—that is, workable numbers in these cases and in the United States—is rather easy. I believe it is necessary to ascertain something more about the nature of the African's arrival in the American nation: At the end of the Civil War in 1865 there were about 4.5 million Africans in the United States, which means there had been a steady flow of Africans into the American nation since the seventeenth century. These Africans and their descendants constitute the proper plaintiffs in the reparation case. Hundreds of thousands of Africans labored and died under the reign of enslavement without leaving any direct descendants. We cannot adequately account for these lost numbers, but we can account for most of those who survived the Civil War and their heirs. In fact, some of the 187,000 who fought in the Civil War did not survive, but their descendants survived. These also constitute a body of individuals who must be brought into the discussion of reparations. Thus, two classes of people—those who survived after the Civil War and their heirs, and those who fought and died in the Civil War and their heirs—are legitimate candidates for reparations. Indeed, the consequences of the residual effects of the enslavement must be figured in any compensation.

One of the issues that must be dealt with is, How is loss to be determined? Since millions of Africans were transported across the sea and enslaved in the Caribbean and the Americas for more than two centuries, what method of calculating loss will be employed? It seems to me that loss must be determined using a multiplicity of measures suited to the variety of deprivations experienced by the African people. Yet the overarching principle for establishing loss might be determined by ascertaining the negative effects on the natural development of people. What this means to me is that the physical, psychological, economic, and educational toll must be evaluated. What were the fundamental ways in which the enslavement of Africans not only undermined the contemporary lifestyles and chances of the people but also destroyed the potential for their posterity? I believe all of the issues of educational deficit, economic instability, poor health conditions, and the lack of estate wealth are directly related to the previous conditions of Africans in this system. Nothing can produce a collective national will but a redress of the enslavement of African people.

Given the fact that African Americans constitute the largest single ethnic-cultural grouping in the United States and will maintain this position in the future, reparations for the enslavement of Africans will have positive benefits on the nation as a whole. African Americans number approximately 35 million people. Occasionally newspapers report that the Hispanic or Latino population will soon outstrip the African population in the United States; this is an imprecise rendering of statistics based on the United States census. It is true that taken together in the aggregate the number of Spanish-speaking Americans will soon outnumber the absolute number of African Americans. However, this is misleading because the Spanish-speaking population includes more than twenty different national origin groups, plus individuals who identify with African, Caucasian, and Native American heritages. Among the Spanish-speaking population, for example, we find people from Mexico, Cuba, Puerto Rico, Dominican Republic, El Salvador, Honduras, Costa Rica, and numerous South American countries. Many of these people will self-identify as white; others will self-identify as black or African.

Africans are an indispensable part of the American nation: history, culture, philosophy, mission, and potential. It is insane to speak of America without the African presence, and the deeper we get into the future the more important the nature of the relationship of Africans to the body politic will become. Reparations would ensure: (1) recognition of the Africans' loss, (2) compensation for the loss, (3) psychological relief for both blacks and whites in terms of guilt and anger, and (4) national unity based on a stronger political will. These are intrinsic values of reparations.

Reparations are always based on *real* loss, not *perceived* loss. Human beings must have been moved completely off their own cultural and social foundations, and against their will, forcibly and without mercy, in order for reparations to be required. Take the case of the Japanese Americans who were taken from their homes in California and other western states during World War II. They were removed against their will from their homes, their property confiscated, and their children taken out of schools. The Japanese Americans lost in real terms and were consequently able to make the case for reparations. Their case was legitimate and it was correct for America to respond to the injustice that had been done to the Japanese Americans.

The case of the Africans in America has some of the same characteristics, but in many ways is different and yet equally significant as far as real loss is concerned. What is similar is the uprooting of Africans against their will by a people who had determined that the African people were the natural target for human slavery. Also similar is the definition that whites created for Africans as culturally and intellectually inferior. From this standpoint it was easy to brutalize, humiliate, and enslave Africans since, as whites had argued, blacks were inferior in every way. What is different about the reparations case for African Americans is that it is much larger than the Japanese American situation, it has far more implications for historical transformation of the American society, and it is rooted in the legal foundations of the country.

It is possible to argue for reparations on the following grounds: (1) forced migration, (2) forced deprivation of culture, (3) forced labor, and (4) forced deprivation of wealth by segregation and racism. However, these four constituents to the argument for reparations are buttressed by several significant factors that emerged from the experience of the enslaved Africans. In the first place, Africans often lost their freedom because of their age. Most of the Africans who were abducted from the continent of Africa were between fifteen and twenty years of age. This was, therefore, the robbery of prime youth. A second factor is based on the loss of innocence where abuse—physical, psychological, and sexual—was the order of the day in the life of the enslaved African. Third, one has to consider the loss in transit that derived from coffles and the long marches, the dreaded factories where Africans were held sometimes as long as seven months while the Europeans waited for a transport ship, and the extreme loss of life in transit where death on board the ships or in the sea further deprived a people. Fourth is the factor of loss due to maimed limbs: that is, the deprivation of feet, Achilles tendons, and hands.

Thus, to deny freedom, will, culture, religion, and health is to create the most thorough conditions for loss. The Africans who were enslaved in America were among the most deprived humans in history. It is no wonder that David Walker wrote in *An Appeal to the Colored Citizens of the World* that the enslaved Africans were "the most abject" people in the world. The corollary to that statement was that "the White Christian Americans" were the most cruel and barbarous people who have ever lived.[18]

One way to approach the issue of reparations is to speak about money but not necessarily about cash. Reparations will cost; it is not free. But although it will cost billions of dollars, it will not have to be the doling out of billions of dollars of cash to individuals. While the delivery of money for other than cash distributions is different from most other reparations agreements, it is possible for reparations to be advanced in the United States by a number of other means. Among the potential options are educational, health care, land or property grants, and a combination of such grants. Any reparation remedy should deal with long-term issues in the African American community rather than a one-time cash payout. What I have argued for is the establishment of some type of organization that would evaluate how reparations would be determined and distributed: The National Commission of African Americans (NCAA) would be the overarching national organization to serve as the clearinghouse for reparations. The NCAA would use reparations as a more authentic way of bringing the national moral conscience to bear on the education of African Americans. Rather than begin in a vacuum, the NCAA would consider various sectors of society, education, health and welfare, and economics and see how Africans were deprived by two and a half centuries of enslavement. For example, by the time Africans were freed from bondage in 1865, whites had claimed all the land from sea to sea and had just about finished the systematic "cleansing" of Native Americans from the land, pushing thousands to Oklahoma on the Trail of Tears or, as in the case of the Oneida, to Wisconsin in a trail of sorrow. Furthermore, there were already five hundred colleges teaching white students a white self-esteem curriculum, when it was still a crime for Africans to learn and illegal for whites to teach them. One likely answer to the reparations issue is full access to public and private education to all descendants of enslaved Africans for the next 123 years, half the time Africans worked in this country for free. This would mean that all expenses of students who qualified for college would be covered, directly or indirectly through vouchers, by the government. Inequities at the elementary and secondary levels that would prevent students from successfully qualifying for higher education would be addressed in two ways. In the first place, the elementary and secondary curricula would be infused with Afrocentric content so that students who sit in classrooms would not feel that they are alien to the subjects being taught. All proper education should attach the pupil to the subject or theme of the class, so that the student appreciates the role that all humans have played in the construction of the contemporary world. At the second level, the educational support needs of the students, including tutoring and mentoring, would be taken care of by the federal government.

In some ways, this temporary program of government reparations and involvement with African Americans as a group mirrors the Native American special case, in that the government recognizes a particular responsibility to the Native Americans for the appropriation of their lands. One is an issue of land and the other is an issue of labor. However, it is important that the graft, corruption of purpose, misuse of Native American resources by the government, and inadequate record keeping be avoided in any reparation scheme devoted to rectifying the crime against African Americans.

The bottom line in race relations in the United States is the unresolved issues surrounding the institution of slavery. At the root of this irresolution is the belief that Africans are inferior to whites and therefore do not deserve compensation for labor or anything else. Indeed, it is this feeling that fuels the attacks on reparations for Africans as well. How whites feel about the condition of servitude forced on blacks and how we feel about that condition, or how we feel about the attachment of whites to the perpetration of that condition, are the central issues affecting race relations in this nation. Once we have overcome the problem of slavery we will have discovered the basis for reparations and, indeed, the end of guilt and anger.

$$\boxtimes \boxtimes \boxtimes$$

The really brave and challenging action is to take the bull by the horns and say: Let us look at this problem that troubles all racial relationships in this country. Thus, this national commission cannot be a group dealing with "minority issues" or "ethnic problems"; it must be centered on the fundamental historical problem: the resolution of the African issue. A bold initiative such as this will benefit from experts in various fields and recommend to Congress actions to be taken that will bring about the resolution of the reparations issue.

Almost all other issues of race, class, and color stem from this basic situation in the sense that should society resolve the issue of reparations, all other ethnic and racial concerns will appear resolvable because they derive from the main issues.

This is not an absolutely new idea but it is new in the age of affirmative action. Because affirmative action, as a conservative agenda item with some national guidelines under President Richard Nixon's administration, was dependent upon local operators, individuals, corporations, and educational institutions, it was doomed to failure. What *real* incentives can be given to a racist to allow him to confront racism and also to work affirmatively to eradicate it by aggressively bringing Africans into the workplace and into education? It would take a thousand years for affirmative action to redress the economic, educational, and social dislocation and deficits of African Americans by virtue of the history of oppression. Of course, to begin to take on this task we must have a rejection of hegemony and domination by whites.

The addiction to hegemony can be neutralized only by a forced feeding of facts. Thus, it will be necessary for every institution, particularly the schools, to undertake a renewed effort to eradicate the basis of racism through proper antiracist education.

Most of the attacks on affirmative action are not justified in light of our nation's history. They are attacks that do not provide alternatives for resolving the national moral deficit. In fact, most often they add to the deficit with meanness, callousness, and an unwillingness to face the circumstances of the African population of this country that has everything to do with enslavement.

To preach equality without preaching justice is like comparing the suburban child whose parents both attended university and hold professional degrees with the inner-city child whose mother did not complete high school—and saying that you will give them an equal chance to do a paper on trade in medieval China. One child's parents may have access to computers, bookstores, and friends might know something about medieval China; while the other student from the inner city might have only an old encyclopedia that was given to him by some junk dealer down the block. Whose paper is going to look better? What does it say about the intelligence of these children? Each had an equal chance—but their support systems were so different. The same can be said about equality without justice, without fair play. Martin Luther King Jr. once said that we must always seek equality *with* justice.

The NCAA, comprised of citizens with unquestioned moral and ethical histories, could create a thoroughly positive environment for national healing. The NCAA would listen to various proposals for resolving the issue through reparations, and many of these ideas will be noncash remedies. I suggest this as an approach to allay the glib remarks of some antireparationists that African Americans are simply looking for cash. While it is true that there is a view that agrees with the popular African American poet Obidike when he says, "Gimme my money," most African Americans want something more than cash. They want an authentic, historic, eternal gesture of national recognition of the wrongs done to our ancestors. This is also why a national apology is necessary.

The nation cannot change its history. African Americans cannot change our history as a part of this nation. We can only embrace our history and culture every day. We can only accept it as a basis for understanding, transformation, and renewal. In my judgment, this provides us with a better orientation to fair play and justice. Our crime has been that we, like a family ashamed, have tried to sweep our history under the rug of ignorance, only to discover that truth cannot be concealed forever. Whites, often with the assistance of confused black intellectuals or, as former President Nixon said, "Uncle Toms," have floated the idea that freedom from oppression would eventually come naturally. But who is an "Uncle Tom" in the African American lexicon?

Uncle Tom was a character in Harriet Beecher Stowe's classic novel, *Uncle Tom's Cabin*. But the appellation has come to mean a black person who is self-deprecating, nonassertive toward whites, and docile in the face of disrespect; an apologist for white abuse, who makes peace with evil for the sake of his own greed or fame; a collaborator against the interests of African people; a weak-kneed Judas who betrays the trust of African people; a joke-making, dumb-acting person who seeks to make white people feel comfortable even when they have committed criminal acts against blacks and who will not stand up for his own or others' rights. One has only to contrast this position, with that of the Afrocentrist to see that the healthier attitude is that of the Afrocentrist.

Afrocentrists have never opposed any racial group or supported any type of discrimination. But the Afrocentrists have been leaders in calling the nation to attention on the issues of racism in the social fabric of the society. We know that blacks can be just as vicious in their attacks on the legitimate demands of Wilderness dwellers as whites can, so the opposition to negative thinking has to be an opposition to oppression, meanness, and ignorance, not to a racial group. The honorable John Brown, in my judgment the most important white man in African American history, was one of the most revolutionary personalities in the American saga. His fight for African liberation from slavery was monumental in terms of his loss, self-sacrifice, and inspiration. The blacks who fought alongside him and his sons thought of John Brown as a brother. This is why the true Afrocentrist cannot support any racist doctrine but must insist on diversity of cultural positions and experiences without hierarchy—that is, without saying one is better than another or more advanced than the other.

How can we make a better nation when many whites, who reap the rewards and advantages accrued over the long period of enslavement and racial discrimination against blacks, act as if they are not accountable to history? What is the future of relationships between the races when the United States government walks out of an international conference on racism because it fears that its treatment of African Americans will be the main topic? Immigrants who come from Europe—whether Albanian, Bulgarian, Hungarian, Irish, Italian, or Greek—join the flow of white America and partake of whatever advantages they see in whiteness, which truly is an American invention, and then claim they are not a part of the enslavement of Africans. Of course it is true that they are not the direct descendants of the Western Europeans who enslaved Africans on this land, but they are the direct beneficiaries of an invisible system of racial hierarcy that is activated by both individual and collective attitudes of white superiority. They learn to think of racism as individual petty acts of overt negation of black rights, freedom, and expression. They are never shown how racism produces ideas of dominance in every sector of American society, so much so that it is possible to say that we live in a racist society. It is true that it is not as dangerous as it once was for an African to express himself, to explore possibilities, and to dream expansive visions of race peace. Yet I must grant the immigrant's point that she was not a slave owner, but neither my great-grandparents, Plenty and Hattie Smith, nor my grandparents, Moses and Willie Maud, nor my parents, Arthur and Lillie, were slaves. I am not a slave, yet I bear the marks of the historic oppression of our people. And those Africans who have come to this nation from Nigeria, Jamaica, Haiti, Cuba, Costa Rica, Ghana, Ethiopia, or Puerto Rico, though they may not have experienced our particular history, have, in fact, become a part of the great body of Africans in this country and often bear the same marks of psychological and social discrimination.

American society is locked into this two-nation syndrome of which Andrew Hacker has written so eloquently.[19] You are either white or black, and if you are neither then you are forced to choose. Thus, recent immigrants prefer "whiteness" to "blackness" because of the privilege it brings. But this complicates their lives and produces in them psychological scenarios that trouble the relationships they have with African Americans. Furthermore, choosing whiteness is no guarantee that one will be seen that way by the dominant culture; thus we see the violence and harassment measured on Asians in the southern states, where they are attending college at a greater rate than in the past. Hacker is probably correct that only whites and Africans really matter, historically and socially, as two racial principals. This is the legacy of America's most defining fact: the enslavement of millions of Africans. Some immigrant whites, Asians, and certain South Americans have found that they must choose whiteness or blackness. Others have been defined by the white society as black or people of color. For European immigrants it is easier to choose white than it is for Asians, though they are all eventually drawn to privilege and status. Some Turks, Albanians, and Greeks quickly abandon their languages, customs, cultures, and heroes to worship at the feet of Anglo-Germanic America. This is the reason some African Americans view immigrants as culpable. There is resentment because the immigrants are able to advance economically and succeed socially in America when blacks, who were here before the colonial government, are locked out often by an invisible system or racism. By failing to interrogate or locate whiteness as privilege, the immigrant becomes, wittingly or unwittingly, an accomplice to the further dispossession of black America. You cannot blame them for taking advantage, on the one hand; yet on the other hand you have to see the cruelty in the fact that an African American could be profiled and stopped on the New Jersey Turnpike while a recent European immigrant would never be threatened with arrest, harassment, or abuse because of the color of his skin. Upon whose broken and bent backs and out of whose cotton pod–pierced hands did these advantages of wealth and privilege accrue in this nation?

The demand to teach an Afrocentric curriculum is more important now than ever in America's history if we want to avoid slipping deeper into two dangerous camps. No nation can long exist that does not teach accurate history to its people so they can have a full under-standing and appreciation of the experience of African Americans. How else can a Korean American or a Turkish American feel what it truly means to be an American if he does not share in the knowledge of how this nation came to be what it is and how it is today?

Every child must understand the enslavement experience of Africans in detail. This will give logic to the Los Angeles conflagra-tion and the many other rages that we have seen—and will see. From this angle we will be able to construct a true future based upon a common knowledge of history.

We do not harbor fury out of some irrational need, some insane desire for anarchy and havoc. Our rage is legitimate and rational. Indeed, if we did not have anger it would be the most illogical, irra-tional, and insane response a people ever had to an oppressive history. This is precisely why African Americans see the "Uncle Tom" char-acter as the most insane of all people. Our anger is not shaped out of a will to harm others, but out of a will to protect ourselves against deceit and lies. This is precisely the reason our children and white children should be taught the truth of our achievements as well as the brutal enslavement of Africans in this country.

Writers like Robert Hughes, with rather opaque views of Amer-ican history—whitewashed to highlight a monocultural reality—would probably find fault with the suggestion that all Americans, including those of the Promise, should study the African enslavement. Hughes would see this as some form of cultural therapeutics.[20] In fact, all culture is therapeutics. But this is a therapy we need in order to move the Wilderness out of the mind of the society. Furthermore, the Wilderness dwellers must study themselves to find a way to break through the walls of the Wilderness.

Both the people of the Wilderness and the people of the Promise should hear the story of how the barbaric treatment of Africans began, how the African's dignity was stolen, and how cultures were destroyed, and how death swam next to the ships in the dreaded Middle Passage. The records are not beautiful. Yet one of the crimes is that neither blacks nor whites in this nation have been exposed to the details of the enslaved person's experience. Often when a person was captured, she was marched to the coast and held in a dungeon until a ship was available for transporting Africans to the Americas and the Caribbean. Once on the ship, she was chained on the deck, made to bend over, and branded with a red-hot iron in the form of letters or signs dipped in an oily preparation and pressed against the naked flesh till it burned a deep and ineffaceable scar. The brand was for identification.

Every African taken aboard a ship had to undergo the same treatment. Those who screamed were lashed in the face, breast, thighs, and back with cat-o'-nine-tails wielded by white sailors. These blows brought the returning lash pieces of grieving and agonizing flesh. It is easy to see how our African ancestors must have felt abandoned when they saw mothers with babies branded, lashed, and scarred. What could be in the tormentors' minds and who would measure out to them the doom they richly deserved for the abuse of men, women, and children?

History is replete with very poignant accounts of the abuse of Africans. The male slaves were chained two by two, at the arm and leg. Women were stowed away without chains, naked; all were packed away in the holes of ships for the five- to eight-week trip across the sea. The Africans could not even sit upright; the space between the decks was only two feet high. On fair-weather days Africans were allowed to come up on deck and dance for exercise. They did this in leg irons and chains to prevent escapes.

Every aspect of life as an enslaved person was harsh, cruel, and difficult. The ships created the situation for the most authentic African American pathos with the most powerful psychological horrors and terrors. Even some of the slave ship captains said the "groans and suffocating cries for air and water coming from below the deck sickened the soul of humanity."

I have faith enough to believe that compelled to moan the long hours of night away, with no water to quench their tormenting thirst and just enough oxygen to prolong their suffering, Africans vowed in those dark, damp, dank hellholes of horror that we would be free one day to teach the world the meaning of humanity. It is true that the weak perished and that the strong stayed alive. Their sleeping and resting places were often covered with blood and mucus, the horrid stench of the dead—breeding yet others for death—was everywhere. Those who survived often looked upon the dead beside them and intoned "gone to she own country" or "gone to he own friends."

The slavers spared neither children nor infants from this terror. Stories were told in the African American community of babies being flogged for crying or because they would not eat.[21] One captain of a ship is said to have placed a baby's feet in boiling water, which dissolved the skin and nails, because the child refused to eat. When the child could not be coaxed to eat, probably too ill, the captain took the infant from its mother and dropped it to the deck of the ship. The child died instantly. The mother was called and asked to drop the dead child overboard into the sea. She refused and was beaten. When she was forced to take the corpse to the ship's side, she averted her head so that she would not see and let the body fall into the sea. In my judgment, the fact that neither blacks nor whites have any real understanding of the horrors of the enslavement means that we have people whose analyses of racism lack historical vigor.

If the children of this nation were educated as they ought to be about the history of Africans in this country, they would find a renewed sense of purpose and vision. Of course, I must believe that if white children knew this, rather than the pablum of deceit normally given to them about the European slave trade, they would rise up and not only see differently but work to create a better place. If high school students knew that one captain of a ship with 440 Africans on board had 132 thrown overboard in order to save water, they might have a different attitude about patriotism, national unity, and social loyalty. Nowhere in this nation filled with the memories of Africans working in the hot cotton fields and being denied the right to drink a cold glass of water in a whites-only restaurant do our children learn about our *real* history. When those slave ships reached land, whether in the Americas or the Caribbean, whatever the condition, nothing, the Africans thought, could be as bad as the Middle Passage, with its long bloody nights of violence and terror. But here, on land, the situation was often worse. Mothers were often forced to leave their children alone in the slave shacks while they worked in the fields. Unable to nurse their children or to care for them, they often returned from work at night to find them dead. This was not suffering produced because of our religion or our previous class (and many were royalty), but because of our race. Neither class nor religion could sustain the level of persecution and violence inflicted against Africans in America.

Our ancestors came ashore to the uncertainty of life but the certainty of pain, drudgery, disrespect, and abuse. Yes, it is true that George Washington held more than one hundred Africans in bondage and brought eight of them—Moll, Christopher Sheels, Hercules, Oney Judge, Austin, Paris, Giles, and Richmond—to Philadelphia when he served as president. Moll had become his wife's personal servant at the age of nineteen. Washington was then twenty-seven. Since an enslaved person had no rights and could appeal to no higher authority than her slaveowner, Moll undoubtedly lived a life of personal terror. Like little Sally Hemmings, who became Thomas Jefferson's sex object at the age of fourteen, Moll, in the White House on Sixth and Chestnut in Philadelphia, was like a trapped animal with no protection from the authority of her slaveowner.

Ignorance is the great cavity that ruins an otherwise healthy nation. If young people, who are most susceptible to violence and the committing of violent actions in the Wilderness, could really read history and understand the relationship of Africans to cotton, they would have a different view of life.

The time was when men, women, and children worked till the blood ran from the tips of their fingers, where they had been pricked by the hard pod of the cotton. I believe that if Wilderness dwellers and Promise dwellers could appreciate how my ancestors dragged their cotton baskets to the scale, trembling for fear their weight should be short and they would be whipped, they would have a common understanding of the trials that made our history.

I know that if Promise dwellers learned about the foundations upon which their privileges were based—that is, on the backs of my ancestors, bent double with constant stooping and scourged on their bare backs when they attempted, for a moment, to stand erect—they would want to treat each human being with respect and dignity.

In the end, however, both the Promised Land and the Wilderness are mythic concepts brought to life by the lives we live. The only promise must be to ourselves, to each other, to eradicate the last vestiges of white supremacy as a doctrine of Promise. The Wilderness must be eradicated as a condition and situation of inferiority, poverty, neglect, and disrespect. When we have achieved these goals we will have defeated the terror in our souls, and that is the most insidious of all terrors.

I offer the suggestion that reparations will free whites from some degree of guilt and liberate African Americans from most of the heavy burden of inferiority and self-hatred rooted in the fact that the nation has never apologized for the historical abuse measured out to their ancestors. It is true that I remain an optimist, a believer in the perfectibility of our national union, based on mutuality, respect, generosity, and *maat*. When the fury is dispelled and the debts paid, the American nation will have found its survival in its own actions.

This nation is one nation only if we make it so; there is no magic to the declaration of unity itself. Those who have tried to declare one nation by insisting that we all become Anglo-Germanics have failed. There is no returning to the past. There is fury everywhere, but it is a righteous anger that seeks to right the wrongs of an unjust society. We are not a one-culture society and we never were. We are a multicultural society—that needs multisystemic solutions to our problems. Do we go forward with a mission for harmony and unity or do we persevere in creating structures of racism and walls between the Wilderness and Promise? This is the national question. The answer can be only that we go forward seeking the path to justice and peace. In this journey, however torturous, together, we can find the maturity to become the nation the Dreamer dreamed and, hence, erase racism.

# NOTES

## INTRODUCTION: EXPANDING THE DREAM

1. Henry Louis Gates Jr., "We Are All Africans," *Ebony* 63, December 2007.

2. Ibid.; "Abraham Lincoln, Race, and DNA" (lecture, Free Library, Philadelphia, PA, February 12, 2009).

3. George Sefa Dei, *Anti-Racist Education: Theory and Practice* (Toronto: Fernwood, 2003), pp. 12–23.

4. Arthur Schlesinger, *The Disuniting of America* (New York: Norton, 1998); Mary Lefkowitz, *Not Out of Africa* (New York: HarperCollins, 1996).

5. "Multiculturalism or Afrocentricity: A Debate with Arthur Schlesinger, Jr., Cornel West, and Molefi Kete Asante" (debate, East Stroudsburg University, East Stroudsburg, PA, March 12, 1992).

6. Marvin Harris, *Theories of Culture in PostModern Times* (Walnut Creek, CA: AltaMira Press, 1999).

7. Ibid., p. 117.

8. Ibid.

9. Ibid.

10. Louis Lomax, *The Negro Revolt* (New York: Harper and Row, 1962).

11. Ama Mazama, "On the Prospects of Black Studies: Theories and Practices" (National Council of Black Studies Annual Conference, Houston, TX, March 2006).

12. Ronald L. Jackson II, *Scripting the Black Masculine Body: Identity, Discourse, and Racial Politics in Popular Media* (Albany: State University of New York Press, 2006), pp. 11–23.

13. Lillian Smith, *Killers of the Dream* (New York: Norton, 1981).

14. Clenora Hudson-Weems, *Emmett Till: The Sacrificial Lamb of the Civil Rights Movement* (Hastings, Sussex, UK: Authorhouse, 1994), pp. 3–25.

15. Patricia Reid-Merritt, *Sister Power* (New York: Wiley, 1996), p. 23.

16. Jean-Bertrand Aristide, *Eyes of the Heart* (New York: Common Courage Press, 2000), pp. 3–4.

# CHAPTER ONE: THE TORTURED DREAM

1. Randall Robinson, *The Debt: What America Owes to Blacks* (New York: Dutton, 2000).

2. "Mornings with Mary," WHAT Radio, Philadelphia, Penn., December 13, 2000.

3. Arnold Schuchter, *Reparations: The Black Manifesto and Its Challenge to White America* (Philadelphia: Lippincott, 1970).

4. Cornel West, *Race Matters* (Boston: Beacon Press, 1993).

5. "Study Finds Disparity in Justice for Blacks," *New York Times*, February 17, 1996, p. 1.

6. West, *Race Matters*. See also Manning Marable, *Beyond Black and White: Transforming African American Politics* (New York and London: Verso, 1995). Both of these books are remarkable in different ways for their optimistic views of race in America. West is a preacher who professes a radical Democrat's vision; he seeks what he calls "a race transcending vision" that is different from Marable's more feet-on-the-ground vision of transforming America by dealing with black political and economic oppression.

7. Arthur M. Schlesinger Jr., *The Disuniting of America: Reflections on a Multicultural Society* (New York: Whittle Communications, 1991).

8. Frantz Fanon, *Black Skin, White Masks*, trans. Charles Lam

Markman (New York: Grove Press, 1967); Albert Memmi, *The Colonizer and the Colonized*, trans. Howard Greenfield (Boston: Beacon Press, 1991).

9. See Derrick Bell, *Faces at the Bottom of the Well: The Permanence of Racism in America* (New York: Basic Books, 1992) and Andrew Hacker, *Two Nations: Black and White, Separate, Hostile, Unequal* (New York: Scribner's, 1992). These two monographs represent studied reflections on the nature of white racial domination in a pluralistic society. They are penetrating accounts of how racism challenges the most fundamental ideas about American unity.

10. Hacker, *Two Nations*, p. 13.

11. Vincent Harding, *There Is a River: The Black Struggle for Freedom in America* (New York: Harcourt Brace Jovanovich, 1981). This monumental work chronicles the struggles of African Americans to overcome the injustices in legal, political, economic, and social arenas. Harding is eloquent in dealing with pathos and brilliant in his analysis of the conditions of life in the Wilderness.

12. Ellis Cose, *The Rage of a Privileged Class* (New York: HarperCollins, 1993).

13. West, *Race Matters*, p. 14.

14. W. E. B. Du Bois, *The Souls of Black Folk* (1903; reprint, New York: Vintage, 1990), pp. 8–9. See also Molefi Kete Asante, "Racism, Consciousness, and Afrocentricity," in *Lure and Loathing: Essays on Race, Identity, and the Ambivalence of Assimilation*, ed. Gerald Early (New York: A. Lane/Penguin, 1993).

# CHAPTER TWO: THE POLITICAL MEMORY

1. A. Birley, *Septimius Severus: An African Emperor* (London: Eyre and Spottiswoode, 1971), pp. 44–46.

2. Stanley Feldstein, *Once a Slave: The Slaves' View of Slavery* (New York: Morrow, 1971), pp. 123–78.

3. "Political Talk" forum on TigerDroppings.com, an independent sports news Web site featuring (but not affiliated with) Louisiana State University, http://www.tigerdroppings.com/rant/messagetopic.asp?p=9633810 (accessed August 10, 2009).

4. "McCain Supporter: 'Obama Is an Arab,'" online video posted by The

Uptake, a nonprofit citizen journalism organization focused on video, http://www.youtube.com/watch?v=0YIq5Q15L1o (accessed August 10, 2009).

5. Ibid.

6. Martin Luther King Jr., "I Have a Dream," Washington D.C., August 28th, 1963, in *The Voice of Black Rhetoric*, ed. Arthur L. Smith and Stephen Robb (Boston: Allyn and Bacon, 1971).

7. Joseph R. Feagin, *Systemic Racism: A Theory of Oppression* (New York: Routledge, 2006); Peggy McIntosh, "White Privilege: Unpacking the Invisible Knapsack," from Working Paper 189, in *White Privilege and Male Privilege: A Personal Account of Coming to See Correspondences through Work in Women's Studies* (Wellesley, MA: Wellesley College Center for Research on Women, 1988); Tim Wise, *White Like Me* (New York: Soft Skull, 2008).

8. Wise, *White Like Me*, p. 2.

9. Ibid.

10. Ibid., p. 3.

11. Ibid.

12. Daniel F. Littlefield Jr., *Africans and Seminoles* (Westport, CT: Greenwood Press, 1977); Richard Prince, "Cherokee Nation Ousts Blacks," *Washington Afro American*, March 10, 2007.

13. Charles J. Kappler, *Indian Affairs: Laws and Treaties* (Washington, D.C.: Government Printing Office), 2:942–45.

14. Ellen Knickmeyer, "Cherokee Nation May Expel Blacks," *Washington Post*, March 2, 2007.

15. Paul Gilroy, *The Black Atlantic: Modernity and Double Consciousness* (Cambridge, MA: Harvard University Press, 1992).

16. Mark Christian, *Black Identity in the 20th Century* (London: Hansib, 2002), p. 126.

17. Ibid., pp. 125–45.

18. K. A. Appiah, *In My Father's House* (New York: Methuen, 1993).

19. Dinesh D'Souza, *The End of Racism* (New York: Free Press, 1995).

20. *Hidden Internment: The Art Shibayama Story*, DVD, directed by Casey Peek (Berkeley, CA; Progressive Films, 2004).

21. Yukyko Takahashi Martinez, "Citizens of Japanese Origin in Peru during World War II: A Review of Current Debates," trans. Andre Soares. *Discover Nikkei: Japanese Migrants and Their Descendants*, March 10, 2009, http://www.discovernikkei.org/en/journal/2009/3/10/citizens-of-japanese-origin-in-peru/ (accessed August 10, 2009).

# CHAPTER THREE: THE MYTHIC CONDITION

1. See Cornel West, *Race Matters* (New York: Vintage, 1993), p. 9. With a prophetic tone, West proclaims, "We have created rootless, dangling people with little link to the supportive networks—family, friends, school— that sustain some sense of purpose in life." As insightful as West tends to be in some matters of race, he misunderstands what constitutes purpose in the community. Family, friends, and schools do not grant purpose; they reflect purpose that inheres in a community of values derived from one's connection to an ancestral story. That is the way all meaningful human purpose is constituted.

2. Andrew Hacker, *Two Nations: Black and White, Separate, Hostile, Unequal* (New York: Scribner's, 1992), p. 13; and Derrick Bell, *Faces at the Bottom of the Well: The Permanence of Racism in America* (New York: Basic Books, 1992), p. 42.

3. National Advisory Commission on Civil Disorders, *The Kerner Report: The 1968 Report of the National Advisory Commission on Civil Disorders* (New York: Pantheon Books, 1988).

4. Jack Forbes, *Africans and Native Americans: The Language of Race and the Evolution of Red-Black Peoples*, 2d ed. (Urbana: University of Illinois Press, 1993), pp. 8–23.

5. Molefi K. Asante, African American History: A Journey of Liberation (Saddle Brook, N.J.: People's Publishing Group, 2002), p. 90.

6. Leon Higginbotham, "An Open Letter to Justice Clarence Thomas from a Federal Judicial Colleague," *University of Pennsylvania Law Review* 140, no. 3 (January 1992): 1005.

7. Ibid.

8. Haki Madhubuti, *Enemies: The Clash of Races* (Chicago: Third World Press, 1978), p. 109.

9. William H. Grier and Price M. Cobb, *Black Rage* (New York: Basic Books, 1968), p. 3.

10. Ellen Goodman, "Those White Males Are Angry!!!" *Philadelphia Inquirer*, December 31, 1994, p. 20.

11. Ibid.

12. One of the most complete accounts of the Dred Scott decision is the book by Vincent Hopkins, *Dred Scott's Case* (New York: Fordham University Press, 1951). A more recent portrait of Roger Brooke Taney is seen in Vin-

cent Harding, *There Is a River: The Black Struggle for Freedom in America* (New York: Harcourt Brace Jovanovich, 1981). Taney's opinion that blacks had no rights that whites had to respect was in line with opinions he had held when he was attorney general. Taney had written that "the African race in the United States even when free, are everywhere a degraded class, and exercise no political influence. The privileges they are allowed to enjoy, are accorded to them as a matter of kindness and benevolence rather than a right." See Carl B. Swisher, *Roger B. Taney* (New York: Macmillan, 1935), p. 154.

13. Bell, *Faces at the Bottom of the Well*, p. 52.

14. Frantz Fanon, *The Wretched of the Earth* (New York: Grove Press, 1965). This is a classic discussion of the severity of psychological disorders that accompany an oppressed people's acceptance of the logic, mannerisms, ethics, and definitions of the oppressor. Fanon's concern is with the oppressed arriving at sanity by exorcising the oppressor from the soul. Since the publication of his book the rationality of his theory has seemed unfaltering.

15. Na'im Akbar, "Psychological Slavery" (lecture at the Afrocentric Conference, Columbus, Ohio, June 1995).

16. James Allen and Hilton Als, *Without Sanctuary: Lynching Photography in America* (Santa Fe, N.M.: Twin Palms, 2000); Ralph Ginzburg, *100 Years of Lynchings* (New York: Lancer Books, 1962).

17. "Two White Girls and Negro Whipped," *New York Times*, April 27, 1903.

18. "Negro Dragged from Cell and Tortured to Death," *New York Herald*, June 18, 1903.

19. "Mob Lynches Negro Man, Flogs Three Negro Women," *Chicago Record-Herald*, July 2, 1903.

20. "Rape Victim Witnesses Lynching," *Chicago Record-Herald*, July 15, 1903.

21. "Mob Terrorizes Negroes After Police Spoil Lynching," *Chicago Record-Herald*, August 13, 1903.

22. "Negro Haters Fire Town," *New York Herald*, March 9, 1907.

23. "15 Negroes Are Shot Down," *Montgomery (Ala.) Advertiser*, August 1, 1910.

24. "Angry Miners Lynch Negro," *Montgomery (Ala.) Advertiser*, October 13, 1910.

25. "Governor Commends Lynchers," *Birmingham (Ala.) News*, November 13, 1911.

26. "4 Negroes Lynched at Once," *Montgomery (Ala.) Advertiser*, January 23, 1912.

27. "African Recruiter Lynching," *Savannah (Ga.) Tribune*, May 4, 1912.

28. "Wrong Man Lynched," *Harrisburg (Pa.) Advocate*, September 13, 1912.

29. "Second Negro Lynched for Crime of One Man," *Atlanta Constitution*, February 9, 1913.

30. "Lynching Bad for Business," *Memphis Commercial Appeal*, August 5, 1913.

31. "Impertinent Question," *Birmingham (Ala.) News*, September 23, 1913.

32. "Negro Powerless to Aid Sister Who Was Raped and Lynched," *New York Age*, April 30, 1914.

33. "Negroes Lynched for Saying 'Hello,' " *Philadelphia Inquirer*, January 3, 1916.

34. "Five Lynched in Georgia," *New York Herald*, January 22, 1916.

35. "Lynched from Courthouse," *Atlanta Constitution*, April 4, 1916.

36. "Burning of Negro in Public Square," *New York World*, May 16, 1916.

37. "Negro Lynched Despite Protests of Rape Victim's Parents," *Philadelphia Inquirer*, August 27, 1916.

38. "Lynching Was 'Humane' Declare Lynch Leaders," *Minneapolis Tribune*, September 3, 1916.

39. "Grim Reminder," *Chicago Defender*, September 8, 1917.

40. "Negro Lynched and Body Mutilated," *Chicago Defender*, October 13, 1917.

41. "Negro Veteran Lynched," *Chicago Defender*, April 5, 1919.

42. "Illiterate Negro Lynched for Writing Improper Note," *Knoxville East Tennessee News*, May 1, 1919.

43. "White Man Blackens Face and Attacks White Girl," *Chicago Defender*, May 10, 1919.

44. "Negro Intruder Lynched," *Vicksburg (Miss.) Herald*, May 15, 1919.

45. "Church Burnings Follow Negro Agitator's Lynching," *Chicago Defender*, September 6, 1919.

46. "Sumter Negro Found Dead after Spreading Propaganda," *Atlanta Constitution*, October 4, 1919.

47. "Denies Rapist Was Black," *Knoxville East Tennessee News*, December 2, 1920.

48. "Lowry Roasted Before Wife and Children," *Memphis Press*, January 27, 1921.

49. "Lynching After Refusing to Dance on White Man's Command," *Knoxville East Tennessee News*, February 3, 1921.

50. "Midnight Terrorist Lynch Negro Brakeman," *Memphis Times-Scimitar*, March 18, 1921.

51. "Mob Respects Woman's Request to Move Lynching from Lawn," *Baltimore Afro-American*, August 19, 1921.

52. "Lynch Victim's Father Clears Away Ashes," *St. Louis Argus*, November 25, 1921.

53. "Whites Display Negro Body Parts," *Chicago Defender*, February 17, 1923.

54. "University Students Help Mob Lynch Janitor," *New York World*, April 20, 1923.

55. "Outspoken Negro Killed," *St. Louis Argus*, June 15, 1923.

56. "Mass Exodus of Negroes," *Washington (D.C.) Eagle*, August 11, 1923.

57. "Wrong Negro May Have Been Killed," *Chicago Tribune*, October 10, 1924.

58. "Darrow Forced to Flee After Anti-Lynch Speech," *Chicago Defender*, March 12, 1927.

59. "Texas Mob Runs Amuck," *New York Sun*, May 10, 1930.

60. "Prison Warden Doubts Guilt of Negro Lynched in Georgia," *New York Negro World*, October 4, 1930.

61. "Lynched for Killing Banker, Negro Was Wrong Man," *Indianapolis Recorder*, March 4, 1933.

62. "Doctor Rescues Negro Lad," *New York Herald-Tribune*, March 27, 1933.

63. "Mysterious Lynching in Mississippi," *Knoxville (Tenn.) Journal*, July 23, 1933.

64. "Wildest Lynching Orgy in History," *New York Times*, October 19, 1933.

65. "Big Preparation Made for Lynching Tonight," *Macon (Ga.) Telegraph*, October 26, 1934.

66. "Lynching Carried Off Almost As Advertised," *Birmingham (Ala.) Post*, October 27, 1934.

67. "Lynched with Hymn on Lips," *Atlanta Constitution*, March 13, 1935.

68. "Lynched before Trial," *Hickory (N.C.) Record*, April 28, 1936.

69. "Lynchers Torture, Burn Two Negroes," *New York Times*, April 14, 1937.

70. "NAACP Says Rape Charge Was Pretext," *Philadelphia Tribune*, December 15, 1938.
71. "Mississippi Minister Lynched," *New York Amsterdam News*, August 26, 1944.
72. "15-Year-Old Is Lynched; Wolf-Whistled at White," *Washington Post*, September 1, 1955.
73. "Negro Is Hanged by Heels," *Birmingham (Ala.) News*, March 8, 1960.
74. "Texas Horror Shocks Nation," *New York Daily News*, June 10, 1998.
75. Hacker, *Two Nations*, p. 13; Bell, *Faces at the Bottom of the Well*, p. 42.
76. William R. Spivey, *Corporate America in Black and White* (New York: Carlton Press, 1993), p. 23.

# CHAPTER FOUR: THE WILDERNESS OF RACIAL DISCONTENT

1. "The Great 'White' Influx," *New York Times*, July 31, 2002.
2. Winston Van Horne, interview with author, University of Wisconsin–Milwaukee, April 12, 1993.
3. "A Day of Fasting," *New York Tribune*, May 4, 1899.
4. Ibid.
5. W. E. B. Du Bois, *The Souls of Black Folk* (1903; reprint, New York: Vintage, 1990), p. 22.
6. Ibid.
7. Ibid.
8. William M. Tuttle Jr., *Race Riot: Chicago In the Red Summer of 1919* (New York: Atheneum, 1970), p. 23.
9. "Wounded Negro Lynched," *Chicago Whip*, August 25, 1919.
10. Ibid.
11. "Uptown Unrest," *New York Times*, July 8, 1992.
12. Maulana Karenga, *Kawaida Theory* (Los Angeles: University of Sankore Press, 1989), pp. 1–30.

# CHAPTER FIVE: THE DISORIENTATION

1. James D. Delk, *Fires and Furies: The L.A. Riots* (Palm Springs, Calif.: ETC Publications, 1995); and Lou Cannon, *Official Negligence* (New York: Random House, 1997), p. 347.

2. "The Melting Pot Thesis," *New York Times*, March 7, 1996.

3. "Judge Rejects Attempt to Free Young Killers," *Beloit Daily News*, December 16, 1999.

4. W. E. B. Du Bois, *The Souls of Black Folk* (1903; reprint, New York: Vintage, 1990), p. 3. Du Bois's full quote is "one ever feels his two-ness—an American, a Negro—two souls, two thoughts, two unreconciled strivings; two warring ideals in one dark boy whose dogged strength alone keeps it from being torn assunder." My contention is that Du Bois's observation, though cast widely, was really autobiographical.

5. Charshee McIntyre, address to the African Heritage Studies Association, Columbus, Ohio, March 21, 1996.

6. Kobi Kambon, *The African-Centered African American Personality* (Trenton, N.J.: Africa World Press, 1983), pp. 2–25.

7. Lerone Bennett, *Before the Mayflower* (New York: Penguin, 1984), pp. 3–7.

8. Carter G. Woodson, *The Miseducation of the Negro* (Trenton, N.J.: Africa World Press, 1990), pp. 12–18.

9. "A New Campus Hero," *Atlanta Journal and Constitution*, November 28, 1992.

10. Elijah Anderson, *Streetwise: Race, Class and Change in the Urban Community* (Chicago: University of Chicago Press, 1992), p. 37.

11. Robert Williams, *Negroes with Guns* (New York: Marzani and Munsell, 1992). This is the report of the historic confrontation when Robert Williams defended his home against a white mob in North Carolina. He later traveled to China and Cuba, where he remained for many years.

12. Michael Moore, *Stupid White Men—and Other Sorry Excuses for the State of the Nation!* (New York: ReganBooks, 2001).

13. Patricia Gaines-Carter, "New Breed on the Streets," *Washington Post*, February 23, 1992.

14. Gregory Freeman, S*t. Louis Post-Dispatch*, September 14, 1990.

15. Mark Naison, "Outlaw Culture and the Black Neighborhood," *Reconstruction* 4, no. 4 (1992): 1–6.

16. Anderson, *Streetwise*, p. 102.

17. Ibid., p. 87.

18. *Jackson Sun*, June 14, 1992.

19. *USA Today*, February 6, 1991.

20. *Journal of the American Medical Association*, November 29, 1991.

21. Andrew Hacker, *Two Nations: Black and White, Separate, Hostile, Unequal* (New York: Scribner's, 1992), pp. 31–35.

22. David Mills, "Sista Souljah's Call to Arms," *Washington Post*, May 13, 1992, p. 6.

23. *New Orleans Times-Picayune*, December 5, 1991.

24. Malcolm X, *The Last Speeches* (New York: Pathfinder, 1989), p. 39.

25. Ibid.

26. Ibid. p. 156.

27. Ibid. p. 195.

28. *The New Negro*, ed. Alain Locke (New York: Atheneum, 1968). Just up from slavery Africans in America found many obstacles to success in the urban areas of the North. Alain Locke understood that the intellectual and artistic work of the various members of the intelligentsia had to become standards for the African race. There were those who saw in the contributions of the authors to the so-called Negro Renaissance true genius, and there were those who derided what they saw as imitation of whites. Nevertheless, Locke's contribution, by gathering in one volume many of the new authors, was to have a powerful impact on the Renaissance centered in Harlem.

29. Maulana Karenga, *Kawaida Theory* (Los Angeles: Kawaida Publications, 1989), p. 29.

30. Malcolm X, *The Last Speeches*, p. 35.

31. Ibid., p. 27.

32. Molefi Kete Asante, *Kemet, Afrocentricity, and Knowledge* (Trenton, N.J.: Africa World Press, 1987), pp. 4–40.

33. Malcolm X, *The Last Speeches*, p. 40.

34. Maulana Karenga, *Introduction to Black Studies* (Los Angeles: University of Sankore Press, 1992), pp. 1–100.

35. Marimba Ani, *Yurugu* (Trenton, N.J.: Africa World Press, 1993), p. 3.

36. Finley Campbell, "Voices of Thunder, Voices of Rage," in *Language, Communication and Rhetoric in Black America*, ed. Arthur L. Smith [M. K. Asante] (New York: Harper and Row, 1972), p. 22.

37. Malcolm X, *The Last Speeches*, p. 40.

38. Many contemporary works examine the interface between culture and language. One work that might be of interest is Molefi Kete Asante and K. Welsh-Asante, eds., *African Culture: The Rhythms of Unity* (Trenton, N.J.: Africa World Press, 1990). See particularly the introduction on language and culture.

39. Malcolm X, "Message to the Grassroots," phonograph record, 1963.

40. John Illo, "The Rhetoric of Malcolm X," *Forum* 9 (spring 1966): 7.

41. Malcolm X, *The Last Speeches*, p. 175.

42. Illo, "The Rhetoric of Malcolm X," p. 24.

# CHAPTER SIX: RACE AND THE RELIGION SITUATION

1. Mark 16:15.

2. James H. Cone, *A Black Theology of Liberation* (Maryknoll, NY: Orbis Books, 1970), p. 23.

3. Samuel Dewitt Proctor, *Substance of Things Hoped For: A Memoir of African American Faith* (Valley Forge, PA: Judson Press, 1999).

4. Molefi Asante and Ama Mazama, eds., *Encyclopedia of African Religion* (Thousand Oaks, CA: Sage Publications, 2009).

5. Eddie Glaude, *Exodus! Religion, Race, and Nation in Nineteenth-Century Black America* (Chicago: University of Chicago Press, 2000).

6. Ama Mazama, "African American Culture: The Stripped Thesis" (lecture at Kean University, Union, NJ, November 31, 2008).

7. Melville Herskovits, *The Myth of the Negro Past* (Boston: Beacon Press, 1990).

8. E. Franklin Frazier, *The Negro Family in the United States* (Chicago: University of Chicago Press, 1939); Frazier, *The Negro in the United States* (New York: Macmillan, 1949); Frazier, *Black Bourgeoisie* (Glencoe, IL: Free Press, 1957); Frazier, *Race and Culture Contacts in the Modern World* (New York: Knopf, 1957).

9. Martin Luther King Jr., "Letter from a Birmingham Jail" (Atlanta, GA: Martin Luther King Jr. Estate, April 16, 1963).

10. Ibid.

11. David Walker, *An Appeal to the Colored Citizens of the World* (Boston: s. p., 1829).

# CHAPTER SEVEN: THE FURIOUS PASSAGE

1. See Haki Madhubuti, *Black Men: Obsolete, Single, Dangerous? Afrikan American Families in Transition: Essays in Discovery, Solution, and Hope* (Chicago: Third World Press, 1990). See also Bobby Seale, *Seize the Time: The Story of the Black Panther Party and Huey P. Newton* (New York: Random House, 1970), for an assessment of some predictable actions and reactions in the Wilderness.

2. Andrew Hacker, *Two Nations: Black and White, Separate, Hostile, Unequal* (New York: Scribner's, 1992), p. 2.

3. Ibid., pp. 3–5.

4. Ibid., p. 5.

5. "Contemporary Police Brutality and Misconduct: A Continuation of the Lebacy of Racial Violence," report issued by the Black Radical Congress, February 28, 2001, p. 1.

6. There are a number of books on race that suggest that the stress of racism is a major factor in black resignation. See, for example, Stephen L. Carter, *Reflections of an Affirmative Action Baby* (New York: Basic Books, 1991); Cornel West, *Race Matters* (Boston: Beacon Press, 1992); and Manning Marable, *The Great Well of Democracy: Reconstructing Race and Politics in the Twenty-first Century* (New York: Basic Books, 2002).

7. Keith B. Richburg, *Out of America: A Black Man Confronts Africa* (New York: Basic Books, 1997).

8. Fred Mazelis, "New Jersey Internal Records Document Widespread Racial Profiling of Black and Hispanic Motorists," *World Socialist Web*, [online], www.wsws.org/articles/2000/dec2000/race-d02.shtml [December 2, 2000].

9. Ibid.

10. Dinesh D'Souza, *The End of Racism: Principles for a Multicultural Society* (New York: Free Press, 1995); Richard J. Herrnstein, *The Bell Curve: Intelligence and Class Structure in American Life* (New York: Free Press, 1994); Mary R. Lefkowitz, *Not Out of Africa: How Afrocentrism Became an Excuse to Teach Myth As History* (New York: Basic Books, 1996).

11. "Three Whites Charged in Attack on Black," *Chicago Tribune*, May 27, 1997.

12. See Molefi Kete Asante, *The Afrocentric Idea* (Philadelphia: Temple University Press, 1999); also Ama Mazama, ed., *The Afrocentric Paradigm* (Trenton, N.J.: World Africa Press, 2002).

13. Dinesh D'Souza, *Illiberal Education: The Politics of Race and Sex on Campus* (New York: Free Press, 1991).

14. Shelby Steele, *The Content of Our Character: A New Vision of Race in America* (New York: St. Martin's Press, 1990). This is Steele's most important work. In this book he argues that the basic problem between blacks and whites is who shall declare the greater innocence. In effect, Steele believes that the black community seeks to declare its innocence on the basis of the past injustices and that whites tend to declare their innocence as well. He fails to say what whites use to declare innocence inasmuch as he is seeking to indict black leadership for seeking group solutions based on making whites feel guilty. There are many things wrong with Steele's construction of the racial issues in the United States, but the most profound error is the idea that there is some equality between black and white innocence and guilt in racism. This belies the historical record and minimizes the thousands of blacks who have died fighting for freedom from oppression over the past five hundred years. Actually Steele's notion that white racism is not the issue, but the belief that racism exists is the issue, is way off target. This strategy seeks to place the burden of economic, cultural, and material dispossession on the dispossessed.

15. Thomas Sowell, *The Vision of the Anointed* (New York: Basic Books, 1995). Sowell's critique of liberal ideology where he supports a tragic view instead of what he calls a perfectible view of humanity.

16. Thomas Sowell, *The Economics and Politics of Race* (New York: William Morrow, 1985).

17. Anne Wortham, *The Other Side of Racism* (Columbus: Ohio State University Press, 1982).

18. Chuck Stone, *Black Political Power in America* (New York: Dell, 1970), p. 45.

19. Ibid., p. 46.

# CHAPTER EIGHT: THE DRAMA OF RACISM

1. Cornel West, "Diverse New World," *Democratic Left* (July/August 1991): 2–4.

2. Malcolm X, *The Last Speeches* (New York: Pathfinder, 1989), pp. 9–10.

3. William Julius Wilson, *The Declining Significance of Race: Blacks and*

*Changing American Institutions* (Chicago: University of Chicago Press, 1978). Wilson established the saliency of class issues in the life chances of African Americans but failed to account for the antipathy of whites toward blacks of the same class. Clearly most whites see race, not class, as the most important factor in their relationships with African Americans.

4. Sidney M. Willhelm, *Who Needs the Negro?* (Cambridge, Mass.: Schenkman, 1970) and *Black in a White America* (Cambridge, Mass.: Schenkman, 1983) are important works in the discourse on racism. Willhelm's analysis is based on radical sociological theory, but to Afrocentrists he is correct in his interpretations of the economic condition of blacks in urban America. His thesis that black progress is a myth because African Americans remain economic hostages, even while receiving the same socioeconomic and political rights as whites, is extremely cogent when you consider the nearly 250-year advantage whites had during the period of enslavement and rigid segregation. Since the end of slavery did not destroy racism, we could not expect the end of segregation to bring about equality.

5. The works of Joe Feagin are important for a thorough understanding of racism in America. Several of his books are useful for our discussion. See particularly *Ghetto Revolts: The Politics of Violence in American Cities*, with Harlan Hahn (New York: Macmillan, 1973); *Racial and Ethnic Relations* (Englewood Cliffs, N.J.: Prentice Hall, 1989); *White Racism: The Basics*, with Hernan Vera (New York: Routledge, 1995); *The Urban Scene: Myths and Realities*, 2d ed. (New York: Random House, 1979); and *Double Burden: Black Women and Everyday Racism*, with Yanick St. Jean (Armonk, N.Y.: M. E. Sharpe, 1998). Feagin's work is at the cutting edge of racism studies in the United States. A prolific author, he has examined white racism in a more thorough way than any contemporary sociologist.

6. Michael Omi and Howard Winant, *Racial Formation in the United States: From the 1960s to the 1990s* (New York: Routledge, 1994). This is a classic work in the field of contemporary sociology. Omi and Winant should be applauded for seeing the dead end within the traditional race theories of sociology. However, they have failed to grapple with the fundamental problem of the ideology of white racial domination, the great generator of racist thinking and behavior. To argue, for example, as they seem to, that world history has been racialized is to beg the question. By whom has it been racialized and for what purpose are issues that Afrocentrists raise in their own literature on racism? It is a euphemism to say the "modern world

system" is responsible when, in fact, it is the continuation of the doctrine of white racial privilege and domination that structures the debates within the field of sociology.

7. John Bunzel, "Affirmative Action," *Chronicle of Higher Education*, March 1, 1989, pp. 31–33.

8. Stephen Carter, *Reflections of an Affirmative Action Baby* (New York: Basic Books, 1991).

9. See Cornel West, *Race Matters* (Boston: Beacon Press, 1992), pp. 30–65.

10. "The Death Penalty in Black and White: Who Lives, Who Dies, Who Decides," in *GAO Death Penalty Study* (Washington, D.C.: US General Accounting Office, 1998). The report was quite clear that racism played a major role in who died and who lived. The race of the defendant is the most determinative factor in the administration of the death penalty. African American defendants are four times more likely to get the death sentence than others who commit crimes of the same severity. Of the thirty-eight states that impose the death penalty, 98 percent of the prosecutors who decide to seek the death penalty are white (African Americans and Hispanics are each 1 percent of the death penalty decision makers). In 93 percent of the states where race and the death penalty have been examined, there was a greater likelihood of death sentences for the murder of a white victim.

11. Andrew Hacker, *Two Nations: Black and White, Separate, Hostile, Unequal* (New York: Scribner's, 1992), pp. 2–13.

12. "Holiday Spa Settles," *USA Today*, July 31, 1990, p. 4. A more recent case of discrimination in the industry was reported in a business wire from Oakland, California, on February 17, 1998, under the headline, "Former Manager Files Lawsuit against Claremont Resort, California." The resort and spa company was accused of racial discrimination and harassment against African Americans in a lawsuit filed in Alameda Superior Court by Gina Carter, a former manager at the resort. She hired and promoted numerous African American employees, according to the lawsuit. Carter alleged that following her hiring and promoting of African American employees, higher management at Claremont discouraged her from hiring additional black front-office employees and lower-level managers because of their race.

The lawsuit claimed that Carter complained about the discrimination to senior management and to Harsch Investments, an Oregon company that owns the Claremont Resort, and that following her complaint she was terminated from employment. According to the lawsuit, this termination was in retaliation for complaining about the discrimination. The aim of the lawsuit was to redress the civil rights violations practiced against Gina Carter and to prevent any further discrimination against African American employees and applicants by Claremont. By February 2003 the University of California, Berkeley, and other institutions had withdrawn from association with Claremont on labor issues.

13. "Denny's Tries to Make Amends for Racial Discrimination," *Lubbock Avalanche-Journal*, January 16, 1997.

14. Lynne Duke, "Buffalo Family Seeking Millions for Fatal Lack of a Bus Stop," *Washington Post*, November 15, 1999, p. A03.

15. Steve Sailer, "Golf Club Discrimination," *St. Louis Post-Dispatch*, December 12, 1990.

16. "Racism and Private Clubs: Editorial," *USA Today*, July 31, 1990, p. 12.

17. Ibid.

18. "Race and Private Clubs: Editorial," *New Orleans Times-Picayune*, August 16, 1990.

19. "GM Will Pay," *Los Angeles Times*, April 4, 1991. Since the General Motors settlement there have been other cases of major corporate legal settlements for racial discrimination. In "Coca-Cola Settles Suit for a Record $192.5 Million" (November 17, 2000), *Michigan Daily* reported that Coca-Cola agreed to settle the suit in order to adjust the salaries of black employees who were discriminated against in promotions and salaries. The agreement surpassed the $176-million settlement of a discrimination lawsuit against Texaco in 1995. Texaco's agreement also included a watchdog panel and established a model for Coca-Cola.

20. See also T. Shawn Taylor, "Joliet-Area Plant Settles Racial Harassment Complaint: $1.8 Million to be Shared by 32 Men," *Chicago Tribune*, March 28, 2002. Apollo Colors, small company in Rockdale, Illinois, settled a racial harassment complaint for nearly $2 million when black men said factory managers had a pattern of harassment dating to the 1980s. A complaint filed with the Equal Employment Opportunity Commission said the harassment included racial slurs and racist graffiti in bathrooms, locker rooms, and break rooms, which made the situation intolerable.

21. Julianne Malveaux, "Blacks Still Face Racism," *Progressive* (September 1998): 3.

22. "Discrimination Suit," *New Orleans Times-Picayune*, December 5, 1991. Of course, it is not just discrimination in employment that plagues

African Americans, it is also the willful harassment of black people. David A. Harris's "Driving While Black: Racial Profiling on Our Nation's Highways," *American Civil Liberties Union Special Report*, June 1999, details the way in which blacks are often robbed of dignity by racist police.

23. "CBS Employees Charge Company Retaliation," *Los Angeles Sentinel*, December 21, 1990.

24. "Discrimination Complaint," *Washington Times*, April 13, 1990.

25. "Police Review Board Idea Attacked," *New York Amsterdam News*, November 14, 1992.

26. "Rendell Vetoes Police Board," *Philadelphia Inquirer*, June 1, 1993.

27. "Black Deputies File Charges," *Los Angeles Sentinel*, April 11, 1991. See also Pamela Johnson, "Discrimination Suit Against Sheriff's Department," *Los Angeles Times*, April 1, 1999.

28. "Texaco Accused of Unfair Practices," *Wall Street Journal*, May 14, 1991. See Ian Springsteel's "A Penny for Your Actions: A Texaco Bonus Plan Stirs Controversy by Rewarding Minority Hiring and Promotions," *CFO* (August 2, 1997).

29. "Blacks Denied Job Opportunities," *Houston Post*, May 5, 1991.

30. "Urban Institute Report Discrimination," *Chicago Defender*, June 17, 1991.

31. "Utility Firm Charged with Bias," *Chicago Defender*, June 17, 1991.

32. "Segregation Persists," *Washington Post*, July 17, 1991.

33. Roger Waldinger and Thomas Bailey, "The Continuing Significance of Race: Racial Conflict and Racial Discrimination in Construction," *Politics and Society* 19, no. 3 (1991): 291–323.

34. "Black Employees Cry Foul," *Michigan Chronicle*, December 11, 1991.

35. Ibid.

36. "Company Agrees to Settle," *Washington Post*, March 3, 1992.

37. Tom Larson, "African American Male Migration and Employment," *Review of Black Political Economy* (winter 1992): 15–30.

38. Derrick Bell, *And We Are Not Saved: The Elusive Quest for Racial Justice* (New York: Basic Books, 1987). Bell's corpus, legal and popular, constitutes one of the most significant statements on race by an African American legal philosopher. Recognized universally in the black academic community for his commitment to antiracism, as indicated by his resignation from Harvard Law School when the school was slow to tenure an African American woman, Bell's actions against racism are taken as a high-water mark for academic resistance.

39. George Anderson, "Race, De Facto Segregation, and the Law," *Journal and Guide*, June 21, 1989.

40. "Black Woman Wins Right to Sue," *Washington Times*, July 10, 1990.

41. Haki Madhubuti, *Enemies: The Clash of Races* (Chicago: Third World Press, 1978).

42. Hacker, *Two Nations*, pp. 23–45. Hacker's position agitated both whites and blacks in a public symposium at City College soon after the publication of his book. It was one of the first times I had to rescue a white author from a series of pointed questions. There was a misunderstanding of Hacker's argument and the audience, largely African American, assumed that the negative assessment of racial relations Hacker was making was a policy he was advocating. My defense of Hacker's position was probably as misunderstood by some in the audience as was Hacker's statement. His point was that America "did not care a damn about black people; it cared, at the policy level, only for those workers and consumers who would continue to support the capitalist system. If it meant importing Asians and Hispanics to do the work, without dissent, that blacks did not want to do, then America would take that option." This statement angered some in the audience. I informed the audience that their faith was longer than Hacker's facts.

43. Martin Luther King Jr., *Where Do We Go from Here: Chaos or Community?* (Boston: Beacon Press, 1968). Ralph Bunche, an African American, was one of the most distinguished leaders of the United Nations.

44. "Sting Operation Shows Discrimination," *Boston Globe*, October 23, 1991.

45. "Landlords Reveal Bias," *Washington Post*, June 24, 1989.

46. "Cab Companies Charged with Racism," *Chicago Tribune*, April 12, 1992.

47. Patrick Reardon, "Sports Inequalities," *New York Times*, August 16, 1992.

# CHAPTER NINE: THE NATIONAL SURVIVAL

1. Cornel West, "Diverse New Worlds," *Democratic Left* (July/August 1991): 2.

2. Ibid.

3. Cornel West, *Race Matters* (Boston: Beacon Press, 1993), p. 43.

4. Maulana Karenga, *Introduction to Black Studies* (Los Angeles: University of Sankore Press, 1992). This is the most authoritative introductory

text to the field of Black Studies. The prolific author has contributed more to building the discipline than any contemporary scholar. His works seek to project African cultural values on the world stage in their own right. For West not to engage Karenga's work in a serious way is to avoid a principal piece of the cultural discourse.

5. "Profiling Black Motorists," *New York Times*, February 27, 1990.

6. "Social Security Discriminates," *Philadelphia Inquirer*, May 12, 1992.

7. "Discriminatory Practices," *New York Times Magazine*, July 12, 1992. See also Alphonso Pinkney's *The Myth of Black Progress* (New York: Cambridge University Press, 1984), for a brilliant discussion of the reality of being black and living in the Wilderness. Pinkney demonstrates that the citizenship gains of the civil rights period were exaggerated as conservatives attempted to reverse them. Much along the lines of the works of Derrick Bell, Andrew Hacker, and, increasingly, Robert C. Smith, Pinkney argues that the conditions of the people of the Wilderness are indictments of the American Promise.

8. Bruce Wright, *Black Robes, White Justice* (Secaucus, N.J.: Lyle Stuart, 1987). Wright's analysis of the justice system from his position as a sitting judge is uniquely revealing. In fact, Wright contends that a white judge who knows nothing of the Wilderness cannot possibly understand the crimes committed by blacks. Regardless of his or her decency, the white judge has never experienced the deprivation, frustration, brutality, and the humiliation of the African American. Citing the system of bail as one instance in which the Wilderness dweller is punished by his inability to pay, Wright argues that bail becomes punishment rather than a guarantee that a person will return to the courtroom to face charges.

9. George G. M. James, *Stolen Legacy* (Chicago: African American Images, 2002). What has agitated many Eurocentric scholars about this book, first published in 1956 and read since that time in the black community, is the contention that many ancient Greek ideas were borrowed from Africa, although that is rarely acknowledged by Europe at this time. The use of the word "stolen" in the title is considered too strong. James, who was a professor of Latin and Greek at the University of Arkansas, Pine Bluff, contended that when you borrow something and then forget that you borrowed it, one could easily say that it is stolen. See Molefi Kete Asante, *The Painful Demise of Eurocentrism: An Afrocentric Response to Critics* (Lawrenceville, N.J.: Africa World Press, 2000), for a further discussion of the Greek debt to Africa.

10. Henry Louis Gates Jr., "Black Demagogues and Pseudo-Intellectuals,"

*New York Times*, July 20, 1992. Compare ADL research report: *The Anti-Semitism of Black Demagogues and Extremists* (New York: Anti-Defamation League, 1992). The real attacks on both Jews and African Americans are enough to suggest what is needed is a concerted effort against anti-Semitism and anti-Africanism rather than any attempt to divide the victims.

11. Letter to the editor, *New York Times*, August 15, 1992.

12. Michael Bradley, *The Iceman Inheritance: Prehistoric Sources of Western Man's Racism, Sexism, and Aggression* (Trenton, N.J.: Africa World Press, 1990), p. 6.

13. Andrew Hacker, *Two Nations: Black and White, Separate, Hostile, Unequal* (New York: Scribner's, 1992).

14. Derrick Bell, *Faces at the Bottom of the Well* (New York: Basic Books, 1992).

15. Richard America, *Paying the Social Debt: What White America Owes Black America* (Westport, Conn.: Praeger, 1993).

16. Randall Robinson, *The Debt: What America Owes to Blacks* (New York: Dutton, 2000).

17. "French Court Rules in Favor of Jewish Depositors," *New York Times*, June 13, 2001, p. A-14.

18. David Walker, *An Appeal to the Colored Citizens of the World* (Boston: Author, 1829), p. 1.

19. Hacker, *Two Nations*, pp. 199–219.

20. Robert Hughes, *The Culture of Complaints: The Fraying of America* (New York: Oxford University Press, 1993). This book rationalizes the responses of the dominant society to the conditions of the oppressed. Wilderness dwellers know full well that there are those who repudiate them for the very conditions the accusers have perpetuated. To name the protest as "complaint" is to dismiss the justice of the grievance. In the end, what is remarkable is that the Wilderness dwellers' calling card has been patience.

21. Stanley Feldstein, *Once a Slave: The Slave's View of Slavery* (New York: William Morrow, 1971), pp. 33–38.

# BIBLIOGRAPHY

Akbar, Na'im. "Psychological Slavery." Lecture at the Afrocentric Conference, Columbus, Ohio, June 1995.

Allen, James, and Hilton Als. *Without Sanctuary: Lynching Photography in America*. Santa Fe, N.M.: Twin Palms, 2000.

America, Richard. *Paying the Social Debt: What White America Owes Black America*. Westport, Conn.: Praeger, 1993.

Anderson, Elijah. *Streetwise: Race, Class, and Change in the Urban Community*. Chicago: University of Chicago Press, 1992.

Anti-Defamation League. *The Anti-Semitism of Black Demagogues and Extremists*. New York: Anti-Defamation League, 1992.

Asante, Molefi Kete. *African American History: A Journey of Liberation*. Saddle Brook, N.J.: People's Publishing Group, 2002.

———. *The Afrocentric Idea*. Philadelphia: Temple University Press, 1999.

———. *Kemet, Afrocentricity, and Knowledge*. Trenton, N.J.: Africa World Press, 1987.

———. *The Painful Demise of Eurocentrism: An Afrocentric Response to Critics*. Lawrenceville, N.J.: Africa World Press, 2000.

————. "Racism, Consciousness, and Afrocentricity." In *Lure and Loathing: Essays on Race, Identity, and the Ambivalence of Assimilation*, edited by Gerald Early. New York: A. Lane/Penguin, 1993.

Asante, Molefi Kete, and K. Welsh-Asante, eds. *African Culture: The Rhythms of Unity*. Trenton, N.J.: Africa World Press, 1990.

Bell, Derrick. *And We Are Not Saved: The Elusive Quest for Racial Justice*. New York: Basic Books, 1987.

————. *Faces at the Bottom of the Well: The Permanence of Racism in America*. New York: Basic Books, 1992.

Bennett, Lerone. *Before the Mayflower*. New York: Penguin, 1984.

Bradley, Michael. *The Iceman Inheritance: Prehistoric Sources of Western Man's Racism, Sexism, and Aggression*. Trenton, N.J.: Africa World Press, 1990.

Bunzel, John. "Race and Education." *Chronicle of Higher Education*, March 1, 1989.

Campbell, Finley. "Voices of Thunder, Voices of Rage." In *Language, Communication, and Rhetoric in Black America*, edited by Arthur L. Smith [M. K. Asante]. New York: Harper and Row, 1972.

Cannon, Lou. *Official Negligence*. New York: Random House, 1997.

Carter, Stephen L. *Reflections of an Affirmative Action Baby*. New York: Basic Books, 1991.

Cose, Ellis. *The Rage of a Priveleged Class*. New York: HarperCollins, 1993.

Delk, James D. *Fires and Furies: The L.A. Riots*. Palm Springs, Calif.: ETC Publications, 1995.

D'Souza, Dinesh. *The End of Racism: Principles for a Multicultural Society*. New York: Free Press, 1995.

————. *Illiberal Education: The Politics of Race and Sex on Campus*. New York: Free Press, 1991.

Du Bois, W. E. B. *The Souls of Black Folk*. 1903. Reprint, New York: Vintage, 1990.

Fanon, Frantz. *Black Skin, White Masks*. Translated by Charles Lam Markman. New York: Grove Press, 1967.

————. *The Wretched of the Earth*. Translated by Constance Farrington. New York: Grove Press, 1965.

Feagin, Joe. *Racial and Ethnic Relations*. Englewood Cliffs, N.J.: Prentice Hall, 1989.

————. *The Urban Scene: Myths and Realities*. 2d ed. New York: Random House, 1979.

Feagin, Joe, and Harlan Hahn. *Ghetto Revolts: The Politics of Violence in American Cities*. New York: Macmillan, 1973.

Feagin, Joe, and Yanick St. Jean. *Double Burden: Black Women and Everyday Racism*. Armonk, N.Y.: M. E. Sharpe, 1998.

Feagin, Joe, and Hernán Vera. *White Racism: The Basics*. New York: Routledge, 1995.

Feldstein, Stanley. *Once a Slave: The Slave's View of Slavery*. New York: William Morrow, 1971.

Forbes, Jack. *Africans and Native Americans: The Language of Race and the Evolution of Red-Black Peoples*. 2d ed. Urbana: University of Illinois Press, 1993.

Gates, Henry Louis, Jr. "Black Demagogues and Pseudo-Intellectuals." *New York Times*, July 20, 1992.

Ginzburg, Ralph. *100 Years of Lynchings*. New York: Lancer Books, 1962.

Goodman, Ellen. "Those White Males Are Angry!!!" *Philadelphia Inquirer*, December 31, 1994.

Grier, William H., and Price M. Cobb. *Black Rage*. New York: Basic Books, 1968.

Hacker, Andrew. *Two Nations: Black and White, Separate, Hostile, Unequal*. New York: Scribner's, 1992.

Harding, Vincent. *There Is a River: The Black Struggle for Freedom in America*. New York: Harcourt Brace Jovanovich, 1981.

Herrnstein, Richard J. *The Bell Curve: Intelligence and Class Structure in American Life*. New York: Free Press, 1994.

Higginbotham, Leon. "An Open Letter to Justice Clarence Thomas from a Federal Judicial Colleague." *University of Pennsylvania Law Review* 140, no. 3 (January 1992).

Hopkins, Vincent. *Dred Scott's Case*. New York: Fordham University Press, 1951.

Hughes, Robert. *The Culture of Complaints: The Fraying of America*. New York: Oxford University Press, 1993.

Illo, John. "The Rhetoric of Malcolm X." *Forum* 9 (spring 1966): 11–23.

James, George G. M. *Stolen Legacy*. Chicago: African American Images, 2002.

Kambon, Kobi. *The African-Centered African American Personality*. Trenton, N.J.: Africa World Press, 1990.

Karenga, Maulana. *Introduction to Black Studies*. Los Angeles: University of Sankore Press, 1992.

———. *Kawaida Theory*. Los Angeles: University of Sankore Press, 1989.

King, Martin Luther, Jr. *Where Do We Go from Here: Chaos or Community?* Boston: Beacon Press, 1968.

Larson, Tom. "African American Male Migration and Employment." *Review of Black Political Economy* (winter 1992): 6–17.

Lefkowitz, Mary R. *Not Out of Africa: How Afrocentrism Became an Excuse to Teach Myth As History.* New York: Basic Books, 1996.

Locke, Alain, ed. *The New Negro.* New York: Atheneum, 1968.

Madhubuti, Haki. *Black Men: Obsolete, Single, Dangerous? Afrikan American Families in Transition: Essays in Discovery, Solution, and Hope.* Chicago: Third World Press, 1990.

———. *Enemies: The Clash of Races.* Chicago: Third World Press, 1978.

Malcolm X. *The Last Speeches.* New York: Pathfinder, 1989.

Marable, Manning. *The Great Well of Democracy: Reconstructing Race and Politics in the Twenty-first Century.* New York: Basic Books, 2002.

Mazama, Ama, ed. *The Afrocentric Paradigm.* Trenton, N.J.: Africa World Press, 2002.

Memmi, Albert. *The Colonizer and the Colonized.* Translated by Howard Greenfield. Boston: Beacon Press, 1991.

Mills, David. "Sista Souljah's Call to Arms." *Washington Post*, May 13, 1992, p. 6.

Moore, Michael. *Stupid White Men—and Other Sorry Excuses for the State of the Nation!* New York: ReganBooks, 2001.

Naison, Mark. "Outlaw Culture and the Black Neighborhood." *Reconstruction* 4, no. 4 (1992): 1–6.

National Advisory Commission on Civil Disorders. *The Kerner Report: The 1968 Report of the National Advisory Commission on Civil Disorders.* New York: Pantheon Books, 1988.

Omi, Michael, and Howard Winant. *Racial Formation in the United States: From the 1960s to the 1990s.* New York: Routledge, 1994.

Pinkney, Alphonso. *The Myth of Black Progress.* New York: Cambridge University Press, 1984.

Richburg, Keith B. *Out of America: A Black Man Confronts Africa.* New York: Basic Books, 1997.

Robinson, Randall. *The Debt: What America Owes to Blacks.* New York: Dutton, 2000.

Schlessinger, Arthur M., Jr. *The Disuniting of America: Reflections on a Multicultural Society.* New York: Whittle Communications, 1991.

Schuchter, Arnold. *Reparations: The Black Manifesto and Its Challenge to White America*. Philadelphia: Lippincott, 1970.

Seale, Bobby. *Seize the Time: The Story of the Black Panther Party and Huey P. Newton*. New York: Random House, 1970.

Sowell, Thomas. *The Economics of Politics and Race*. New York: William Morrow, 1985.

———. *The Vision of the Anointed*. New York: Basic Books, 1995.

Spivey, William R. *Corporate America in Black and White*. New York: Carlton Press, 1993.

Springsteel, Ian. "A Penny for Your Actions: A Texaco Bonus Plan Stirs Controversy by Rewarding Minority Hiring and Promotions." *CFO* (August 2, 1997).

Steele, Shelby. *The Content of Our Character: A New Vision of Race in America*. New York: St. Martin's Press, 1990.

Stone, Chuck. *Black Political Power in America*. New York: Dell, 1970.

Swisher, Carl B. *Roger B. Taney*. New York: Macmillan, 1935.

"The Death Penalty in Black and White: Who Lives, Who Dies, Who Decides." *GAO Death Penalty Study*. Washington, D.C.: US General Accounting Office, 1998.

Tuttle, William M., Jr. *Race Riot: Chicago in the Red Summer of 1919*. New York: Atheneum, 1970.

Waldinger, Roger, and Thomas Bailey. "The Continuing Significance of Race: Racial Conflict and Racial Discrimination in Construction." *Politics and Society* 19, no. 3 (1991): 291–323.

Walker, David. *An Appeal to the Colored Citizens of the World*. Boston: David Walker, 1829.

West, Cornel. "Diverse New World." *Democratic Left* (July/August 1991): 2–7.

———. *Race Matters*. Boston: Beacon Press, 1993.

Willhelm, Sidney M. *Black in a White America*. Cambridge, Mass.: Schenkman Publishing, 1983.

———. *Who Needs the Negro?* Cambridge, Mass.: Schenkman Publishing, 1983.

Williams, Robert. *Negroes with Guns*. New York: Marzani and Munsell, 1992.

Wilson, William Julius. *The Declining Significance of Race: Blacks and Changing American Institutions*. Chicago: University of Chicago Press, 1978.

Woodson, Carter G. *The Miseducation of the Negro*. Trenton, N.J.: Africa World Press, 1990.

Wortham, Anne. *The Other Side of Racism*. Columbus: Ohio State University Press, 1982.

Wright, Bruce. *Black Robes, White Justice*. Secaucus, N.J.: Lyle Stuart, 1987.